THE
Tristran
OF BEROUL

T. B. W. REID

—

THE

Tristran

OF BEROUL

===

A TEXTUAL
COMMENTARY

1972
OXFORD
BASIL BLACKWELL

ISBN 0 631 14350 5

Printed in Great Britain by
Western Printing Services Ltd. Bristol

Contents

Preface

My interest in the text of the *Tristran* of Beroul goes back to 1925, when at the University of Montpellier I attended a course of lectures on the romance given by Georges Millardet, then Professor of the Romance Languages there; the edition we used was of course that of Ernest Muret, in its 1922 version, and Muret has remained for me one of the great names in medieval textual studies. Later, as a colleague at the University of Manchester of Eugène Vinaver, Mildred K. Pope and, from 1939, Frederick Whitehead, I could not fail to become aware of the wider problems, both linguistic and literary, presented by this perennially fascinating work. At Oxford between 1958 and 1968 I lectured at intervals on aspects of the language of the poem (now naturally in the edition of Alfred Ewert), and learnt much from both the perplexities and the occasional inspirations of students. Most valuable of all were my frequent discussions of questions of emendation and interpretation with Ewert, especially during the last years of his life when he was completing the second volume of his edition. It is true that I very rarely succeeded in converting him to my point of view, and there is much in the present volume that he would have uncompromisingly rejected (some of my suggestions, indeed, have already been rejected by him); yet I would venture to dedicate it to his memory, for he was one with whom it was always possible, on the more subjective matters of scholarship, to 'agree to disagree'.

My thanks are due to Manchester University Press for permission to incorporate much of the substance of my article 'On the Text of the *Tristran* of Beroul' in *Medieval Miscellany presented to Eugène Vinaver* (Manchester and New York, 1965).

Finally, I am deeply indebted to my friend and colleague Mr. F. J. Barnett (himself a pupil of Ewert), who read the typescript with a care and attention which resulted in several wise deletions and a number of valuable additions.

T. B. W. R.

References and Abbreviations

Line-references are to the text in *The Romance of Tristran by Beroul*, edited by A. Ewert (Basil Blackwell, Oxford; Vol. I, 1939; Vol. II, 1970), which is in this respect identical with Muret's later editions; the quotations constituting the lemmas are given in the form in which they appear in the latest reprint (1967) of Ewert's first volume.

Muret's editions are referred to by the sigla used by Ewert (M^0 = S.A.T.F. edition of 1903; M^1, M^2, M^3 = C.F.M.A. editions of 1913, 1922, 1928 respectively; M^4 = C.F.M.A. edition of 1947 revised by 'L. M. Defourques'); a reading attributed to 'Muret' is one to be found in all or most of Muret's own editions from 1903 to 1928. The two volumes of Ewert's edition are referred to as E (I) and E (II). The editions used for the other Old French texts most frequently cited are: Chrétien de Troyes, ed. W. Foerster and A. Hilka (*Erec, Yvain, Lancelot, Guil. d'Angl., Perceval*); *Chanson de Roland*, ed. F. Whitehead (*Rol.*); *Eneas*, ed. J.J. Salverda de Grave (C.F.M.A.); *Thebes*, ed. L. Constans; *Romance of Horn*, ed. M. K. Pope (*Horn*); Marie de France, *Lais*, ed. A. Ewert; *Twelve Fabliaux*, ed. T. B. W. Reid.

Abbreviations are used for other frequently-cited works as follows:
F.E.W. = W. v. Wartburg, *Französisches Etymologisches Wörterbuch*, Bonn-Leipzig, 1922–.
F.S. = *French Studies*.
Fouché = P. Fouché, *Le Verbe français*, Paris, 1931.

Foulet = L. Foulet, *Petite Syntaxe de l'ancien français*, 3e éd., Paris, 1930.

Gdf. = F. Godefroy, *Dictionnaire de l'ancienne langue française*, Paris (reprint 1937–8).

Lerch = E. Lerch, *Historische französische Syntax*, Leipzig, 1925–34.

M.L.R. = *Modern Language Review*.

Morawski = J. Morawski, *Proverbes français antérieurs au XVe siècle*, Paris, 1925.

Pope = M. K. Pope, *From Latin to Modern French*, Manchester (revised reprint 1952).

Pope Studies = *Studies in French Language and Mediaeval Literature presented to Professor Mildred K. Pope*, Manchester, 1939.

Rom. = *Romania*.

S.O.E.D. = *Shorter Oxford English Dictionary*, 3rd ed., Oxford (reprinted 1964).

T.–L. = Tobler-Lommatzsch, *Altfranzösisches Wörterbuch*, Berlin, 1925–43, Wiesbaden, 1954–.

V.B. = A. Tobler, *Vermischte Beiträge zur französischen Grammatik*, Leipzig (I, 3rd ed., 1921; II, 2nd. ed., 1906; III, 2nd ed., 1908).

Vinaver Misc. = *Medieval Miscellany presented to Eugène Vinaver*, Manchester and New York, 1965.

Introduction

Not only is the *Tristran* of Beroul 'a text which, in spite of its obscurities—and no doubt often because of them—continues to hold the attention of students and critics' (E II v); it presents in an acute form a problem of great interest for medievalists. The two outstanding modern editions of the poem approach it with very different preconceptions and editorial principles. In his S.A.T.F. edition of 1903 Ernest Muret, in accordance with the usual practice of the time, took the text of the sole manuscript as a starting-point and sought to penetrate behind it and to arrive at an approximation to the original work as it left the hands of its author (or rather authors, 'Béroul et un anonyme').[1] On the other hand, Alfred Ewert, faithful to the principles of the Bédierist revolution, in the first volume (1939) of his edition printed the text of the manuscript with 'the minimum of change'; his second volume (*Introduction, Commentary*, 1970) admits only a few further corrections. Muret in his C.F.M.A. editions (1913, 1922, 1928)

---

[1] Muret afterwards removed from his title-page the reference to an anonymous collaborator; but he maintained his belief in the existence of an 'interpolateur ou continuateur anonyme' until his edition of 1928, when he rather reluctantly abandoned it in favour of the hypothesis that there was an interval between the composition of the first part of the poem and its completion. The hypothesis of dual authorship was revived in 1958 by G. Raynaud de Lage, and has been supported with evidence from phonology and morphology by the present writer (*M.L.R.* 60 (1965), 352–8). Though certain further differences between the two parts of the poem in respect of vocabulary or syntax are referred to incidentally in the following notes (e.g. in those on 131, 3223–7, 3486–90), the question of single or dual authorship has in general been avoided for the sake of simplicity.

came under the same influence and progressively abandoned many of his early corrections; the fourth edition of 1947, revised by 'L. M. Defourques' (i.e. Lucien Foulet and Mario Roques), goes much farther in the same direction and presents a text much closer to that of Ewert than to the original version of Muret.

The vast majority of those whose first acquaintance with the poem has been made in the last twenty-five years have therefore met it under the auspices of Ewert or Muret-Defourques in an extremely conservative form. These editors, like other uncompromising followers of Bédier, tend to make certain assumptions —conscious or unconscious—which medievalists of Muret's and earlier generations would not have considered justified. They assume that the scribe 'knew his own language'—that since his native speech was (presumably) a form of Old French, he is automatically a better authority (except when caught out in a purely palaeographically motivated error) on what could and could not be said in Old French than any modern student; the most strenuous efforts must therefore be made to attach an acceptable sense to what he has written. They also assume that Old French literary works were composed in accordance with principles of construction, narrative consistency etc. which are not necessarily ascertainable today, and that the usages of grammar and the rules of versification which have been established for the period by modern scholars were subject to arbitrary and equally unascertainable licences; we are therefore warned that, however odd the MS. text may seem, it would be dangerous to conclude that it does not represent what the author wrote. In the particular case of Beroul, Ewert makes criticism or correction even more hazardous; for in his opinion the poet was 'a well-informed but non-conforming deviationist in grammar and style no less than in his treatment of received narratives and of the moral, legal and literary questions which exercised the minds of his contemporaries' (II 44).

But these assumptions are surely in danger of distorting our understanding of poems such as the *Tristran* no less disastrously than the editorial practices against which Bédier was reacting. First of all, the scribe of MS. Fr. 2171 of the Bibliothèque Nationale cannot be taken as an authority on the language or the wording of the original romance. He was working at least half a century, and possibly much longer, after the date of its composition. Though he may himself have belonged to the Western dialect region in which the poem was written, there had been between him and the original at least one copy containing forms and spellings derived from a quite different dialect tradition.[1] What is even more important, 'he was but imperfectly acquainted with the subject-matter of the romance, possessed a very inadequate command of the literary language, and was a copyist of very limited intelligence . . . at times transliterating the graphies of his model without regard to meaning, at others interpreting them to the best of his ability though wrongly' (Ewert, *Pope Studies*, p. 97). But if all this is true of the sole extant manuscript text of the poem, it is hard to believe with Ewert that the elimination of those errors, and only those, 'which on palaeographical grounds can be safety attributed to the scribe or which a study of his habits and failings justifies one in ascribing to him' will leave us with a

---

[1] Many of the spellings of the MS. correspond to the features of the original as attested by the rhymes, whether Western (e.g. *-us* for Central *-uis*, *-or* for *-eur*, *el* for *ele*, 1st pl. *-on* for *-ons*, 1st conj. impf. indic. 3 sing. *-ot* etc.) or Central. Other spellings are inconsistent with these, and in at least two different directions. Some are markedly Western (notably *lié*, *mié*, *prié* for *li*, *mi*, *pri* etc., *soier*, *voier* for *seoir*, *veoir* etc.). Others are, compared with the usage of the original, more Central (e.g. *-oi-* for Western *-ei-*, *feme* for *fene*, occasional *-an-* for *-en-*, *-eur* for *-or*, *-uis* for *-us*) or more Northern (*-ie* for *-iee*, occasional *-ch-* for *-c-*, *g-* for *j-*, *ca-* for *cha-* etc.), together suggesting the mixed forms of the literary Franco-Picard of the 13th century. It is not certain which (if either) of these two groups of non-original spellings has been introduced by the scribe of MS. 2171. Muret credited him with the Central and Northern features (M[2] pp. x–xi, M[4] pp. ix–x), but Ewert thinks these are due to an intermediate copyist (*Pope Studies*, pp. 97–8) and attributes to the final scribe the Western features like *lié*, *mié*. This does in fact seem the more probable explanation of the varied forms in the MS., provided that we make an additional assumption about the scribe of MS. 2171: that he was trying to curb his own Westernizing tendencies (he did actually write *li*, *mi* etc. much more frequently than the forms with *-ié*), and that it was by hypercorrection that in a limited number of words he sometimes wrote *i* where not only the Centre (and Franco-Picard) but also the West had *ie* (*live* 722, 745, 827 etc. for *lieve*, and similarly *brif* 3227, *briment* 997 etc., *escrive* 731; *fire* adj. 1186, vb. 1764, *arire* 1527 etc., *legirement* 556; *crime* 1538 for *crieme*; *pice* 1218 etc.).

version which can fairly be considered 'a substantially faithful reproduction of the original' (ib. p. 98).

If, however, we reject this view of the authenticity of the manuscript text as presenting 'an "unvarnished" Beroul' (Ewert, II 43)—a view evidently shared by 'Defourques'—acceptance of Ewert's estimate of the author's personality and attitude to his work may still debar us not only from attempting to reconstitute the original but even from venturing to interpret the version that we have. If the author were indeed a thoroughgoing 'deviationist', we should have no hope of understanding what he wanted to convey to his audience. Unless we are prepared to abandon Beroul altogether, we must assume that in most respects he conformed in matters of substance, grammar and style to the principles that applied to other writers of his time, and that if occasionally he deviated from those principles he did so systematically. The sequence of letters that stands in the manuscript must be interpreted by reference to systems of orthography, of phonology, of morphology and syntax, of versification and of literary structure established by examination of the practice of writers of the period —including Beroul: in other words, we must at all points seek for parallels. Ewert, it is true, declares that the 'circumspect editor' will resist 'the fear of the *hapax legomenon* which an undiscriminating reliance on parallelism might otherwise have relegated to the variants' (II 46); but discrimination must be exercised in both directions (and circumspection in all). Anything for which no parallel can be found must be prima facie suspect. If parallels are found within the manuscript text itself, but not elsewhere, it may be possible to deduce, with due caution, that they indicate an idiosyncrasy on the part of the author; but evidence of system, of one kind or another, there must be if the text and its meaning are to be established.

In attempting to interpret, and if necessary correct, the words of the manuscript in terms of attested linguistic and literary systems we are of course liable to be hampered by the lack of a reasonably complete classified repertory of available evidence. That a form, a meaning or a construction is not to be found either elsewhere in the text or in existing grammatical and lexicographical works is obviously no proof that its presence in the manuscript is due solely to scribal error. In the commentary that follows, however, such absence of attestation has often been taken as justifying, or at least confirming, doubts about the reading or interpretation of the text. Some of these doubts may in due course be proved unwarranted by the discovery of parallels not yet registered by the dictionaries and grammars; but I venture to suggest that my scepticism may nevertheless have been justified as a first step towards the establishment of the facts.

It is not perhaps superfluous to emphasize once more the peculiarly delicate situation of the reader of a medieval text which like the *Tristran* is preserved in a single manuscript copy. Whether his approach is that of editor or critic, he comes to the examination of its content with a body of conscious or unconscious preconceptions. He translates the letters of the manuscript into tentative phonemes, and as these begin to build up into words and clauses he supplies, in accordance with probabilities based on his previous experience, all those essential elements of discourse that are simply not represented in the manuscript, from the distinction between vocalic *i* or *u* and consonantal *j* or *v* to the whole range of varied intonation patterns corresponding to a modern system of punctuation, and, in the case of dialogues, to the distribution of speeches between the interlocutors (if this is not expressed in words in the text). Now, different editors or critics may here supply the missing elements in different ways: see, for example, for the choice between *u* and *v* the note below on 1991; for punctuation those listed under this heading in the Index; for the distribution of speeches that on 4308; for the distinction between narrative text and quoted words that on 1467. In each case of this kind, however, only one alternative can be in accordance with the intentions of the author—the others are simply wrong; and the only way to establish which is correct (if indeed it can be established) is to see which is in accordance with the linguistic systems of the author and of his contemporaries and with the contextual probabilities imposed by the narrative and expressive conventions of the time and in particular by those of romance as a genre and of the Tristran legend as subject-matter.

But this is true not only of what does not stand in the manuscript, but also of what is written there and should perhaps have been written differently. Again, judgments may differ; but they are perhaps least subjective in the strictly linguistic domain, and in particular in that of grammar (morphology and syntax). Here the principles of Old French usage can sometimes be decisive (especially if confirmed by the general usage of the text itself) in imposing the conclusion that what stands in the manuscript cannot be accepted as representing the original. I suggest, for example, that in *Que ançois que il s'esvelleront* 2021 the indicative *esvelleront* makes it certain that *ançois que* is corrupt; that in *Ainz berseret a veneor N'ert gardé* . . . 2697–8 the collocation of *ainz* . . . *ne* 'never' and the imperfect (or future) *ert* is impossible; that *ne lairai mie* . . . *Ne face con que il dira* 2717–19, with its unattested use of *con que*, should not be attributed to the author; that the reading *Ja ne voist il sanz paradis* 3454 cannot be justified by punctuating *s'anz* (whether *s'* is understood as for *se* or *soi* reflexive or for *si* adverb) and taking *anz* as a preposition; that in *Ou soit a voir ou set enfance* 224 we must assume, as long as the existence of an adjectival locution *a voir* 'reasonable' has not been demonstrated, that this reading is an error. Less frequently, phonological principles can be invoked in the same way: it is most unlikely, for example, that the author rhymed the product of closed *o* tonic free with *eus* in 2677–8, contrary to his invariable practice elsewhere. Similar considerations will sometimes enable us to reject a correction that has been adopted by one or more of the editors: thus *Que ce vos di por averté* 231 must not be emended to *Ne ce vos di*, since 'Nor do I say this to you', the meaning intended by the editors, could be expressed only by *Ne ce ne vos di* (or in the South-West *Ne ce n'os di*); again, in *Vos savez bien, beaus oncles, sire, Vos vosistes ardoir en ire* 2581–2 the pronoun object *nos* required by *vosistes ardoir* cannot simply be substituted for *vos*, since a weak personal pronoun could not occupy the initial position in its clause.

In some of the instances where for these or other reasons the manuscript text is seen to be corrupt, it is possible to state with some confidence what must have stood in the original, or at the very least in the scribe's model, and can therefore be justifiably introduced into the edited text of the poem. Thus the scribe's *traient* 42 is undoubtedly an error for *raient*, his *por Deu* 658 for *por ce*, his *par soi* 1326 and 3313 for *par foi*, his *Çaint s'espee* 1780 for *Çaint' espee*, his *Qanuit* 2449 for *La nuit*, his *N'ert gardee* 2698 for *Ne fu gardé*, his *seront* 4241 for *seroie*, his *espesse li jagloiʒ* 4318 for *espés li jagloloiʒ*, and so on. More frequently, however, the nature of the correction required remains uncertain, or two or more alternatives seem equally plausible; here there is of course no question of modifying the edited text, but only of annotating it.

The interpretation of the transmitted text in those passages where there is no positive reason to suppose that it is corrupt is again a matter of annotation or glossing; but here also it is important to view the letters of the manuscript in relation to the linguistic systems of the period. I suggest, for example, that in *S'il les trovout, nes vilonast* 1107 the contracted form *nes* cannot represent *ne* (< NEC)+ *les*, an enclisis of which no instance has been adduced (it must therefore represent *ne* (<NON)+*les*, and *nes vilonast* must be, not a second alternative in the conditional clause, but its apodosis—and therefore, in the context, a question). In matters of syntax in particular, I suggest that the text must be understood in accordance with established principles of Old French usage as regards mood and tense, word-order, negation etc.: that, for example, in *Ne savon el qel voie tienge* 2636 the subjunctive *tienge* makes it impossible to take the subordinate clause as a simple indirect question 'whither he goes'; conversely, that in *qui voloit faire* 4149 and *qui ara tort* 4158 the indicative excludes the possibility of a concessive interpretation, 'whoever might wish to do so', 'whoever may be at fault'; that Old French restrictions on the position of weak pronoun objects make it impossible to take *qui* in *ce qui avenir lor dut* 822 as *qu'i*, or *l'en* in *deus seetes . . . ot l'en menees* 1283-4 as *li+en*; that in *Ainʒ que n'en fust prise venjance* 1114 the presence of the negation *ne* precludes the interpretation 'before my vengeance would be satisfied'.

The comments which follow concern a relatively small proportion of the text of the *Tristran*. In a considerable majority of passages the text presented by Ewert and Muret-Defourques may be accepted as definitive and as correctly interpreted by both editors. On these passages I make no comment, any more than on those where the text is agreed to be corrupt beyond recovery. My commentary is devoted to the intermediate category of

B

passages where the two most recent editions disagree, or fail to discuss what seems to me to be obscure, or where both appear to be at fault. In each case I have briefly summarized the views of the editors and the principal commentators; the prominence given to those of Ewert is due to the fact that his commentary is the most recent and the most explicit.

Commentary

29–30. (*li felon* . . .) *Li font acroire, ce me senble, Que nos amors jostent ensenble.* E comments (II 82) 'Here, as at ll. 83, 289, 429, 2859, the M⁰ reading *a croire* (replaced in later editions by *acroire*) is hardly possible'. There is some ambiguity about the term 'reading'; but E seems here to recognize that the word-divisions made by the scribe are often arbitrary or random, and that they are in no way binding upon an editor (as is indeed shown by his own practice: compare, for example, the scribe's spacings on f. 25ʳ as reproduced in *Pope Studies*, p. 89, with those in lines 3360–3429 of E's edition; see also his note on 1055). It is therefore surprising that in some other comments he attaches a quite unjustified importance to the scribe's word-divisions: see below notes on 789–90, 2243–6, 3933–4, 4219–20.

In saying that 'the reading *a croire* . . . is hardly possible' E appears to be imposing on O. F. a Mod. F. distinction that is merely a matter of orthographical convention; for within O. F. *faire acroire* (which does not contain the verb *acroire*) is indistinguishable from *faire a croire*, *faire assavoir* from *faire a savoir* (cf. *faire a entendre*) and *avoir afere* (3913) from *avoir a fere*. If, however, an artificial distinction is to be made between *font acroire* and *font a croire*, it is, as E says, the first that is required here, but not for the reason he gives, that *font a croire* would imply an impersonal meaning; for the construction *faire a* +infin. is commonly used personally, as in *Mout font andui a redoter* 'both are much to be feared' (*Yvain* 5586; other examples in T.-L. III 1587–8). For *Bien lor faisoit a redouter* 1664, cited by E as an instance of the impersonal use of the construction, see note.

40. *Je puis dire: de haut si bas!* As E says (II 82), *de (si) haut si bas* is a well authenticated proverbial expression. Muret's later eds. and M⁴ have a glossary entry *Proverbes*, which lists only those at 40, 42–3 and 3428–9, but as might be expected in view of the general character of the style there are in the text other proverbs and proverbial expressions; see the notes on 911 (*Ne vieat pas mort de pecheor*), 1035 (*Chascun aime mex soi que toi*), 2682 (*Molt est dolenz qui pert s'amie*), 3211 (*Chascun puet dire ce qu'il pense*).

41–3. *Sire, molt dist voir Salemon: Qui de forches traient larron, Ja puis nes amera nul jor.* The MS. has *nel amera*, corrected by all editors because of the pl. *traient*; but I have shown in *Vinaver Misc.*, pp. 279–80, that *nel* should be retained and *traient* corrected to *raient*, pres. indic. 3 of *raiembre* 'redeem, rescue' (cf. *Lerres n'amera ja celui qui le respite des fourches*, Morawski 1048, with variant *qui lui reynt*), a reading which is now accepted by E (II 82–3). Muret had been misled by the reference to Solomon into associating Beroul's lines with a passage in *De Marco e de Salemons, Qui en sa meson Atret lou larron Domage i reçoit*; but this is quite a different proverb (analogues of it are cited by Morawski under 39, 977, 1180, 1526). It is true that the proverb about the ingratitude of the thief rescued from the gallows is not in *De Marco* or any of the other collections attributed to Solomon; but this is of no significance. In 1461–2 Beroul tells us that *Salemon dit que droituriers Que ses amis, c'ert ses levriers*, which as E notes (II 168–9) is equally unauthenticated; evidently he had adopted the convention of attributing to Solomon any proverb to which he wished to give an air of authority.

56–9. *Et il ont fait entendre au roi Que vos m'amez d'amor vilaine. Si voient il Deu et son reigne! Ja nul verroient en la face.* Lines 58–9 are obscure, and have been variously punctuated and interpreted. E cites 58 as an example of 'the concessive or conditional clause being given an exclamatory turn' (II 78), and sees some kind of parallel with *se onques point du suen oi* 211 (see his note) and *Ja ne voie*

Deu en la face, Qui ... 841; but he seems to decide finally that the line constitutes an independent exclamation, 'Let them come into the presence of God and his kingdom!' (II 83). A better explanation is that of M⁴ (Index, s.v. *Deu*), somewhat modified: with a comma for the full stop after 57, 'they have made the king think that you love me with a wicked love, so may they see God and his kingdom!', the asseverative formula *si*+subjunctive+subject (cf. *si m'aït Dex* 628, 4201) being put into the mouths of the hostile barons; then Iseut, by contradicting the asseveration, denies the truth of the assertion it supports: '(But) never would they look upon his face!'

60–1. *Tristran, gardez en nule place Ne me mandez por nule chose.* E (II 84) says that *mandez* is a subjunctive (as the same form may well be in *s'il vos vient, sire, a corage Que me mandez rien* 2712); but it could also be an imper., with the common transition from indirect to direct speech, as in *Gardez, se vos pansez folie, Que por ce ne la feites mie* (*Yvain* 1323–4).

65–8. *S'or en savoit li rois un mot, Mon cors seret desmenbré tot, Et si seroit a molt grant tort; Bien sai qu'il me dorroit la mort.* I have suggested (*Vinaver Misc.*, pp. 275–6) that 67–8 might be one of the couplets in which the lines have been interverted by the scribe: it would be more logical to mention both of the physical consequences of the king's being informed—the dismemberment and the killing—before the reflection that they would be unjustified. There is no doubt that such interversions have often taken place; they have been recognized and corrected by both editors in 857–8, 1879–80, 3365–6, by Muret in 1379–80, 2825–6, 3115–16 (the corrections in these three cases abandoned by M⁴), by Ewert in 1505–6 (the correction also adopted in M⁴), 3029–30, 4285–6. I have suggested that there may have been additional interversions in (besides the present couplet) 2611–12, 3169–70 (now accepted by E, II 225), 3441–2; a similar suggestion has been made by B. Blakey for 1173–4 (see note) and by F. J. Barnett for 1175–6 (see note). The correction or retention of such couplets is discussed in notes on 1173–6, 1378–80, 2610–12, 2824–7, 3028–30, 3114–18, 3440–3, 4285–7, 4308–12.

69–70. *li rois ne set Que por lui par vos aie ameit.* The MS. has *pas vos aie ameit*, retained by M⁰ and M²; M⁴, like E, corrects to *par.* Grammatically, *pas* is possible in such a clause, itself affirmative but depending on a negative principal, cf. *N'i a celui qui pas l'en creie* (*Thebes* 3773); but its meaning would be 'in the slightest degree, at all', which is out of the question here. Though *pas* could easily be a scribal error for *par*, this is hardly more appropriate in the context. Elsewhere in Beroul, and almost invariably in O.F. (cf. T.-L. VII 180–3), *par* intensive is accompanied by another intensive adv. (*trop par* 133, 1152, *tant par* 834, *molt par* 962, *a mervelle par* 1157). Here *pas* is therefore probably a slip (perhaps induced by *por*) for a monosyllabic intensive adv. other than *par*; cf. in similar contexts *Sire, molt t'ai por lui amé* 79, *Por vos l'ai je tant amé, sire* 426.

73–5. *Je quidai jadis que ma mere Amast molt les parenz mon pere, Et disoit ce* . . . According to E (II 85) 'the mood of *disoit* indicates that logically the statement attributed to Iseut's mother is not a matter of opinion'. Neither the sense nor the sequence of words, however, requires *disoit ce* . . . to be understood as grammatically dependent on *quidai*; it is more probably a principal clause co-ordinated with *je quidai.*

75–7. *Et disoit ce que la mollier Nen avroit ja* [*son*] *seignor chier Qui les parenz n'en amereit.* In 75 the MS. has *que ja mollier*, corrected only by E; in 76 M⁰ read *avroit pas seignor* and corrected to *avroit pas son seignor*, but Muret's later editions read *avroit ja seignor* and correct to *avroit le suen s.*; E and M⁴ correct to *avroit ja son s.* M⁴ thus retains *ja* in both lines, and though noting (p. 141) that *ja* is rarely found repeated in the same clause, cites in support *ja sunt il ja si luinz!* (*Rol.* 2429). E rightly comments (II 85) that *Rol.* 2429, even if accepted as the correct reading, is not a true parallel (it is an affirmative sentence, and the two *ja* are not synonyms). Elsewhere in Beroul, however, the MS. has *Qar ja corage de folie Nen avrai ja jor de ma vie* 2323–4, where, though Muret and E correct to *je jor*, M⁴ considers (p. 146) that the second *ja* ought perhaps to be retained. This passage somewhat strengthens the case for the repeated *ja* in 75–6; and there is certainly no positive requirement in O. F. for the *la* which E introduces in 75.

76. *Nen avroit ja [son] seignor chier.* Muret also printed *Nen*, but M⁴ has *N'en*. The editors sometimes find it difficult to decide whether scribal *nen* before a vowel is to be understood as *nen*, the unreduced prevocalic form of *ne*, or as *n'en*. E (II 26) admits *nen* in only eight instances (76, 137, 1131, 1501, 2324, 2573, 4103 twice); M⁴ agrees about all these except 76, but prints *nen* also in 620 (with a different emendation from that of E), 816, 1022; M² had even more cases of *nen*, e.g. 793, 1153. The fact is that in nearly every case it would be just possible to understand *n'en*, with *en* either used rather vaguely in the respective sense of 'with regard to it, in the matter' (e.g. 2324), or in the causal sense of 'because of it, consequently' (e.g. 1131), or accompanying a verb of motion (e.g. 1501), or used proleptically (e.g. 137; see note on 1944–7). In *Mestier nen est dont la nen ait* 4103 (so printed in M², E and M⁴) it seems essential to understand at least the first *nen* as *n'en* (see note).

89–90. *Mais l'en puet home desveier, Faire le mal et bien laisier.* M⁴ retains the correction, adopted by Muret in his later editions from Tobler, to *Faire mal faire et . . .* E (II 85) justifies the MS. reading by saying that 'the idea conveyed by the modal *faire* "to cause to" is already implied in *desveier*', and translates 'a man may be misled into doing evil and . . .'. No such use of *desveier* appears in Gdf. (II 679–80, 681, IX 367) or T.-L. (II 1820–22); it is sometimes constructed with *de* in the sense of 'lead away from', but to give it the sense here required we should need at least to correct to *A faire mal et . . .* (which would be less likely than *Faire mal faire et . . .* to be miscopied as *Faire le mal et . . .*). There are, however, several passages in the text which suggest the existence in the author's language of a factitive use of certain verbs, especially *faire*. It is perhaps possible to interpret *faire le mal* here as equivalent to *(lui) faire faire le mal*; similarly *de s'ire face pardon* 166 (see note) may be understood as *de s'ire li face faire pardon*, *Fai grant senblant de toi proier* 543 as *de toi faire proier*, *A beste prendre sanz crïer* 1605 as *A beste faire prendre* or *A lui faire beste prendre*; *Iré le fait* 1992 (see note) should perhaps be read as *Ire le fait* or *Ire li fait* and understood as *Ire li fait faire*; *Qu'il metra lance par astele* 3526 (see note) was already interpreted by M⁴ as *Qui fera metre lance par astele*; see also 1051–4. This usage is no doubt to be associated with the converse use of *faire* +infin. as a periphrasis for the simple verb, cf. note on 3221.

109–11. *Qar j'ai tel duel c'onques le roi Out mal pensé de vos vers moi Qu'il n'i a el fors que je muere.* On *out . . . pensé* E comments (II 87): 'O. F. syntax allowed of this use of the indicative, which has the effect of presenting as a fact what is grammatically dependent on a verb of feeling (*j'ai tel duel*); or is *c'* (= *que*) causal?' In fact, O. F. syntax not merely permitted but almost universally required the indic. in this construction (cf. Lerch, I 290, II 79 ff.), no doubt precisely because in origin the *que* was causal; cf. *qel duel que la roïne N'avot les dras du lit ostez!* 750–1, and with other expressions of emotion, judgment etc. *Gel blasmé que il me mandot* 357, *Liez est que ore ra son esse* 548 (cf. with explicitly causal conjunction *Molt li fu bel . . . De ce qu'il sont en lait tripot* 3857–8), *quel damage Qu'a si grant honte estes l'iez!* 904–5 (cf. 835–6), *poise m'en . . . Que il la mort a ici quise* 1565–6 (cf. 1653–4), *Quel mervelle que l'en si toise* 3072. For apparent cases of the subjunctive in similar contexts see 629, 1570, 1655, 3255 and notes.

131. *Il ne me lait sol escondire.* E (II 88–9), discussing the terms *escondit, escondire, deraisne, deraisnier, esligier* and *alegier*, says that *escondit* and *escondire* denote 'the defence against a charge or, in a wider sense, the hearing of a case', and that the other four words denote 'specifically a successful defence or acquittal'. The contexts in which the terms are used in the poem do not seem to bear out these definitions: with the exception of *escondire* 3720, 3915 in the non-technical sense of 'refuse, demur', and *escondire* 3252 and *les escondiz* 4176, for both of which see note on 4223–5, they all refer to the action of clearing an accused person of a charge (an action which, as Ewert says, may take the form of a judicial duel, trial by combat or a sworn declaration of innocence—all involving an appeal to supernatural powers). There is no passage in which any of these words necessarily means 'the hearing of a case'. The terms

also seem to be practically synonymous. The only apparent distinction is that the noun *deraisne* (of which there are ten instances, all in the second part of the poem) is applied only to Iseut's clearing of herself by oath; this is not, however, the case with the verb *deraisnier*.

139–40. *Molt vi mon oncle iluec pensis, Mex vosist estre mort que vis.* Muret corrected to *pensif: vif*; M⁴ follows E in restoring the MS. forms. It is hardly possible to accept E's justification (II 89) of the nom. sing. *pensis*, viz. that it 'might well have been induced by a sort of ellipsis ("who was")'; this would imply a breakdown of the case-system, but in the opposite direction to what actually happened (cf. E II 19–20). On the other hand, his justification of the nom. *vis*, that 'the oblique is by no means obligatory after the comparative *que*', is a marked understatement: the noun or adj. after *que*, when its function is, as here, that of a complement of *estre*, is normally in the nominative. However, the oblique does occur in such comparative constructions; and taking the couplet as a whole it is therefore probable that Muret's *pensif* and *vif* represent the original text.

143–6. *Ne deüst pas mis oncles chiers De moi croire ses losengiers . . . Pensë il que n'en ait pechié?* For *avoir pechié*, rather than 'be guilty, do wrong', E (II 89) prefers to understand 'suffer damage', referring to the loss of Tristran's services. There is, however, no authority for this interpretation (the nearest attested sense of *pechié* to it is 'misfortune', 'a pity', cf. 700, 720, 1415 etc. and T.-L. VII 533–4); the context concerns not Tristran's possible departure but Mark's unjust suspicion and Tristran's innocence, and the meaning of *pechié* is clearly 'guilt' (the line is correctly cited by T.-L., VII 532, under 'Unrecht, Frevel'). The sense of *en* is therefore 'in so doing' rather than 'as a result'.

147–50. *Certes, oïl, n'i faudra mie, Por Deu, le fiz sainte Marie. Dame, ore li dites errant Qu'il face faire un feu ardant . . .* E punctuates thus, with a comma after *mie* and a full stop after *Marie*. It is true that in the MS. the word *Dame* has a large red initial; but these large initials are placed almost at random. E himself says (I x) 'they do not correspond to divisions in the narrative', and Muret, followed by M⁴, disregards them altogether and introduces his own paragraphing (in the first 500 lines he has 11 paragraph insets, only two of which coincide with any of the 16 large initials in that part of the MS.). The presence of one of these initials does not necessarily even mean that a sentence ends with the preceding line, and all editors print a comma at the end of 3122 in spite of the large initial of 3123. I therefore suggested (*Vinaver Misc.*, pp. 265–6) that the lines should be punctuated, as in M⁴, according to the obvious sense, with full stop after *mie* and comma after *Marie*; the formula *Por Deu* . . . 'for God's sake' is clearly intended to reinforce the imperative, as in *Dame, por Deu qui en pucele Prist por le pueple umanité, Conselliez moi* 198–200 (cf. 797–8 etc.). E (II 89) says that there is no compelling reason for thus breaking the couplet; but he admits himself (II 33) that Beroul does break the couplet, and in fact this happens so often (see 198–9 quoted above, also 32–3, 52–3, 124–5, 128–9, 188–9, 262–3 etc.) that the metrical argument can never be invoked against the requirements of the sense. See also 304–5 and note, 783–5 and note.

155–6. *Qar je sai bien n'a de sa cort Qui a batalle o moi s'en tort.* The MS. has *o batalle*, corrected by all editors to *a b.* (*n'a* 155 is not clear, and was at first read by Muret as *n'ert*: M² (p. 141) says '*n'ert* illisible'). The sense of the couplet is summarized by E (II 72) as 'for I know that none of his court will accept combat' (his glossary gives for *torner* v.refl. 'come forth, go away 156' and for *en* adv. 'thence, away . . . 156'); M⁰ and M⁴ render 156 'qui se risque à combattre contre moi' (Glossary s.v. *torner*). It is difficult to see how these interpretations are arrived at. The verb *soi (en) torner* normally means 'turn away, go away, depart'; in a negative context, as here, it can mean 'get away, extricate oneself, escape' (cf. Gdf. X 789), which would make sense in our passage if the prep. *o* (evidently due to anticipation of *o moi*) were corrected not to *a* but to *de*: 'he has not at his court anyone who will escape from a combat with me'. But as the editors have seen, this is not the meaning to be expected in the general context; what is stressed in several parallel passages is the refusal of Mark's knights even to accept Tristran's challenge: (Tristran) *bien savoit et bien quidoit,*

S'a escondit peüst venir, Nus n'en osast armes saisir Encontre lui, lever ne prendre 814-17; '*N'offri Tristran li a defendre? Ainz n'en osastes armes prendre*' 3063-4; cf. also 3422-3. It therefore seems possible that in the original the line ran *Qui de* (or *a*) *batalle o moi s'atort*: for *soi atorner de* (or *a*) 'equip oneself for, prepare for' see Gdf. I 483, T.-L. I 649; for scribal confusion of *torner* and *atorner* see 4472, also 1985 as emended by Muret's later editions and M⁴.

160-2. *Tenez moi bien a mon ami; Qant je vinc ça a lui par mer, Com a seignor i vol torner.* Muret, followed by M⁴, assumes that there is a lacuna between 161 and 162. Since *mer* and *torner* rhyme, this would mean either that the omitted portion comprised at least four lines (and it is difficult to see how so long a development could be inserted) or that it consisted of two lines also ending in -*er*, the original text having had two successive couplets on this rhyme. But such a sequence is abnormal in Continental O. F. (cf. E II 4), and apparent instances in our text are probably not to be attributed to the author (see notes on 725-8, 2313-18, 2702-6, 3947-50; in 1729-30 -*ie* is merely scribal for -*iee*).

E is no doubt right in believing (II 90) that there is no need to assume a lacuna between 161 and 162. He suggests that the lines should be understood as signifying 'I wish to return there' (i.e. across the sea to his native land) 'in lordly fashion as when I crossed hither' (i.e. to take service with Mark). But this involves several serious difficulties. E says that *com* is taken 'to apply to both clauses (sc. *comme quand* . . .)': in fact, it has to be taken to apply only to the clause in which it does not occur, as if the sentence ran *Com quant je vinc ça, a seignor i vol torner*. The adv. *i* has to be taken as conveying the notion of the land across the sea from which Tristran had come to Mark, a land to which there has been no other reference. The phrase *a seignor* has to be understood as accompanying *torner* in adverbial function, 'in lordly fashion', but the passages cited as parallels contain quite different constructions: in *Estre o le roi Marc a seignor* 2308 *a s.*, which E himself (II 202) translates 'as my liege-lord', and in *Toi retenir a soudeier* 2670 *a s.* 'as a serving-man', both have a predicative function of a well-known type (cf. T.-L. I 18). The verb *torner* has to be taken as meaning intrinsically 'return', of which there is no other example in the text. Finally, the whole couplet 161–2 must be taken to refer to a plan of Tristran's to leave Mark's court and return to his native land, of which there has been no previous mention: all he has so far proposed to do is to clear himself by judicial combat (131, 155–6) or by ordeal by fire (149–54), and no departure from the court is mentioned in the extant text until 204 ff. It is therefore more probable that, if there is indeed no lacuna, the meaning of the couplet is the literal one, 'When I came here across the sea to him, I wished to come to him as my lord' (with *i* = 'to him' as in 517 etc., and *vol* not pres. I as stated by M⁰ and E, but scribal for *voil* (cf. *çole* 669 for *çoile* etc.), pret. I, as in 445, 453.

163–6. *grant tort avez, Qui de tel chose a moi parlez Que de vos le mete a raison, Et de s'ire face pardon.* E (II 91) comments '*Et* might well be a mistake for *Que*'; if his translation is to be accepted, 'that I should intercede in your favour with him to pardon you his wrath', the correction to *Que* must be introduced into the text. Muret and M⁴ have the same text, but do not indicate how they understand it. If *face pardon* can be taken as equivalent to (*li*) *face faire pardon* (see note on 89–90), *Et* will of course be retained: 'that I should speak to him about you and cause him to renounce his anger'.

181–3. *Se il vos pardounot . . . son mautalent et s'ire, J'en seroie joiose et lie.* E's glossary gives for *pardoner* only the translation 'pardon'; but its meaning in all the passages cited (181, 539, 554, 2226), like that of *faire pardon de* in 166, is 'renounce, lay aside, abandon (one's anger or ill-will)'. The sense 'pardon' also occurs in the text, e.g. in 865.

204–5. *Engagiez est tot mon hernois; Car le me faites delivrer.* With these lines compare *Envers mon oste m'aquitez* 218; *Se il en ot un mot parler Que vos gages face aquiter . . .* 227–8; *Dist moi que l'ostel l'aquitasse* 444; *il vos requist quitance De ses gages* 487–8. E's notes (II 91–2, 93, also 77, 95, 108) speak of the release of Tristran's pledged arms (mentioned also by Eilhart) and the payment for his lodgings (not in any other version) as two different things; Muret and M⁴ (s.v. *ostal*) also gloss *aquiter l'ostel* 444 'payer les frais d'hôtellerie, de logement'. There seems, however, to be no reference in Beroul to any 'confiscating of (Tristran's) arms' (E II 92) or to 'the release of any sureties held by Mark' (E II 92 n. 2, 123). All the references are consistent with the assumption that some of Tristran's arms are held by his host as a pledge for the payment for his lodging. It is true that at a later stage Governal seems to have no difficulty in obtaining Tristran's sword (971–4; the hauberk was apparently not Tristran's own, 1015; the bow was 'taken' from a forester, 1280–2), and, still later, his shield and lance (3586, 3989).

207–10. *Bien sai que j'ai si grant prooise, Par tote terre ou fol adoise . . . Bien sai que u monde n'a cort, S'i vois, li sires ne m'avot.* E mentions (II 92), though he does not here positively adopt it, the explanation of certain apparently repetitive passages as being due to 'variant redactions' or 'alternative variant readings' standing in the scribe's model and mistakenly incorporated in his copy: so also in 697–8 (II 128), 867–70 (II 135), 1834 (II 181), 2315–18 (II 202). This hypothesis (put forward by Muret and retained in M⁴) seems to imply that the scribe of MS. 2171 had access either to the author's original draft or to an exact copy of it, which is surely very unlikely. It is more probable that the irregularity is purely scribal in origin: a careless copyist has dropped out one or more lines (at 208–9, 2314–16) or has duplicated the substance of a line (697–8, 1833–4; see notes). The mere repetition of the initial words of a line (*Bien sai que* 207 and 209, *Li rois* 867 and 869) is not evidence of corruption; there is no reason to doubt the authenticity of such repetitions as *Bien sai* 201 and 203.

210. *. . . li sires ne m'avot.* See note on 1030–1.

211–14. *Et se onques point du suen oi, Yseut, par cest mien chief le bloi, Nel se voudroit avoir pensé Mes oncles, ainz un an passé.* The sense of 211, and its relation to 213, is obscure. M⁴ makes no comment. E (II 93) translates 'I never had anything belonging to king Mark and even if I did, my uncle would wish before the year is out that he had never harboured such a thought', and comments 'The conditional clause postulates the thing denied'; but such an interpretation of the conditional clause is hardly justified, and in the only passage cited as a parallel (*Si voient il Deu et son reigne!* 58) there is no conditional clause (see note on 56–9).

218. *Envers mon oste m'aquitez.* See note on 204–5.

219–20. *Par Deu, Tristran, molt me mervel, Qui me donez itel consel!* (so also Muret and M⁴, but without the exclamation mark). It is hardly likely that *Qui* is a relative depending on *Tristran* or an absolute pronoun in some way related to *molt me mervel*; it is probably an error for *Que* (introducing a clause with indicative verb, cf. note on 109–11). An alternative, however, would be to punctuate *molt me mervel! Qui me donez itel consel, Vos m'alez porchaçant mon mal*, with *Qui* relative depending on *Vos*.

224. *Ou soit a voir ou set enfance.* The correction of *a voir* to *savoir* (Muret, M⁴) seems indispensable; cf. *Ou soit savoir ou soit folie* 2718 (and other examples in Gdf. X 636). E (II 94) defends the MS. reading on the grounds that 'there is no need to suppose absolute uniformity or parallelism: *a voir* "truthful", "genuine", "serious" may stand as the opposite of *enfance*'; but he has not shown that *a voir* existed as an adjectival locution 'truthful' or that *voir*, either as noun or as adj., could be used in this construction with *a* as complement of *estre*.

227–9. *Se il en ot un mot parler Que vos gages face aquiter, Trop par seroit aperte chose.* The reference is to 204–5 (cf. note). E (II 94) questions whether *face* is 1st person or 3rd person, but in the context it must be 1st person: the only person who has been asked to redeem Tristran's pledge is the speaker, Iseut. For the construction cf. *S'un mot en puet li rois oïr Que nos fuson ça asenblé . . .* 190–1.

230–1. *Certes, je ne sui pas si osse, Ne ce vos di por averté.* The MS. text is *se je sui pas si osse Que ce vos di*; the corrections of Muret (M², M³) are retained by E and M⁴. It is true that, as E says (II 94), the MS. reading does not make sense; but while Muret's correction in 230 is no doubt right, that in 231 is highly question-able. The use of *ne* in the negative sense of 'nor', unaccompanied by the negation *ne* before the verb, is unparalleled in the text and extremely unusual in the O. F. of the period. The minimum acceptable correction of 231 would be *Que ce n'os di* (with the South-Western enclisis of *vos*, cf. *Se il n'os laisent en present* 1243); but the *Que* 'For' is not very plausible, and the original may well have had *Ne ce n'os di* or *Ne nel vos di* or even (as in M⁰) *Ne le vos di*.

254. *Petit savroit a mon corage.* Both E (II 96, 264) and M⁴ (glossary) take *savoir* in the sense of 'have a savour' and so 'be pleasing': 'Little would it be to my taste'. In the absence of a context (the line begins a new development, and the following three lines are illegible), it seems difficult to justify this comparatively rare sense, which is attested chiefly with *mal* in disjunctive locutions like *Ou bel nos soit ou mal nos sace* (*Eneas* 4727). A more probable reconstruction of the argument of 254–6 might be '[Anyone who had such a suspicion about me] would know little of my heart'; for *a* introducing the complement of *savoir* 'know about, have knowledge of' cf. *i* in *A ceste foiz je n'i sai plus* 2427.

269–70. *De mon nevo me fist entendre Mençonge, porqoi ferai pendre.* The meaning is undoubtedly 'wherefore I will have him hanged', and M⁰ corrected to *porqoil.* E (II 98, 250) prefers to consider this and *qui voloit faire* 4149 as examples of the idiomatic non-expression of the complement of the verb *faire*; but this usage is confined to a limited range of cases where *faire* is used as verbum vicarium (as in *Dex! porqoi fist?* 728), or in the sense of 'finish' (as in *Qant il out fait* 2431). Quite different are the numerous cases where the scribe, no doubt influenced by his own pronunciation, has omitted before a word beginning with a consonant the *l* representing the enclitic form of the pers. pron. obj., and it would be more in accordance with normal editorial practice to print *porqoi[l] ferai pendre* 270, also *Ne[l] sot que il* 1308, *por ce[l] t'os bien loer* 2371, *Si que[l] virent ti chevalier* 2564, *Je[l] vos pramet* 2722, *qui[l] voloit faire* 4149 etc. (see also note on 1190–1); similarly with the *l* of the def. art. masc. sing. after the preps. *a* and *de: A[l] terme* 3248 (cf. *Au terme* 3305, 3334), *De[l] tot* 1403, 2693 (cf. *du tot* 168, 397 etc.), *de[l] segroi* 1325 (see note) etc. Where the scribe has in the same way dropped the *l* of the subject pron. *il*, as in 865 where M⁴ prints *Qu'i li pardonast*, E does supply it with *Qu'i*[*l*] *li pardonast* (but see 1690–2 and note); it should be noted that by hypercorrection the scribe has sometimes added a meaningless unpronounced *l* to *Qui*, as in *Qui*(*l*) *n'a hueses, s'en a soffrete* 3683 (see also notes on 3045–7, 3525–9, 3581–2, 3663–5).

303–5. *Bien les veïse entrebaisier; Ges ai oï si gramoier. Or sai je bien n'en ont corage.* The case is even stronger here than at 147–50 (see note) for following Muret's later editions and M⁴ and deleting E's full stop at the end of 304 (to which he still adheres, II 99), in spite of the breaking of the couplet that this entails, and in spite of the presence in the MS. of a large initial at 305. The meaning is clearly 'I have heard them so lament that now I know well that they have no thought of it' (cf. *Vinaver Misc.*, pp. 265–6).

306. *Porqoi cro je si fort outrage?* The spelling *cro* is obviously intended to represent a form of the pret. 1 of *croire*. For this form E (II 99) refers to Fouché, pp. 313–14; but the first person forms there cited are written with *ou* (or Northern *au* or *eu*), not *o*, and correspond to third persons in *-out*, not *-ut*. It is much more probable that *cro* is scribal for *croi* (cf. *çole* 669 for *çoile*, *ro* 600, *ros* 757 for *roi*(*s*) etc.), itself scribal rather than phonetic for *crui* (273; cf. *amedoi* 1677 beside *andui* 88 and *endui* 828, *apoie* 3928 beside *apuie* 236, *ennoie* 3927 for *enuie*).

349. For E's reference (II 106) to the extent of Mark's kingdom see note on 2231–2; for the importance of Arthur's presence at Iseut's *escondit* see note on 3233–64.

357. *Gel blasmé que il me mandot.* For E's note (II 106) see note on 109–11.

373–6. (*Dex*) *vos a fait desevrer Du parlement sanz plus outrer, Que li rois n'a chose veüe Qui ne puise estr'e*[*n*] *bien tenue.* On the construction of 375 E comments (II 107) '*Que* consecutive, or possibly causal? "So that (*or* Since) the king has seen nothing . . .".' The *Que* is

certainly not causal; it could be described as consecutive, taking
this term in a wide sense, but is more precisely modal: 'in such
circumstances that the king has seen nothing . . .', 'without the
king's seeing anything . . .'. Cf. 1005–7 and note.

386. *Dex! tant ert a Tristran sordois!* E comments (II 108) ' "So
much the worse for Tristran", *ert* being either imperfect or
future'. The forms *ert* and *iert* are used for both impf. and fut.,
and must be understood according to the context. E says (II 110)
that here and in *li cuvert Qui vos dïent ce qui ja n'iert* 422 'either tense
fits the context'; but if a past tense were intended it is the pret.
rather than the impf. that would be expected. In view of the
author's fondness for prophetic declarations there can be little
doubt that it is the fut. that is intended in 386; and in 422 *ja n'*
'never' implies the future ('what never was' would be *ce qui ainz
ne fu*; cf. note on 2697–9). See also note on 1061–3. The lists of
forms of *estre* should therefore be corrected in E's glossary and
II 24–5 (in line with M⁰'s glossary, which gives *ert* 386 and 422 as
fut.).

389. *Sire, por Deu, dont venez vos?* According to E (II 109–10)
'Mark only half answers Iseut's questioning . . . Iseut's "dont
venez vos?" remains unanswered'. In O. F., however, the locution
dont venez vos?, dont viens tu? commonly means 'Why are you here?',
i.e. 'What is the matter?' (see, e.g., *Roman du Comte d'Anjou*, ed.
Roques, 2433; *Du Prestre qu'on porte* 58, Montaiglon et Raynaud
IV 3); and here it is fully answered by Mark's *Roïne, ainz vien a vos
parler Et une chose demander.* Cf. Arthur's words to a squire, *Va,
dont viens tu?* 3390, to which the reply is *J'aport novele.*

412–14. *Je t'ai voir dit; si ne m'en croiz, Einz croiz parole [fole et] vaine;
Ma bone foi me fera saine.* E, punctuating thus, takes *si* as the adv.
and translates (II 110) 'I have told you the truth and yet you do not
believe me'. But Iseut has at this stage no reason to suppose that
Mark does not believe her, and 414 as an independent sentence
seems curiously isolated. It is much more probable that the
passage should be punctuated as in Muret and M⁴, with a comma
after *vaine*, *si* being taken as the conj. *se*: 'if you do not believe me,

C

but rather believe foolish and empty talk, my good faith will save me'. The scribe has elsewhere interchanged *si* adv. and *se* conj.: *si* stands for *se* in 2301 (though not, as E implies, in 906), and *se* for *si* in 669 (see notes on these passages).

418–19. *Ne me dist rien, mais je li dui Anor faire.* E translates (II 110) 'He said nothing but that I should pay him honour'. But this sense is inappropriate in the context, and there is in any case no authority for taking *mais* as a conj. introducing a restrictive clause (even *mais que* in such a function is rare, cf. T.-L. V 865). There is no subordination here; *mais* is the co-ordinating conj., and the meaning is 'He said nothing to me (about his reason for wishing to speak to me), but I felt bound to pay him honour'.

421–2. *li cuvert Qui vos dïent ce qui ja n'iert.* See note on 386.

432–5. *A ton nevo parlai ersoir; Molt se conplaint com angoisos, Sire, que l'acordasse a vos. Ge li dis ce qu'il s'en alast.* The context, with the prets. *parlai* and *dis* in the contiguous principal clauses and the dependent impf. subj. *acordasse*, makes it almost certain that *conplaint* is for *conplainst*, pret. (cf. *fraint* in *Cil fraint la cire et lut le brief* 2513). The sense must be, not 'complain' (E, glossary), but 'implore' (cf. T.-L. II 629 and note on 2321–4).

439–41. *Sire, de rien ne mentirez! Il n'i ot plus; se vos volez, Ocïez moi, mes c'iert a tort.* Muret and M⁴ correct *mentirez* to *m'en creirez*; E (II 111) attempts to justify the MS. reading by interpreting 'You will not be in any way mistaken (if you accept my statement that) there was nothing more', assuming an extension of the meaning of *mentir*, 'speak falsely'—'report incorrectly'—'be mistaken, be misled'. But this extension, which he describes as 'very slight', goes far beyond anything attested in Gdf. V 244 or T.-L. V 1444–50. It seems essential to accept Muret's emendation, which, as E admits, 'presupposes a highly probable scribal misreading'.

444. *Dist moi que l'ostel l'aquitasse.* For the substance see note on 204–5. As regards the form of *l'aquitasse*, E (II 26) says that in the text the weak dat. pron. *li* is elided not only, as is common,

before *en* but also in five other instances (444, 798?, 1206, 1946, 3434); he adds (II 27) that *ne li* is reduced to *nul* in 810, but see the note on this line. The elision of *li* before words other than *en* is unusual in O. F., and in 798, 1206, 1946 and 3434 another interpretation is possible (see the notes on these passages). It therefore seems conceivable that in the remaining case the pheno-menon is scribal, and that *l'ostel l'aquitasse* 444 is for, e.g., *l'ostel aquitasse* or *l'ostel li quitasse*; and it is undesirable to introduce *l'* for *li* into passages which can be otherwise accounted for, e.g. to emend *prist l'a la main* 1220 and 3157 to *pris l'a* (= *li a*) *la main*, mentioned as a possibility by E (II 153).

450–3. *Je li feïse l'aquitance, Se je osase, volentiers; Ne sol quatre besanz entiers Ne li vol metre en s'aumosniere.* E's translation of 452–3 is 'Not even four whole sovereigns was I prepared to place in his wallet'; this somewhat forces the sense of the conj. *ne* 'nor' (cf. T.-L. VI 557), and it seems possible that *Ne sol* is scribal for *Nes sol* (*neis, nis*, other monosyllabic forms of *neïs* 'not even', occur in 1038, 1548, 4255).

487–8. *il vos requist quitance De ses gages.* See note on 204–5.

491. *Pitié m'en prist a l'arbre sus.* There are many passages such as this where the scribe has written *a* but the preposition one would expect in the context is *en*; since *en* is sometimes written *an* (652, 996, 1503, 1987 etc.), it is a natural assumption that in such cases the titulus has been omitted (a common error of the scribe's, cf. Ewert, *Pope Studies*, p. 91). Muret accordingly often corrected to *an*; M² prints *an* in 491, 805, 1438, 1729, 2260, 2419, 2599, 2664, 3268, 3464, 3470, 4089, 4339, 4394. E, however, restores the *a* of the MS. wherever this preposition seems to him even remotely possible, and prints *a[n]* only in 1438, 2419, 2599, 3470. M⁴ goes much less far in this direction, restoring *a* for M²'s *an* only in 2664, 3268, 4394, and actually introducing *an* where M² and E had agreed in retaining *a* in 765, 772, 1111, 1447. In the great majority of all these lines it seems probable that the original had *en*; so also in 1467, where all editors keep the *a* of the MS. (see the note).

498–9. *Ainz, par ma foi, ne tant ne quant Ne veïstes qu'il m'aprismast.*
E translates (II 113) 'But rather (*or* instead) you did not see . . .'.
Though the sentence-adv. *ainz* can of course mean 'but (rather)',
as in 296, 413 etc., *ainz* accompanying a negated verb in the preterite (T.-L. I 241–2, under the head-forms *ainc, ains*) is normally
a synonym of *onc, onques,* and the sense here is 'Never . . . did
you see . . .' (cf. *Ainz nu pensames* 561, also 582, 1545, 1787–8,
1928 etc.). See also note on 1033–4.

506–7. *Brengain—que Dex anor te donst!—Por mon nevo va a l'ostel.*
There is no reason why Mark should at this point invoke a blessing
on Brengain (and if he did it would most probably take the form
Dex te donst anor! or *Anor te donst Dex!*). What the context requires
in the king's request is the formula of adjuration *se Dex anor te
donst* 'so may God grant you honour'. The same scribal error,
que for *se* (see also note on 1382–4), occurs in a variant of the same
formula, *que Dex t'enort* 2832, again used in adjuration; the correct
form of this is preserved in *Amis, di moi, se Dex t'anort, Fus tu
donc pus a la roi cort?* 2497–8. Other examples of the construction
in the form *se + Dex +* verb in pres. subj. are (in asseveration) *se
Dex me saut* 2587, *se Dex joie et bien me donge* 2860, *se Damledeu mon
cors seceure* 3232, *se Dex me gart au suen* 4433; for the alternative
form *si +* verb in pres. subj. *+Dex* cf. *Si m'aït Dex* 628, 4201 (both
forms are discussed and illustrated in *F.S.* 8 (1954), 193 ff.). For
the form *anort* 2497, *enort* 2832, see note on 2497–8.

515–16. *por vos le laisera Bien tost que ne me tochera.* For *bien tost* 516
E's glossary (s.v. *bien*) gives 'very soon', but his note (II 114)
concedes that it 'may here (as in 711) mean "perchance"'. In
view of the context there can be little doubt that the meaning is
in fact 'perchance, perhaps' (cf. M², glossary s.v. *bien tost*); so too
not only in 711 but also in 3093, for which see note. For 711 M⁴
(p. 142) gives a somewhat fanciful explanation: '*Bien tost* marque
l'imminence d'une action présentée par le conditionnel suivant
comme très probable et très conforme au caractère du nain';
this overstates the significance of the conditional, since in 516
and 3093 the verb is in the future.

526. *Va tost poroc et ça l'amaine.* For *poroc* E's glossary gives 'therefore'; but *va poroc* means 'go for him, go and fetch him' (cf. T.-L. VII 1614–15).

543. *Fai grant senblant de toi proier.* See note on 89–90.

556–7. *Legirement vos defendez Vers moi, qui ce m'avez mis sure.* E translates (II 116) 'you who have brought this upon me': more accurately, 'who have laid this charge against me', cf. in his glossary s.v. *sure* '*metre sure* lay upon, accuse of'.

557–9. *ce m'avez mis sure, Dont li mien cor el ventre pleure, Si grant desroi, tel felonie!* E translates (II 116) 'have brought this upon me whereat my heart weeps within me, such great wrong, such wickedness!', taking *desroi* and *felonie* as nouns in apposition with *ce* (. . . *dont* . . .). In a comment on 4219–20 (for which see note) I suggested (*Vinaver Misc.*, p. 267) that 559 should be understood as an independent exclamation. E objects that putting a full stop after *pleure* 558 'would obscure a characteristic feature of Beroul's style'; but elsewhere he stresses the poet's 'exclamatory and declamatory presentation' (II 44, cf. 78), and though there seem to be no other exact parallels to 559 and 4219, taken as I suggest, exclamations of the same grammatical structure, but with *quel* instead of *si* or *tel*, occur commonly throughout the text: *quel pechié!* 700, *quel aventure!* 1237, *quel mervelle que . . .!* 3072, 3230 etc.

560–1. *Dannez seroie et el honie; Ainz nu pensames, Dex le set.* E explains (II 116) 'I should have been damned and she disgraced (sc. if you had given effect to your intention). Never did we harbour such thoughts, God knows'. But there has been no reference to Mark's intentions: Tristran clearly means 'I should be damned and she disgraced (if this accusation were well founded; but) never did we . . .'.

565. *Ne portë ire a la roïne.* So also M², M⁴; but perhaps rather *Ne porte irë a la roïne* (hiatus seems to occur much more frequently after the fourth or fifth syllable than after the second or third).

576. *Sovent cline l'un vers son per;* cf. *Perinis l'oit, le chief li cline* 3482; *Dinas estoit o la roïne, Aperçut soi, de l'uiel li cline* 3853–4. The verb in 3482 is clearly *cliner* 'nod, bow', that in 3854 *cl(u)ignier* 'wink'; for that in 576 E's glossary as reprinted in 1967 gives 'wink' (though his note in II 117 says '*cline* may be for *cligne* "winks", and not "bows" as the glossary has it'), and this sense alone is given by Muret and M⁴ and T.-L. II 505. To judge by the other examples in T.-L. s.vv. *cliner* and *cluignier*, a verb followed by *vers* and unaccompanied by *de l'ueil* is more likely to be *cliner*.

601–2. *Ou il nos aint ou il nos hast, Nos volon son nevo en chast.* The pres. subj. form *hast* is not given by Fouché (p. 160) or Pope (§960), and there is no other example in T.-L.; E therefore suggests (II 24) that the poet may have written *hace*, the usual form, and *chace* with analogical -*e*. But *chast* is confirmed by *Qui chast sa beste por ataindre* 1875 (where *chace* is metrically impossible) and by the first person form *chaz* 3067 (see note); and in any case, if the original had had analogical *chace*, it seems unlikely that a later scribe would revert to *chast*. Perhaps, therefore, *hast* was a localized form developed (on the basis of pres. indic. 1 *haz*, *has* etc. and on the vague analogy of *chaz*, *chast*) in this particular disjunctive locution, to correspond with *aint*.

612. *Ne set qu'il die, sovent erre.* Opinions differ about the identification of *erre*. E (glossary), like M⁰, takes it as from *errer* < ITERARE (as in *tant ont erré* 2290, also 2454, 2481 etc.) 'walk, travel'; M⁴ (glossary) appears to hesitate between ITERARE 'marcher' and ERRARE 'être perplexe'; T.-L. (III 775) cites the line under *errer* < ERRARE and translates 'unschlüssig hin und her gehen' but gives no other example of this sense. Indeed, it seems doubtful whether the verb *errer* < ERRARE was in use at all as early as the twelfth century; the only other passage of this period cited by Gdf. or T.-L. is *S. Thom.* 4569, where *les justises erranz* appears to be correctly interpreted by Walberg as referring to the itinerant judges ('justices-errant' or 'judges justices in eyre'). The sense of *sovent*, as often elsewhere in the poem (1985, 3928 etc.), is 'repeatedly, continually', and *sovent erre* may be translated 'he keeps walking up and down'; E's 'he walks up and down (dis-

tracted?)' (II 121) may perhaps be justified if we can assume a certain semantic influence of the noun *error*, which occurs in the text (360, 2217) in the not uncommon sense of 'uncertainty, anxiety' (cf. T.-L. III 781–2).

628–9. *molt me mervel Que mes niés ma vergonde ait quise.* The MS. has *meuergonderoit* with the second *r* crossed out and the second *o* converted into *a*. Muret's emendation is plausible in substance, but the subj. *ait* is abnormal in this construction in O. F. (see note on 109–11).

646–8 *Dehé aient tuit cil devin! Qui porpensa tel felonie Con fist cist nain, qui Dex maudie?* The lines are so punctuated also by M⁴; but 'who planned (thought up) such wickedness as did this dwarf?' hardly makes sense. There was therefore much to be said for the emendation *porpensast*, proposed by G. Paris and adopted by Muret (M⁰–M²), 'who (else) would (ever) have devised such wickedness as did this dwarf?'; cf. *Qui pensast mais tel traïson?* 678 (there are other cases where the scribe has dropped the final *-st* of a verb-form, e.g. *tenti* 1530 for *tentist* : *s'esbaudist, Fu* 1726 for *Fust*, and see note on 4111–13). In the general context, however, it is perhaps more probable that the curse in 646 was not directed against all soothsayers without exception, that *cil* has determining force, not merely that of a def. art., that *porpensa* is an error for *porpensent* and that the lines should be punctuated *Dehé aient tuit cil devin Qui porpensent tel felonie Con fist cist nain, qui Dex maudie!*

649–51. *Di ton nevo q'au roi Artur, A Carduel, qui est clos de mur, Coviengne qu'il aut par matin.* The MS. has *qu'il alle*, corrected in all recent editions to *qu'il aut* on metrical grounds and because the 3rd person sing. pres. subj. form *alle* does not occur elsewhere in the text (1 *alle* 1933, 3344 etc., 2 *alles* 2818, 6 *allent* 465, but 3 *aut* 1501, 1958 etc., *voist* 4321). However, the 3rd person sing. form *a(i)lle* is well attested in O.F., especially in the Western region, while on the other hand there is no justification here for the subjunctive *coviengne*, since the meaning is 'Tell your nephew that it *is* necessary . . .', requiring the pres. indic. of *covenir*. The scribe's

version may have been suggested by his awareness of the alternative possibility of saying *Di ton nevo qu'il alle a Carduel* 'tell your
nephew (that he is) to go to Carlisle'; but the original text was no
doubt the grammatically and metrically correct *Di ton nevo q'au
roi Artur . . . Covient qu'il alle par matin* (as in M⁰ and M¹); cf.
Di je li mant (pres. indic.) *qu'il vienge a moi* 510. There is, however, a
difficulty of substance here: when that evening Tristran is given
the order prescribed by the dwarf, he agrees to do exactly what is
stated in 651: '*Rois, ge irai bien par matin*' 691, yet this is rejected
by Mark: '*O vos, ainz que la nuit ait fin*' 692. It would therefore
appear that *par matin* 651 may be corrupt.

656–8. *Anevoies, en ceste nuit, Sai que voudra a lui parler, Por Deu, que
devra la aler.* E (II 123) explains *que* 658 as 'causal'; but the only
causal function it could have would be that of co-ordinating
que = *car* 'for', which is unsatisfactory in the context. E does not
account for the use of parenthetical *Por Deu* 'in God's name', 'for
God's sake', which occurs frequently in the text, but usually in
supplication or adjuration with an imper. or its equivalent (see
note on 147–50, also 217, 517, 784, 797, 804 etc.), more rarely in
emotional asseveration (5, 219 etc.), and never in a context like
this. Muret's emendation to *Por ceu que* (retained in M⁴) gives not
merely a 'smoother reading', as E says, but the only acceptable
construction. The form *ceu* was no doubt chosen in order to
reduce the correction to one letter (E equates it with *ço*, but it is
surely intended as the vocalized form of neuter *cel*, used in 185); it
is more probable that the reading should be *Por ce que*, as in 71,
3111. For the sense of *parler* 657 see note on 1933.

663–4. *Et s'il i vient, et ge nul sai, Se tu nu voiz, si me desfai.* M³'s
correction to *s'il n'i vient* is rightly rejected by E and M⁴. For
et ge nul sai M⁴ (glossary s.v. *savoir*) gives 'je n'en sais rien, je n'y
entends rien', which seems fanciful. The couplet is clumsy, but
the meaning is no doubt covered by E's translation (II 123) 'If he
comes there (*or* to her) without my knowing it and without your
seeing it (*or* him), then kill me'.

669. *Et se li çole l'envoier.* *Se* here stands for *si* < SIC; E says (II 124)

that it is unnecessary, with Tanquerey, to correct the text to *si*, because the form *se* is often used for *si*, particularly if the following word contains an *i*. This is true of O. F. generally, but there is no other example of *se* for *si* in the text (the *se* in 2863, given in the glossary under *si*, is correctly taken as *se* in II 215). On the other hand, *si* is elsewhere used for *se*: see notes on 412–14 and 2301–2.

697–8. *En son cuer dist qu'il parleroit A la roïne, s'il pooit.* E and M⁴ retain this couplet, corrected by Muret from the three lines in the MS., *En son cuer dist qu'il parleret A la roine parleroit Al ajorner se il pooit;* E also mentions (II 128) the possibility that the scribe had omitted one line out of two couplets on the same rhyme (but see note on 160–2). In favour of the alternative single couplet *En son cuer dist que s'il pooit A la roïne parleroit* (based on comparison with the MS. readings at 1631–2 and 1833–4) see *Vinaver Misc.*, pp. 274–5. For the explanation of such MS. readings as 'variant redactions' see note on 207–10. For the sense of *parleroit* 697 see note on 1932–4.

711–13. *Bien tost a ceste place Espandroit flor por nostre trace Veer, se l'un a l'autre iroit.* For *bien tost* 'perhaps' see note on 515–16. The punctuation adopted by Muret, E and M⁴ brings together *por nostre trace veer* 'to see our tracks', and thereby separates off *se l'un a l'autre iroit*, making it look like a conditional clause, 'in case the one should go to the other'. But such a sense could be expressed in Continental O. F. only by the impf. subj. *alast* or the impf. indic. *aloit*; and the MS. reading *iroit* is confirmed by the rhyme-word *feroit* 714. The clause *se l'un a l'autre iroit* must therefore be an indirect question, 'whether the one would go to the other', depending on *veer*. Unless it is assumed that this can simultaneously have as complements the noun *nostre trace* and the clause *se l'un a l'autre iroit*, it seems necessary to punctuate with a comma after *trace* instead of after *veer*: 'would be sprinkling flour for our footprints, to see whether the one would go to the other'.

725–8. *Dedenz la chanbre n'out clartez, Cirge ne lanpë alumez.*

Tristran se fu sus piez levez. Dex! porqoi fist? Or escoutez! E comments (II 128) that these are 'four consecutive lines rhyming together, a common feature in Norman and Anglo-Norman works'. It is true that as written in the MS. all four lines end in *-ez*; but while this is the normal grammatical ending for *levez* : *escoutez* 727–8, it is probable that 725–6 originally ended in *-é*: *Dedenz la chanbre n'out clarté, Cirge ne lanpë* (or perhaps rather *Lanpe ne cirgë*) *alumé*. (M⁰ had suggested, pp. xxxi and 253, correcting to *Cirges ne lanpes*; but in a generalizing negative sentence of this kind the singular is normal). This passage should not, therefore, be cited in support of hypothetical sequences of four lines on the same rhyme elsewhere (see note on 160–2).

731–5. *Sa plaie escrive, forment saine; Le sanc qui(en)n ist les dras ensaigne. La plaie saigne; ne la sent, Qar trop a son delit entent. En plusors leus li sanc aüne.* If *saine, sanc, ensaigne, saigne, sanc* all mean 'bleed', '(cover with) blood', the repetition seems excessive; it is possible that *ensaigne* 732 is to be taken, not as 'cover with blood' (Muret, E and M⁴) but as 'mark' (cf. T.-L. III 517).

755. *Molt grant miracle Deus i out.* So also M⁰ and M⁴; Muret's later editions corrected *Deus*, nom., to *Deu*, obl., 'miracle of God'. E admits (II 129) that *Deu* is probably the original reading, but thinks it is possible to take *Deus* as a nom. and *out* as the equivalent of *fist*; in the absence of cited evidence, such a use of *avoir* seems unlikely.

771–2. *Li troi baron sont en la chanbre, Tristran par ire a son lit prenent.* The MS. text is retained by E, and also by M⁴ with the sole correction of *an* for *a* (cf. note on 491); but E now says (II 130) that *chanbre* and *prenent* 'cannot possibly rhyme'. Instead of assuming, with Muret, that there is a lacuna between the two lines (though this is mentioned as a possibility in II 13), he tentatively suggests correcting 772 to *Tristran pensent a son lit prendre.* If, however, the tonic vowels in *chanbre* and *prendre* can assonate, there seems to be no reason why *chanbre* : *prenent* should not form an assonance comparable to those admitted by E and M⁴ in *asente* : *enfle* 331–2, *roïne* : *oïe* 2627–8 etc.

783–5. *Il li crie: 'Sire, merci! Por Deu, qui pasion soufri; Sire, de nos pitié vos prenge!'* E's punctuation, with semi-colon after *soufri*, must be inspired by his reluctance to accept the 'broken' couplet; but see note on 147–50. The sense is better satisfied by the punctuation of Muret and M⁴, with comma after *soufri*.

789–90. *Ne fust por vos acorocier, Cist plez fust ja venduz molt chier.* Muret, followed by M⁴, prints *a corocier;* in justification of his retention of the MS. form *acorocier* E (II 131) refers to Gdf. I 79, but the only other two examples there cited could also be read as *a correcier* and *a corrocié* respectively, and T.-L. has no article *acorocier*. An editor is not bound by the scribal word-divisions that appear in the MS. (cf. note on 29–30), and the construction *por* (. . .) *a*+infin. is well attested in O. F. (cf. T.-L. I 24); though it is in general North-Eastern, it is more widespread in the concessive sense which it has here (cf. *Twelve Fabliaux*, note on 12. 530).

798. *Tristran l'encline.* E's glossary, like that of M⁰, lists *encliner* here as *v.n.*, and his note says that the verb 'more commonly' takes an indirect object; but both Gdf. (III 106) and T.-L. (III 212) give many examples of the transitive use, and in spite of *La roïne li enclina* 3158 it is probable that *l'* here stands for *le*, not *li* (cf. note on 444).

809–12. *Ja, se Tristran ice seüst, Que escondire nul leüst, Mex se laisast vif depecier Que lui ne lié soufrist l'ier.* E's glossary, s.v. *ja*, cites 809 under the gloss 'well, truly, of course, so much as'; but none of these translations seems possible here. If *Ja* can be understood as associated with the clause in 812, this would mean 'than he would *ever* have allowed himself or her to be bound' (i.e. the sentence begins with *Ja* on the assumption that it will conclude *Ne soufrist lui ne lié l'ier*). Alternatively, *Ja* may be an error for *Quar*; cf. 821.

810. *Que escondire nul leüst.* E hesitates about the interpretation of *nul*. In his note (II 132; similarly M⁴, glossary) he says that it stands for *ne le*, *le* being the personal object of *escondire* and

impersonal *leüst* being used without an indirect object of the person: 'that there would be no leave to defend himself'. In II 27, however, it is stated that *nul* stands for *ne li* (similarly M², glossary). Neither of these analyses is satisfactory: as to the first, *loisir* is not used without an object of the person (cf. T.-L. V 615–17), and the personal object of *escondire*, if expressed, would take the reflexive form (*ne li leüst (soi) escondire*); as to the second, *ne li* is not elsewhere reduced to *nul* (see note on 444). As Gdf. and T.-L. have a few examples of *loisir* with a direct object of the person (i.e. an accusative and infin. construction), e.g. *S'ensemble les leüst ester* (*Troie* 19787), it is probable that *nul* here stands for *ne le*, the *le* being the personal direct object of *leüst* and the refl. object of *escondire* remaining unexpressed.

813–16. *en Deu tant fort se fiot Que bien savoit et bien quidoit, S'a escondit peüst venir, Nus n'en osast armes saisir.* E says (II 132) that '*Que* 814 might be interpreted as causal (with comma after *fiot*)'; but this would make 813 less than plausible, and there is no difficulty about the obvious interpretation implied by the punctuation in the text of all editors, with *Que* consecutive: 'he trusted so firmly in God that he knew . . .'.

819–20. *Por ce ne vout il vers le roi Mesfaire soi por nul desroi.* In 819 the MS. has *ne se vout vers le roi*; the reflexive object of *mesfaire* is thus expressed twice over. Both Muret and E consider that it is the *se* in 819 that is redundant, and emend to exclude it (Muret, followed by M⁴, to *ne vout envers le roi*). In fact, it is this *se* accompanying the finite verb, and not the *soi* with the infin., that is in accordance with normal O. F. syntax; and though in this respect Beroul's usage is sometimes irregular (notably in *se mes oncles veut soufrir Moi a sa cort* 2311–12) it is most probably here the *soi* that is corrupt. It may well have been substituted for another monosyllable under the influence of the rhyme-words *roi* : *desroi* (cf. notes on 1987–90, 2365–70, 3870–2, 4241–6). E suggests (II 132) that it might perhaps be a graphy for *ç'oi*, used parenthetically as in *il est vostre niés, ç'oi dire* 425; but although the scribe's spelling would be no bar to this (cf. note on 3044), such a use of *ç'oi* alone, without *dire*, seems unlikely.

821–3. *s'il seüst ce que en fut Et ce qui avenir lor dut, Il les eüst tüez toz trois*. E says (II 132) that *qui* 822 might be interpreted as *qu'i* (so also M⁰, pp. 224, 253); but if the *i* is intended as the pronominal adv., it could not come in this position (the only possible O. F. word-order would be *ce qu'avenir lor i dut*). Apart from *qui*, rel. pron. nom. (as in the editions), the only other interpretation of the MS. reading would be *qu'i* standing for *qu'il*, with *il* impersonal pron. subject; but this reduction is unlikely before a vowel (for *qu'i = qu'il* before consonant see note on 269–70).

830. *Et que li rois destruire eus veut*. The scribe's *destruire eus veut* probably stands for *destruires veut*, with -*s* representing the weak pron. obj. *les* enclitically attached to the infin. before the finite verb (cf. T.-L. IV 1330); this was by the later twelfth century a South-Western peculiarity (Pope §838), like the commoner parallel treatment of the masc. sing. *le* as in *Cil li dïent que faire el* (i.e. *fairel*) *doit* (*Eneas* 2235; cf. 1852, 5855 and T.-L. IV 1324–5).

835–6. *Qel damage qu'e[n] traïson Vos ont fait prendre cil gloton!* It is possible that *ont fait prendre* here = *ont pris*; cf. note on 3221.

856–7. *Il vos navra d'un javelot, Sire, dont tu deüs morir*. E translates (II 133–4) 'of which you were like to die', but then goes on to add 'i.e. were doomed to die (had you not been miraculously healed by Iseut)'; similarly on *dut estre ars* 1500 'was to be burnt' (II 169), *dut mort recevoir* 1733 'was to have met his death' (II 177). For *par lui . . . Durent il estre tuit destruit* 1705, however, the glossary (s.v. *devoir*) gives 'be about to, be on the point of'. In all these passages, and in *Con deüstes por moi morir Et je redui por vos perir!* 1239–40 (where the glossary, s.v. *redevoir*, gives 'be destined to'), in *Tant lor dut estre pesme et dure!* 1836 and in *a tort dut por moi morir* 2596, the sense of the pret. of *devoir* is merely 'came near to (doing), narrowly failed (to do)'; cf. the glossaries of Muret and M⁴, which give for 1705, 1733 and 1836 'être sur le point de, faillir', and T.-L. II 1891 'nahe daran sein etw. zu tun, was aber nicht getan wird; beinahe etw. tun', with many examples including Beroul 857. The rarer corresponding use of the impf. is probably to be seen in *Ses niés, qui il devoit ardoir* 1067 'whom he was about to burn'.

867–70. *Li rois conmande espines querre . . . Li rois . . . Par tot fait querre les sarmenz*. According to E (II 135), 'Once again it would seem that an unsatisfactory text has resulted from the incorporation of alternative variant readings'; but see note on 207–10.

891–2. *Por estre moi desherité Ne lairoie nes arde en ré*. See note on 3564–5.

892–4. *Ne lairoie nes arde en ré; Se j'en sui araisnié jamais, Laisiez m'en tot ester en pais*. (The MS. has *nel arde*, corrected by M³, E and M⁴). E mentions (II 136) the suggestion in M⁴ (p. 142) that, with a comma after 892 and a full stop after 893, these lines might be understood as 'je ne renoncerais pas à les brûler sur le bûcher, quoi qu'on puisse m'en dire maintenant ou plus tard'; but it is hardly conceivable that *se . . . jamais* could have the pronominal and concessive sense of 'whatever . . . at any time'. E's own tentative proposal is to take 893 as 'exclamatory, i.e. postulating a condition with an implied threat, the same thought being repeated imperatively in 894'. This presumably means that it would constitute an aposiopesis, *Se j'en sui araisnié jamais . . .!*, which is no doubt a possibility, though there seems to be no parallel in the text (211 and 1055 contain logically uncompleted conditional clauses, but could not be similarly explained). Elsewhere E speaks in general terms of 'the concessive or conditional clause being given an exclamatory turn' (II 78), but the only examples he cites are 23 and 58, neither of which contains a concessive or conditional clause (in *Qui sor mon cors mete flaele* 23 the exclamation is a relative clause with verb in the optative subjunctive, and the conditional clause in 24–5 is not itself exclamatory; in *Si voient il Deu et son reigne!* 58 the exclamation is an asseverative formula introduced by *si* < sic, cf. note on 56–9).

906–7. *Qui m'oceïst, si garisiez, Ce fust grant joie, beaus amis*. E's glossary cites *si* 906 under *se* 'if' (so also M⁰), and his note (II 136) translates 'provided you were safe'. But although the spelling *si* does occur in the text for *se* 'if' (see note on 412–14), what we have here is the adv. or sentence-conjunction *si* 'and', the conditional notion being expressed by the impf. subjunctive alone: 'if I were to be killed and you were safe'.

911. (*Damledé*) *Ne vieat pas mort de pecheor.* This is, if not a pro-verbial locution (see note on 40), at least a familiar quotation, based on Ezekiel 33, 11 (*Nolo mortem impii, sed ut convertatur impius a via sua et vivat*). The best-known instance in medieval French is perhaps Villon's *Je suis pecheur, je le sçay bien; Pourtant ne veult pas Dieu ma mort, Mais convertisse et vive en bien* (*Test.* 105–7; earlier versions cited in ed. Thuasne, II 104 f.).

923. *S'uns escureus de lui sausist.* Neither E nor M⁴ comments on the form *sausist* as impf. subj. of *salir*, *saillir* (as against the usual *salist*). It is not mentioned in Fouché or Pope, but Gdf. has an example (VII 287) from *Les Loherains* (*Anseïs de Metz*). It may have arisen by analogy with *fausist*, itself abnormal for *falist* but attested in, e.g. *Erec* 35, 4225.

955–8. *La chapele ert plaine de pueple. Tristran saut sus; l'araine ert moble. Toz a genoz sont en l'iglise; Cil l'atendent defors l'iglise.* E has emended the MS. text only to the extent of printing *en l'iglise* 957 for *en ligliglise*; M⁴ retains Muret's correction to *chiet en la glise* 'falls in the mud' (with comma, not full stop, after *moble*), and suggests (p. 142) that *sus* may be an error for *jus* 'down'. E (II 139) explains his text of 956–8 as meaning 'Tristran leaps to his feet, (uninjured because) the sand was soft and yielding; all (the worshippers; *toz* for *tuit*) continue their orisons (while) the captors wait outside the chapel'; he considers the identical rhyme *en l'iglise* : *defors l'iglise* to be acceptable (II 5–6). While admitting that the narrative is here disjointed, he does not discuss any of the emendations or alternative interpretations that have been pro-posed. Even assuming that there has been no other corruption of the actual words, it might be suggested that the scribe has inter-verted 955 and 956 (cf. note on 65–8): the present 956 would follow on naturally from 948–54, and the sequence 955–957–958 would give a much less disjointed narrative. But the rhyme *l'iglise* : *l'iglise* is unlikely to go back to the original; since elsewhere the scribe has regularly copied *tuit* correctly as the masc. nom. pl. form (except in 4183, where he wrote *Quit*), it is probable that *Toz* in his model was nom. sing.; and *sus* could easily be an error for *jus* (the scribe has often confused the preps. and advs. for 'on, over' and 'under', e.g. 404, 3919, 3945, and indeed other pairs of words of opposite meaning, see note on 2020–3). On the whole, therefore, the most probable reading for 956–7 seems to be that proposed by M⁴, *Tristran saut jus; l'araine ert moble, Toz a genoz chiet en la glise.*

971–4. *Molt ot li mestre Tristran chier, Qant il son brant ne vout laisier, Ançois le prist la ou estoit; Avoc le suen l'en aportoit.* In 974 the MS. repeats *la ou estoit*; Muret's correction *l'en aportoit* is adopted by M⁴ as well as E. Rhymes such as that in the MS. here, or in *Doner ne puet nus penitance A pecheor souz penitance* 1391–2 (MS.), and in 1553–4, 1693–4 etc., (ten in all) are described by E (II 4, 7) as 'instances of homoeoteleuton'. This seems to be a rather imprecise use of the term homoeoteleuton, which is surely better restricted to the sense in which it is applied to medieval texts by scholars such as E. Vinaver ('Principles of Textual Emendation', *Pope Studies*, pp. 355–7)—i.e. to the case where the copyist, turning his eyes back to his model, picks up the text, not from the place at which he left it but from another place at which the same feature occurs, and then copies on from there. A good example in Beroul is 1807, where the model must have read *Sa chemise out Iseut vestue* but the scribe, after writing the -*ut* of *out*, erroneously looked back to the -*ut* of *Iseut* and consequently wrote only *Sa chemise out vestue.* The ten rhymes listed by E are obviously not 'instances of homoeoteleuton' in this sense; nor are they, indeed, clearly distinguishable from the ten other repetitive rhymes described by E (II 5) as 'identical in the strict sense of the term' (193–4, 957–8, 1301–2 etc.). E, however, has corrected the first group but left the second as they stand on the ground that we cannot be certain that they were not tolerated.

982–4. *Qant n'ai Yseut, rien ne me vaut, Dolent, le saut que orainz fis; Que dut ice que ne m'ocis?* Muret emended *le saut* to *el saut*, and punctuated with full stop after *vaut*, exclamation mark after *Dolent* and comma after *fis*: 'in the leap that I made why did I not kill myself?' M⁴ restores *le saut*, but puts an exclamation mark after *fis*: 'Malheureux que je suis! Le saut que j'ai fait! Comment ne me suis-je pas tué?' (p. 143); but this implies a much more disjointed and exclamatory style than is attested elsewhere in the poem. E's interpretation, in which *le saut que orainz fis* becomes the subject of *vaut*, breaks the couplet but is otherwise preferable: 'it avails me nothing, wretch that I am, the leap which I made but now. What did it portend that I did not kill myself?' (II 140).

984–6. *Que dut ice que ne m'ocis? Ce me peüst estre molt tart! Eschapé sui! Yseut, l'en t'art!* 985 is translated by E (II 140) 'It might yet be a matter of regret to me' (his glossary, s.v. *tart*, gives '*estre t. a* be displeasing to 985'), which corresponds to Muret's 'j'aurai peut-être à le regretter' (glossary s.v. *tart*); M⁴, however (p. 143), gives 'ç'aurait bien pu m'arriver trop tard', or in a freer rendering 'il n'était que temps'. The locution *estre tart a aucun* (usually followed by *que*+subjunctive or *de*+infin.) is rare in this absolute form, but cf. *Antre vos m'estuet ci morir, Tart me sera, molt le desir* (*Eneas* 1061–2, cf. 10082–3); for the hypothetical use of *peüst* cf. *Il me peüst trop loin sanbler Sol a demain a demorer* (*Eneas* 10011–12). The meaning of Beroul 985 therefore appears to be 'I might well be impatient, eager, for it (*sc.* death)'.

994. *Par ci trespasse maintes genz* (: *dedenz*). M⁴ comments (glossary s.v. *trespasser*) 'emploi impersonnel: par ici il passe maintes gens', but this is a modern rather than an O. F. construction; E (II 141) is no doubt right in tentatively proposing correction to *trespassent*.

996–8. *Et se en l'art, jamais an cele Ne montez vos, se vos briment N'en prenez enprés vengement.* At first sight *enprés* 'afterwards' is unexpected; Muret corrected it to *aspre* (cf. *s'or n'en prens aspre venjance* 1903); E and M⁴ restore *enprés*, which according to E (II 141) is to be taken closely with *briment*, 'quickly thereafter, without delay'. It is also possible that *enprés* is an error for *senpres* 'immediately' (cf. *A lui seus senpres se repent* 2160).

1005–7. *S'or estïez, beau sire, ocis, Que vengement n'en fust ainz pris,*

D

Jamais nul jor n'avroie joie. In E's glossary *que* 1006 is described as '(concessive) = *sans que*'; but while *que . . . ne* can be considered as equivalent to Mod. F. *sans que*, the function of both conjunctions is not concessive but modal ('in such circumstances that vengeance were not taken', 'without vengeance being taken'); cf. note on 373–6.

1007–9. '. . . *Jamais nul jor n'avroie joie.*' *Tristran respont:* '*Trop vos anoie: Beau mestre, n'ai point de m'espee.*' There is no obvious reason why, in reply to Governal's declaration that he would never again be happy if his master were killed, Tristran should say 'It distresses you too much (*or* greatly)'. In any case, the strong forms of the verb *enoier* normally have in O. F. the diphthong *ui*, and elsewhere in the poem they rhyme only with words in *ui* (*ennuit* 2819 : *nuit*; the noun *ennui* 2422 : *je sui*, 3146 and 3469 : *pui*; the rhyme *ennoie : apoie* 3927–8 is scribal for *ennuie : apuie*). M⁰ had already expressed the suspicion (p. xxxviii) that the end of 1008 might be corrupt. It may be conjectured that its original form was *Dex vos an oie!* 'May God hear you with regard to it!', i.e. 'May God grant your wish (that I should be avenged)!' *Deus vos en oie!* is a very common formula in O. F.; T.-L. (VI 1035) gives half a dozen examples (to which may be added *Atre per.* 2648), nearly all, as here, rhyming with *joie* (cf. *joie : oie* 3507–8). It is not clear why the scribe should have written *trop* for *dex*; but some of his other errors are equally inexplicable.

1009. *Beau mestre, n'ai point de m'espee.* E comments (II 141) '*de* being due to the fact that *point* still retained some of its original substantival force, or by analogy with partitive uses (*pas de*, etc.)?' The use of *mie* or *point* with partitive *de* and a noun designating a specific individual (thing or person) is quite normal in O. F.; a close analogue is *de s'espee ne volt mie guerpir* (*Rol.* 465), and many other examples are cited in T.-L. VI 16–17, VII 1315–17 (numbered 2115–17). There is no question, however, of analogy with *pas de*, for *pas* was not at this period used with partitive *de* (cf. G. Price in *Archivum Linguisticum* 14 (1962), 16).

1030–1. *Avoé sont tuit li borjois Et trestuit cil de la cité.* The MS.

has *Avoc sont*, which was emended by Muret first to *Avoc lui sont*, then at Acher's suggestion to *Avocques sont* (*avoques, ovocques* occurs in 2174, 2867 as prep., but not in the text as adv.). Tanquerey proposed the less extensive correction (*e* for *c*) *Avoé*, which he understood as a spelling of *Avoié* 'directed, instructed'; E retains the form *Avoé* but interprets it quite differently, as the representative of ADVOCATI. In order to have the sense of 'retainers' which he attributes to it (II 141), it must be taken to be, not the well-attested noun *avoé* 'protector, (feudal) lord', but the past part. of the verb *avoer*. E's glossary gives this as '*v.a.* avow, acknowledge as vassal'; but in fact the normal sense of the trans. verb is 'acknowledge as (feudal) lord', and the only example of the converse sense given by T.-L. (I 749) is Beroul 210 (*u monde n'a cort, S'i vois, li sires ne m'avot*), where M⁴ (p.141) suggests the not unplausible correction to *anort*. The past part. *avoé* in 1030 may, however, be taken as that of the refl. verb *soi avoer* 'acknowledge oneself as vassal' (T.-L. I 750); this is normally followed by a complement introduced by *de*, *a* or *par* indicating the feudal superior acknowledged, but T.-L. has one example where the past part. is used absolutely, *A li se fet bon avoer, Car bien garde ses avoez* (*Miracles de N.-D. de Chartres* 2).

1033–4. *cil qui ainz te porra prendre, S'il ne te prent, fera le pendre.* For *ainz* here E's glossary gives 'ever', that of M⁰ 'jamais' and that of M⁴ 'en un temps, un lieu quelconque'; they therefore identify it with the *ainc, ains, ainz* of T.-L. I 241–2, which is a synonym of *onc, onques* (cf. note on 498–9). Like *onc*, however, *ainc* or *ainz* 'ever' is not found with a verb in the future tense (see note on 2697–9). The meaning of *ainz* here (T.-L. I 247–9) is 'first, most quickly', as in the common idiomatic expression *qui ainz ainz* and in proverbs of the type *Qui ainz nest ainz pest* (Morawski 1797). There seems to be no justification for the second element in M⁴'s glosses 'en . . . un lieu quelconque; avec une négation, . . . nulle part'; in all the lines quoted the sense of *ainz* is purely temporal, or (as in *ainz n'i ot rue Ne fust de paile portendue* 2967–8) temporal-intensive.

1035. *Chascun aime mex soi que toi* (: *le hui*). E (II 141) now accepts

Muret's emendation (retained by M[4]) *qu'autrui*; apart from the suspect rhyme *toi* : *hui*, what is required by the context is a sententious statement of general application, and the corrected text corresponds to the proverb *Qui mielz aime autrui que soi au molin fu morz* (var. *murt, mora*) *de suef* (corr. *de soi*) (Morawski 1992, cf. 1993.)

1051–4. *Si l'avoit fait lïer li rois . . . Qu'il li out si les poinz estroiz Li sanc li est par toz les doiz.* In the MS. text, as printed by E and M[4], *il* 1053 must refer to Mark, though in view of 1051 it can hardly be implied that he personally bound Iseut's hands (see, however, note on 89–90). M[0] and M[1] had very plausibly emended to *il li ont*, with the indeterminate use of the third person plural, 'they', 'people' (no doubt those indirectly referred to in 1051). The tense of *ont estroiz* also corresponds better to the present *est* 1054.

1054. *Li sanc li est par toz les doiz.* E (II 144) describes *est* as an Eastern dialectal form for *ist*. The Central form *ist* has *i* representing the reduction of the triphthong *iei* arising from the breaking of tonic open *e* followed by yod in EXIT (Pope §§410–11). In the East and North-East breaking before palatal did not occur, and here the form to be expected is *eist* (Pope §§1321, i and 1322, x). In that part of the West which Miss Pope calls the 'South-Western Region' (§1327: Anjou, Maine, Touraine, Brittany and S. Normandy—quite different from the 'S.W.' of Ewert, II 29, which is south of the Loire and belongs to Miss Pope's 'Southern Border Dialects', §1329), the form to be expected is *iest* or *eist* (Pope §1327, i), cf. spellings in the text such as *lié, liez, mié* (Central *li, liz, mi*). However, spellings with *e* alone are also found in both East and West (see, e.g., Schwan-Behrens, *Grammaire de l'ancien français*, tr. O. Bloch, Leipzig, 1913, §50 R. 1 and III 96); and the spelling *est* for *ist* in the Beroul MS. is at least as likely to be a Western as an Eastern form (it is characterized as Western by, e.g., M[2], p. xi and M[4], p. x). In this context, however, there are also other possible explanations: *li est* may be scribal for *li iest* (with clearly Western *ie*), or it may be by differentiation from *li ist*, like the well-attested sequences *li era, i era* for *li ira, i ira* (see *Twelve Fabliaux*, note on 7.110).

1055–9. '*Par Deu!' fait el, 'se je mes jor . . . Qant li felon losengeor, Qui garder durent mon ami, L'ont deperdu, la Deu merci, Ne me devroit l'on mes proisier*'. All editors assume a lacuna between 1055 and 1056; since in the language of the poem *jor* and *losengeor* rhyme, this would mean the omission either of two lines also rhyming in *-or*, or of at least four lines (see note on 160–2). I have therefore suggested (*Vinaver Misc.*, p. 280) that more probably there is no lacuna, but *mes jor* 1055 is corrupt; and I proposed to correct it to *m'esplor* 'if I burst into tears' (both the rhyme *esplor* : *losengeor* and the construction with present indic. in the protasis and conditional in the apodosis are paralleled elsewhere in the text). B. Blakey (*F. S.* 21 (1967), 99) has since suggested *m'escor*, for *m'acor* 'grieve', which is, as he says, palaeographically closer to *mes jor*; but *mesplor* could easily have been mistaken by the careless scribe for the common sequence *mes jor* 'ever again'. E (II 144) rejects these suggestions on the grounds that 'the context, and particularly l. 1059, indicates a lacuna at this point'. He also mentions a suggestion of Professor Woledge that the scribe's *mesproisier* 1059 should be taken, not as *mes proisier* (cf. note on 29–30), but as the infin. *mesproisier* 'undervalue, despise'; this would invalidate both the proposed emendations, but it is difficult to see what possible insertion between 1055 and 1056 could lead up through the present 1056–8 to a line *Ne me devroit l'on mesproisier*.

1061–3. *li plain d'envie, Par qui consel j'ere perie, En avront encor lor deserte*. E (glossary and II 24) takes *ere* as impf. indic., as do also M⁰ (glossary, with *iere*) and M⁴ (p. 143); but the past tense one might expect here is not the impf. but the pret., and a much better sense is made by the future: 'by whose counsel I shall be destroyed'. Forms of the fut. of *estre* with final *-e* are well attested elsewhere: 1st person sing. *ere* in *Auc. et Nic.* 2.23, 8.22, *Horn* 5054, *iere* in *Jeu de S. Nicolas* (ed. Henry) 380, 1190, *Horn* 1173, *C* 2910a (see also Fouché p. 416). The verb *perir* here is given by E's glossary as *v.a.* 'kill, destroy' (cf. 168); it is also possible to take it, with T.-L. VII 760, as *v.n.*, 'I shall have perished'.

1067. *Ses niés, qui il devoit ardoir*. See note on 856–7.

1069. *De duel ne set con se contienge.* See note on 2636.

1075–6. *Qui ot le duel qu'il font por li, Com il crïent a Deu merci!* This exclamatory construction with absolute *Qui* and the pres. indic., and without expressed principal clause, is without parallel in the text as punctuated by the editors, and there is no other example in T.-L. VIII 87–8 (the usual form of the same construction, with absolute *Qui* and the impf. subj., is illustrated in *Qui donc veïst henap casser!* 3820, cf. 1253–4). It seems possible, however, that it is a genuine form of expression, of a particularly lively character, ('You should see . . .!', 'You should hear . . .!', as against 'You should have seen . . .!'), likely to have appealed to the poet, and that it should be recognized also in 1151–3 and 1226–7 (see the notes on these passages).

1091–5. *Ja n'avras home en tot cest reigne . . . Qui por vostre seneschaucie . . . Me donast une beauveisine.* E paraphrases (II 145–6) 'You will not find a single person in all this kingdom . . . who because of my office of seneschal . . . had given me so much as a farthing'. His interpretation of *avoir* as 'find' must be right; but the use of *donast*, depending on a future, in the sense of 'had given' would be abnormal, and it should be taken rather in the hypothetical sense of 'would give'.

1105–8. *A vos ne mesferoit il mie. Mais vos barons, en sa ballie S'il les trovout, nes vilonast, Encor en ert ta terre en gast.* (The MS. has *vos ballie* 1106, corrected by all recent editors; M⁴ omits the comma after *trovout* but has otherwise the same text as E). E translates (II 147) 'But if he got your barons in his power or assaulted them, your land will yet be laid waste (*or* left lordless?) in consequence'. This implies that *nes* represents *ne* < NEC (which could of course be used in the sense of 'or' in a conditional clause) combined with the pron. obj. *les* (cf. II 27); but M⁴ notes (p. 143) that 'l'enclise de la conjonction *ne* et du pronom personnel est insolite' (it appears to be unknown, and there is no instance of it in T.-L.'s article *ne*, VI 552–65), and Muret had in fact corrected *nes*, first to *sis* (M⁰), then to *ne* (M²). Moreover, the disjunction 'got your barons in his power' (with impf. indic.) 'or assaulted them' (with impf.

subj.) is both illogical and asymmetrical (contrast *S'il nos trovout ne pooit prendre* 1557); and the assumed hypothetical construction *s'il les trovout . . ., Encor en ert . . .* is abnormal both in tense-structure and in the use of *encor* in the apodosis. I have therefore suggested (*Vinaver Misc.*, pp. 264–5) that there is no grammatical relation between 1106–7 and 1108, that 1106–7 constitute a rhetorical question of a type common in the poem (cf. 146, 158, 1784 etc.), and that *nes* represents the common enclisis of *ne* < NON with *les*. The passage would then run: *A vos ne mesferoit il mie; Mais vos barons, en sa ballie S'il les trovout, nes vilonast? Encor en ert ta terre en gast;* 'To you he would do no harm; but your barons, if he found them in his power, would he not ill-treat them? Your land will yet be ravaged as a result'. The general structure of the passage, thus punctuated, is very similar to that of *Pensez que de si franche feme, Qu'il amena de lointain reigne, Que lui ne poist s'ele est destruite? Ainz en avra ancor grant luite* 1115–18.

1110–14. *Qui avroit sol un escuier Por moi destruit ne a feu mis, Se iere roi de set païs, Ses me metroit il en balence Ainz que n'en fust prise venjance.* The editors' interpretations of 1113 are divergent. E translates (II 147) 'yet would he have to throw them all into the scales'; M[0] and M[4] gloss *balence* 'contrepoids, opposition', to which M[4] adds the rather vague explanation 'Dinas . . . ne craindrait pas d'entrer en conflit avec un puissant souverain'; T.-L. (I 813) cites the passage under *balance* 'Wage, Wagschale', with the explanation 'als Ersatz bieten'. But all these renderings (perhaps influenced by a misunderstanding of 1114, for which see next note) appear to misrepresent the point of Dinas's speech. He is drawing a parallel between the actual situation of Tristran, Iseut, Mark and his kingdom on the one hand, and on the other the imaginary situation of Dinas himself, his squire, an unnamed ruler and his seven kingdoms: if that ruler were to treat the squire as Mark is treating Iseut, his seven kingdoms would not be 'thrown into the scales' or 'offered in exchange'—they would be laid waste by Dinas's righteous vengeance, and so too will Mark's kingdom be laid waste by Tristran. The meaning of *metre en balence* here must therefore be 'set at risk, endanger' (T.-L. I 813–14).

1114. *Ainz que n'en fust prise venjance.* E translates (II 147) 'before my vengeance would be satisfied'. But *ainz que*, temporal conj., 'before' does not take an expletive *ne* either in O. F. generally (cf. Lerch II 48) or in particular in Beroul (cf. *ainz que la nuit ait fin* 692, and 1021, 1598, 1621, 1783 etc., also with *ainz . . . que* 309–11). The meaning here is 'rather than that my vengeance should not be satisfied'; cf. with similar negative clauses depending on *ançois . . . que* and on *mex voloir que, ançois s'osast laisier crever Qu'il nu preïst* 1886–7 and *mex veut estre mis au vent Que il de lui n'ait la venjance* 1702–3 (cf. 1019–22, 1954–5). Where the sense of the dependent clause is affirmative, there is no *ne*: *Ainz que m'i doignes, art moi ci* 1222 ('rather than that you should give me to him'), also with *ainz . . . que* 128–30 and with *mex voloir, mex estre* etc. 35–8, 811–12, 946–7, 1563–4.

1115–17. *Pensez que de si franche feme . . . Que lui ne poist s'ele est destruite?* For this and *Et poise moi de la roïne* 2179 E refers (II 148) to W. M. Hackett's comparison with certain passages in *Girart de Roussillon* (*Vinaver Misc.*, pp. 158–60), but he says that her interpretation of the syntax differs from his in respect of the use of *de* after impersonal *peser*. In fact, there appears to be no difference except in so far as Miss Hackett associates the construction in *poise moi de la roïne* or *d'iste donne me pese* with A. Tobler's '*de* ein "logisches Subjekt" einführend' (*V. B.* I³ 5 ff.), which is, however, of a different character and in Tobler's view of a different origin.

1118. *Ainz en avra ancor grant luite.* For *ainz* here E's glossary gives 'yet'. In fact, its meaning is the common one of 'rather, on the contrary' (cf. 296, 413 etc.); the notion of 'yet' is expressed solely by *ancor*.

1146–8. *En un bliaut de paile bis Estoit la dame estroit vestue Et d'un fil d'or menu cosue.* There is no need to consider either the emendation of M¹ (*vestu : cosu*) or the first of the alternative translations mentioned by E (II 151); he rightly prefers *menu cosue* (of the lady) 'sewn (in) with small stitches' (cf. T.-L. II 925 and V 1461).

1151–3. *Qui voit son cors et sa fachon, Trop par avroit le cuer felon*

Qui n'en avroit de lié pitié. As punctuated by the editors, these lines mean 'Whoever sees her figure and her face', or perhaps 'If one sees her figure and her face' (E's glossary gives for *façon* only 'shape, image', but see T.-L. III 1550), 'whoever did not feel pity for her would have a very wicked heart'. It is difficult to take both 1151 and 1153 as simultaneous subordinate clauses to 1152; it therefore seems possible that 1151 may have been intended as an independent exclamatory clause, 'You should see . . .! (see note on 1075–6).

1161–2. *Ainz ne veïstes tant si lait Ne si boçu ne si desfait.* E (II 151) tentatively suggests correcting to *laiz* : *desfaiz* (spelt, by a slip, *laits* : *desfaits*); but this is hardly necessary. The qualificative use of *tant* adj. in the singular in the sense of 'so many a' is well known, and its pronominal use in the sense of 'so many a one', accompanied by singular adjectives, is also attested, e.g. *Tant an gist mort desor le pont Que n'i püent li vif passer* (*Eneas* 5514–5).

1165–8. *Sire, tu veus faire justise, Ta feme ardoir en ceste gise. Granz est; mes se je ainz rien soi, Ceste justise durra poi.* (All recent editors correct the *nen soi* of the MS. to *rien soi*). E translates *Granz est* (glossary and II 152) by 'It is a grievous matter' and compares the use of *en grande* in the *Folie Tristran de Berne*; M⁴ (glossary) says 'sans doute "cela est dur" '. But the words here have nothing in common with the locutions *estre* or *soi metre en grande* (also *en grant*, cf. T.-L. IV 561–3) 'be eager, strive'. The adj. *grant* here refers to *justise* 1165: 'it is high, terrible, punishment (indeed)'; for *grant justise* see the quotations in T.-L. IV 1906–7 from Wace, *Brut* 14418, Marie de France, *Milun* 60 etc.

1171–2. *Cest feu charra, en ceste brese Ceste justise ert tost remese.* (All editors correct the *prise* of the MS. to *brese*). E (II 152) translates 'in these embers the punishment will remain'. The literal meaning is rather 'will soon have come to an end', cf. T.-L. VIII 708–9 and *les mervoilles del palés Sont remeses a toz jorz mes* (*Perceval* 7879–80); but E's explanatory paraphrase 'the punishment will not outlast the fire itself' is acceptable.

1173–9. *Tel justise de li ferez; Mais, se vos croire me volez . . . Et que voudroit mex mort avoir, Qu'ele vivroit, et sanz valoir, Et que nus n'en orroit parler Qui plus ne t'en tenist por ber. Rois, voudroies le faire issi?* All editors print *Et que* in 1175 for the *Et qui* of the MS. All editors also assume a lacuna between 1174 and 1175, part of the missing text being conjecturally supplied by E (II 152) as meaning 'you would give her such a punishment that she would . . .'. E's translation continues 'and that she would rather die and that she would live without reputation'. There is, however, no *Et* in the text before *Qu'ele vivroit* 1176; this is no doubt why M⁴ (p. 143) attempts to render these words by 'que si elle devait vivre', i.e. 'than that she should live' ('she would rather die than live dis-honoured'). The objection to this is that in O. F. the construction in question would require not the condit. but the impf. subj., *Qu'ele vesquist* (cf. 1114 and note); the *et* before *sanz valoir* would also be meaningless. B. Blakey (*F.S.* 21 (1967), 99–100) there-fore proposes to assume a scribal corruption rather than a lacuna. He suggests that 1173 and 1174 have been interverted (cf. note on 65–8), and that *Et qui* in 1175 is an error not for *Et que* but for *Qu'ele*; the text thus corrected, *Mais, se vos croire me volez, Tel justise de li ferez Qu'ele voudroit mex mort avoir (Qu'ele vivroit, et sans valoir), Et que nus n'en orroit parler . . .*, is satisfactory if 1176 is taken as a parenthetical causal clause ('For she would live . . .'). However, F. J. Barnett now points out to me that both Blakey's correction of *Et qui* to *Qu'ele* and the interpretation of 1176 as parenthetical become superfluous if we assume that not only 1173 and 1174 but also 1175 and 1176 have been interverted. The orig-inal would then have read *Mais, se vos croire me volez, Tel justise de li ferez Qu'ele vivroit, et sanz valoir, Et que voudroit mex mort avoir, Et que nus n'en orroit parler . . .* (it is not absolutely necessary, with Barnett, to correct the *Et qui* of the MS. in 1175 to *Si que* rather than to *Et que*). This constitutes a clear and logical statement (like that in the preceding lines, 1167–72), and the emphasis placed by the altered word-order on the notion of life without honour is confirmed by Mark's reply, *Se tu m'enseignes cest, sanz falle, Qu'ele vivë et que ne valle, G[r]é t'en savra[i]* 1181–3. Granted that the scribe has not infrequently interverted the lines of a couplet, there is no reason why he should not on occasion have done so in two successive couplets. Whatever correction or interpretation of this passage is adopted, it should be noted that the meaning of *se vos croire me volez* 1174 is not 'if you would believe me' (E) but 'if you will take my advice' (cf. 2534, 3119).

1177–8. *nus n'en orroit parler Qui plus ne t'en tenist por ber.* E (II 20, n. 3) justifies the use of the nom. *ber* by saying that the nominative appears regularly after *tenir por.* The fact is that the nom. appears regularly after the passive *estre tenuz por* and the refl. *soi tenir por,* but not after *tenir por* as an active verb (see A. Tobler, *Vrai Aniel,* note on 147); this line therefore provides a genuine example of the use of an imparisyllabic nom. sing. form in accusative function, and it is correctly so listed by E in II 21. E's footnote includes a similar remark about *si avoit a non Husdanz* 1444: after *avoir a non* both cases are found, but the nom. appears to be commoner than the oblique (cf. T.-L. VI 745–7).

1190–1. *Ivains respont: 'Si con je pens Je te dirai, asez briment . . .'.* The punctuation (the same as in Muret and M⁴) makes *si con je pens* complement of *dirai,* 'I will tell you the way I think'. Comparison with *Or voi je bien, si con je quit, Qu'il ne voudroient . . .* 123–4 and *Tu es vestu de beaus grisens De Renebors, si con je pens* 3721–2 suggests that in 1190 as in these passages *si con je pens* is a mere cheville without any significant grammatical role in the construction, that there should be a comma after *pens,* and that 1191 should probably be printed *Je[l] te dirai* (cf. note on 269–70).

1194. *Paior fin dame n'ot mais une.* The meaning is, as E says (II 153), 'a worse end did never any lady have', and the MS. text is not impossible (for *ne . . . mais* 'never before' cf. *Si beles meures mais ne vit* and other examples in T.-L. V 860). It is perhaps more probable, however, that *mais une* is for *nesune;* cf. *Ne troverez mais qui vos die . . . Nis une rien se amor non* 4253–5, also *N'i aveit plus hardi nisun* (Wace, *Brut* 12186), *A la cort n'ot baron nesun* (*Violette* 699), *Qu'il n'i a seürté nesune* (*Rose* 4904) etc., in T.-L. VI 613–14.

1204–6. *Qant el verra nos bas bordeaus Et eslira l'escouellier Et l'estovra a nos couchier . . .* The obscurity of 1205 resides not only in *escouellier* but also in *eslira*. Muret (M⁰) considered emending *l'escouellier* to *le connillier* 'kennel', but later printed *escüellier*, for which E and M⁴ restore the MS. spelling, odd though it is. The meaning of this word is given by Muret and M⁴ as 'vaissellier', E 'dishes, utensils', T.-L. 'Schüsselbehälter'. This is not particularly plausible, and one considers also other senses: 'maker or seller of dishes' (T.-L. III 1022); 'dishwasher, scullion' (Gaimar, *Estoire* 152); 'officier de bouche chargé de la surveillance de la vaisselle' (Gdf. III 450). For *eslire* M⁰ gives 'apercevoir' and E 'perceive'; but there is no evidence that it ever had this sense, which could hardly arise except through confusion with *choisir* 'perceive' and 'choose'. The line may be corrupt.

1206. *Et l'estovra a nos couchier.* E (glossary s.v. *il* and II 26) lists *l'* here as elided form of the dat. *li*; but although the construction with *estovoir* has a dat. of the person in 484, 580, the acc. was also used, cf. T.-L. III 1429–30 and P. Rickard in *The French Language: Studies presented to L. C. Harmer*, London, 1970, pp. 65 ff. See note on 444.

1211–12. *Qant or verra la nostre cort, Adonc verra si desconfort.* All editors correct the *verrez* 1212 of the MS. to *verra*. Muret also corrected *si* to *son*, which gave a comprehensible though not very satisfactory sense. E restored *si*, which he understands as the adv. of degree (II 153; cf. glossary, 'so much'); but it is hardly possible to imagine such a use of *si*, especially in the absence of any determinant with *desconfort* (the situation is quite different in *Ja n'avrai si le cuer dolent* 2702, cited as an analogue). E points out that M⁴ also restores *si*, but omits to say that it is there taken (glossary, where it is in error attributed to 1262) as an analogical form of masc. acc. sing. of the possessive adj., derived from the nom. sing. *sis* by dropping the -*s*; this is equally unacceptable. We are therefore forced back to Muret's correction *son*; but the correction of *verrez* to *verra* is much less indispensable (if the model had *verra* in both 1211 and 1212, why should the scribe have changed it in 1212?). The line may have been intended to mean 'Then you will see her distress!'; it is true that the leper generally addresses Mark in the 2nd person sing., but he also uses the pl. form in 1173–4 and 1203. The passage may, however, be corrupt: the repetitions *verra* 1211, *verrez* 1212 and *Adonc* 1212, *Donc* 1213, *Donc* 1214 are somewhat suspect.

1220. *Cort a Yseut, prist l'a la main.* For the locution *prendre aucun a la main* cf. *Prist l'a la main, si l'en leva* 3157; for the word-order (normal at the period) and the elision of the weak pron. obj. before a following preposition cf. also *Pren t'a la main a mon baston* 3840, *Fiert l'en l'escu* 4041. It is not clear why E (II 153) suggests that *prist* may be a scribal error for *pris; pris l'a la main* = *pris li a la main* does not appear to have any advantage over the MS. text, and involves the unusual elision of *li a* to *l'a* (see note on 444).

1226–7. *Qui ot le brait, qui ot le cri, A tote genz en prent pitiez.* (Muret, followed by M⁴, corrects *genz* to *gent*; E compares 994, but it is not clear to what purpose). E says (II 154) '*Qui* generic: "All are filled with pity, all those who heard [*read* hear] the wailing and the crying"'. If '*qui* generic' means what is often called 'absolute *qui*' or the 'indefinite relative' (cf. II 235), it is perhaps misleading to translate as if *tote genz* were its antecedent. It seems possible, however, that the two lines form independent sentences, and that the first should be printed *Qui ot le brait, qui ot le cri!* (cf. 1075–6 and note).

1239–44. *Con deüstes por moi morir Et je redui por vos perir! Tel gent vos tienent entre mains . . . Se il n'os laisent en present, Tel i ara ferai dolent.* Muret's later editions and M⁴ punctuate with a comma after *perir* 1240 and take *con* (glossary s.v. *conme*) as 'aussi vrai que'. This interpretation of 1239–40 as constituting an asseverative formula is not called for by the context, and in any case such a formula would not be introduced by *con* alone, but by *(ain)si com* (cf. *F. S.* 8 (1954), 194–5); the editors have perhaps been misled by a misunderstanding of the force of *deüstes, redui* (cf. note on 856–7). E's punctuation is undoubtedly correct; *con* is simply exclamatory.

1248–9. *Laisiez la tost, qu'a cest'espee Ne vos face le chief voler.* E comments (II 154) '*qu'* concessive: "lest . . ."'. The conjunction taken together with *Ne* may be translated 'lest'; but it is final, not concessive.

1257-8. *Tristran n'en [v]ost rien atochier Ne entester ne laidengier.* E glosses *rien* '*advl.* at all', and translates (II 154) 'Tristran did not wish to touch them in any way . . .'; but this is appropriate only to the line as emended by M⁰, *nes vost rien atochier* (cf. *je nes vuel noient ocire* 2025). In the line as it stands, with *en*, *rien* must mean 'any (one) of them'; this is unusual, though in O. F. *rien* s.f. is commonly used in the sense of 'creature, person'.

1265-6. *Li contor dïent que Yvain Firent nïer.* E has deliberately allowed *contor* here and *asur* 4252 to stand 'as possible isolated instances of the reduction of *contëor* and *aseür*, a reduction which began in the North before the end of the twelfth century' (II 28). There is no evidence of such a reduction at this period in the region to which the *Tristran* belongs (cf. Pope §§243, 268), and the line should be corrected with Muret and M⁴ to *Li contëor dïent qu'Yvain* . . . (cf. note on 1569-70).

1281-4. *Governal en ot un toloit A un forestier, quil tenoit, Et deus seetes enpene[e]s, Barbelees, ot l'en menees.* E says (II 159) that *l'en* 1284 = *li+en*, and this is implied also by the glossary entries of M⁰ and M⁴ under *mener*; E consequently translates 'two feathered, barbed arrows he (*sc.* Governal) had brought for him (*sc.* Tristran)'. But this assumes an unparalleled position of the weak pron. objects *li* and *en*, placed after the finite verb *ot* although this is preceded by the direct object. As an analogue for the word-order E cites *prist l'a la main* 1220; but this is quite different, since here the finite verb *prist* is the first word in its sentence. If the meaning of *l'en* were what the editors allege, the order would have to be *deus seetes . . . l'en ot menees*; as the line stands, *l'en* must be the subject, = *l'on* (as frequently in the text, e.g. 89, 1036, 1209, 4332). The only oddity about this is the use of *mener*, without *en*, in the sense of 'bring (a thing) with one' (for *en mener* in this sense cf. *N'en merré armes ne cheval* 241).

1301-2. *Somel li prist, dormir se vot, Sor son ami dormir se vot.* The repetition of the words *dormir se vot* (retained also in M⁴) seems just as unlikely to be attributable to the author as some of those corrected by the editors (e.g. *home haï* : *du roi haï* 1553–4, *soz un arbre* : *a un arbre* 1693–4); the only difference is that here the correction is less obvious. Muret introduced the verb *estoveir* into 1301 (M⁰ *dormir l'estot* : *dormir se vot*, M² *dormir l'estut* : *dormir se veut*, M³ *dormir l'estuet*: *dormir se veut*); but one would expect the infin. also to be different, e.g. *couchier se veut* 1302.

1303–5. *Seignors, eisi font longuement En la forest parfondement, Longuement sont en cel desert.* So also M⁴; but in view of the improbability of *faire* in this context, and the frequent scribal confusion of *f* and *s* (cf. note on 1325–6), Muret's correction of *font* to *sont* seems fully justified.

1307–8. *Un consel sot li nai[n]s du roi, Ne sot que il.* See note on 269–70.

1325–6. *Ce que dirai, c'ert du segroi Dont je sui vers le roi par soi.* E now (II 162) accepts the correction adopted by Muret and M⁴ of *de* to *du* (perhaps better to *de[l]*, cf. *del pain* 1644, *del ladre* 3838 and other examples of scribal omission of final *l* before consonant cited in note on 269–70). He does not, however, accept the more significant correction (also in Muret and M⁴) of *soi* to *foi*, although there is ample evidence that the scribe often wrote *s* for *f* (all editors correct *saint* 2321 to *faint*, *sait* 1039 to *fait*, and *soi* 1318 itself to *foi*). His translation of 1326 is 'which I share with the king alone', and he actually speaks of 'an effective use of *par soi*'. But though it is well known that in O. F. *par soi* could mean 'by oneself, on one's own', it always refers either to the subject of the sentence or to a term such as *chascun*; moreover, no evidence has been adduced to suggest that *estre vers aucun d'aucune chose* could ever mean 'share something with someone'. On the other hand, as I have pointed out (*Vinaver Misc.*, p. 273), there was in O. F. (and especially in texts of the Western region to which Beroul belongs) a well-attested locution *estre par foi* (or *serement*) *vers* (or *a* or *o*) *aucun* (*d'aucune chose*) 'be bound in loyalty (or by oath) towards someone (in respect of something)'; T.-L. (III 1966) cites, besides Beroul 1325-6, *Ceus qui d'est plait li sont par fei* (*Thebes* 1424), *od le duc esteit par fei* (*Rou* III 10982; cf. ib. 10804), and further examples are *Si'n es vers moi par seirement* (*Eneas* 3848), *Bele, jeo sui par serement A vostre pere* (Marie de France, *Eliduc* 685-6); cf. also *Troie* 26255. The line must therefore be read *Dont je sui vers le roi par foi* and understood 'about which I am bound in loyalty to the king' (not, as in the glossaries of Muret and M⁴, 'dont j'ai reçu la confidence du roi'). See also note on 3313-14.

1336-7. *S'en vint un jor, aprés disner, Parlout a ses barons roi Marc.* E translates (II 163) 'And it happened one day'; but though *S*, as he says, represents *si* < SIC, it would need to be shown that *en venir* (*que*) could be used in the sense of 'happen (impers.) that'; failing this, it seems necessary to emend with Muret and M⁴ to *S'avint*.

1341-5. *Au roi dïent priveement: 'Rois, nos savon ton celement.' Li rois s'en rist et dist: 'Ce mal, Que j'ai orelles de cheval, M'est avenu par cest devin . . .'.* E gives (II 161) a tentative but acceptable justification for retaining (with M⁴) the MS. text, instead of adopting from M¹ and M² the interversion of 1343 and 1344 and other corrections: '. . . ton celement, Que as orelles de cheval.' Li rois s'iraist et dist . . . E does not, however, explain why the king should laugh (1343); perhaps Muret's *s'iraist* should be salvaged.

1374-6. *En ceste terre n'a baron, Au roi ne l'ait plevi en main, Vos rendre a lui o mort ou sain.* E says (II 165) that the infin. *rendre* 'depends loosely on *l'ait plevi*'. In fact, it appears to depend directly on *plevi* (an unusual construction as compared with a dependent *que*-clause, but T.-L. has one example, VII 1157, 21, though with *de*+infin.); what is most striking is that here the infin. is announced by the pron. obj. *l'*, but this is probably an example of prolepsis, which occurs in the text in other forms (see note on 1944-7).

1378-80. *Par foi! Tristran, qui se repent, Deu du pechié li fait pardon, Par foi et par confession.* E says (II 165) that 1380 'may be taken to depend on the preceding line, *par* having practically the meaning "in virtue of" '. But to make sense of the passage the meaning attributed to *par* would have to be more like 'in recognition of', which implies an unattested extension of its semantic field. It is perhaps preferable to assume, with Muret, that 1379 and 1380 have been interverted by the scribe (see note on 65–8).

1382-4. *Que ele m'aime en bone foi, Vos n'entendez pas la raison: Q'el m'aime, c'est par la poison.* E (II 165) explains the *Que* in 1382 as 'loosely dependent on *raison*', which might in itself be accepted; but he offers no explanation for the *Q'* in 1384, which is surely parallel to it. The only natural construction in 1384, and therefore also in 1382, is that introduced by Muret, who corrected to *Se ele* and *S'el* (the correction is abandoned in M³ and M⁴). All editors agree that the scribe was careless in his syntax and especially in his use of conjunctions, and all emend his *Que* initial of the line in 231, 2449, 4003 (cf. also 2423). The *se* proposed here (which might be called the 'argumentative *se*') is one which introduces not a hypothesis but a statement of fact (cf. Lerch, I 283–91). It occurs frequently elsewhere in the text; the closest parallels, with the same concessive nuance, are *Si longuement l'avon menee, Itel fu nostre destinee* 2301-2 and *Ç'a esté fait, c'est sor mon pois* 4180 (see the notes), but a related use is seen in *Se vos m'en erïez ami, N'ert pas mervelle* 54-5, cf. 1849; *Que püent il, se color müent?* 1646; more remotely in *S'onques l'amastes, donc l'amez* 2780; *S'il se mesfist, il est en fort* 3073; see also notes on 2209–10 and 4096–100.

1387–90. *Et quel confort Puet on doner a home mort? Assez est mort qui longuement Gist en pechié, s'il ne repent.* E (glossary s.v. *asez*) renders *assez* here by 'quite'. The meaning is in fact one which, although illustrated in T.-L. I 593 by a single example (inaccurately glossed), *Assez est morz, puis que l'avomes pris*, occurs in a number of O. F. proverbs such as *Assez dort qui riens ne fet, Assez otroie qui se taist* (Morawski nos. 136, 140; cf. also nos. 133-4, 137-9, 145). The translation will vary from case to case, but might in 1389 be 'is as good as dead' or 'might as well be dead'.

1399–400. *A Tristran dist par grant desroi: 'Que feras tu? Conselle toi.'* The word *desroi* is glossed by M⁰ (p. 254) 'impétuosité, violence',

E

by M⁴ 'vivacité', and the phrase *par grant desroi* is translated by E (II 165) 'in great perturbation'. But the word occurs in four other passages in the text (559, 820, 1308, 2574), always in its normal sense of 'disorder, wrong' (so in E's glossary for 559, 820, 2574, with 'distress' 1399; cf. T.-L. II 1732 'Durchbrechung der Ordnung, Auflehnung, Aufruhr; Übermut, Ungestüm'). These senses are obviously inappropriate here, but there is no authority elsewhere for the renderings of M⁰, E and M⁴; they are clearly based entirely on the context, which requires something like 'with great urgency', 'insistently'. I have therefore suggested that *desroi* 1399 may be an error for *destroit* (with fall of final *t* as in certain other rhyme-words in Beroul, *quit* : *lui* 123–4 etc.: see *M.L.R.* 60 (1965), 353–4). This word occurs in 846 and 1676 in the sense of 'distress'; it is in fact the noun corresponding to the verb *destreindre* 'press, oppress, urge on', and it is found in other texts with a meaning close to 'insistence, pressure', e.g. *Tant par destreit, tant par amur Li fist cunuistre la verur* (Marie de France, *Fables*, ed. Warnke, 42, 23), and other examples in T.-L. II 1802–3.

1405. *vivre d'erbes et de glan.* In the plural *erbes* is 'herbs' rather than 'grass' (E, II 163), which suggests Nebuchadnezzar.

1407. *De lié laisier parler ne ruis.* E translates (II 165) 'I would not have anyone speak of my leaving her', and Muret (M²–M⁴, glossary s.v. *ruis*) 'je ne veux pas entendre parler'. The meaning is in fact simply 'I will not (*or* I refuse to) talk of leaving her' (M⁰ correctly glosses 'ne pas vouloir'); cf. *Se cele vie lor durast, Nus d'euls changier ne la rouast* (*Floire et Bl.*, ed. Pelan, 2288–9), *Il ne voleit nule espuser, Ja n'en rovast oïr parler* (Marie de France, *Equitan* 199–200), and other examples in Gdf. VII 255, especially under the erroneous heading *'en rover, se rover, s'en rover'*.

1431–6. *Seignors, oiez con por Tristran Out fait li rois crïer son ban— En Cornoualle n'a parroise Ou la novele n'en angoise—Que, qui porroit Tristran trover, Qu'il en feïst le cri lever.* Muret and M⁴ print this passage as two independent sentences, with an exclamation mark after 1432; this leaves *ban* hanging in the air, and makes 1435–6 depend very awkwardly on *novele*. E's punctuation, making the construction the well-attested *crïer son ban que* . . . (with 1433–4 parenthetical), is much to be preferred.

Both M⁰ (glossary) and E (glossary and II 24) take *angoise* 1434 as an example of the pres. subjunctive of an *-er* verb with analogical *-e*. In O. F. the subjunctive is certainly to be expected in a relative clause depending on an antecedent whose existence is denied (cf. *Nus ne le voit qui pitié n'ait* 1522); but our text also admits the indic., cf. *N'i a un sol grant duel ne fet* 2964, and it would be rash to assume that *angoise* must be meant as subjunctive. See also note on 2403–5.

1449. *Ne vout mengier ne pain ne past.* For *past* E (glossary) gives 'paste (prepared for feeding dogs)', a translation based on that of Muret and M⁴ 'pât, mélange de farine et de son que l'on détrempe dans des lavures pour nourrir les chiens de chasse', which in turn is borrowed from Littré, s.v. *pât*. There seems, however, to be no authority for assigning this specialized sense to the O. F. word, which according to the examples in Gdf. VI 31–2 and T.-L. VII 459–60 meant simply, like PASTUS, food for men or animals, in the latter case not necessarily prepared by human agency. The alliterative locution *ne pain ne past* may be an adaptation by the poet of the well-attested locution *ne pain ne paste* (T.-L. VII 47 and 461), literally 'either bread or pastry', which means merely 'food of any kind'.

1455–6. *Gel metroie du landon fors; Quar, s'il enrage, ce ert deus.* The rhyme *fors : deus* has been much discussed. E lists it (II 11) as joining blocked open *o* and *eu* from open *o*+*l*+cons. But the ŏ in FŎRIS is not blocked; although much the commonest form of the O. F. adv. is *fors* (no doubt through extension to the adv. of the unstressed development in the word used as prep. or prefix), the diphthongized form *fuers, feurs* does occur (Pope §597; examples in T.-L. III 2140) and may have been used here (for the only other instance of a rhyme cited by E as between blocked and free open *o* see note on 4479–80). Another possibility, however, is that *ce ert deus* is, as suggested by A. Holden (*Rom.* 89 (1968), 390), an error for *c'ert dolors*, forming a rhyme similar to that between *dolors* and *cors* in 843–4.

1467–9. *Li rois a dit, a son corage—Por son seignor croit qu'il enrage—* '*Certes, molt a li chiens grant sens . . .*'. Muret had very plausibly corrected *croit* to *croi* (cf. *doit* 346, corrected by all editors to *doi*) making 1468 part of the king's speech; but the retention with E and M⁴ of the MS. reading, interpreting the line as parenthetical, is certainly possible. For *a son corage* Tobler had tentatively suggested emending to *a son barnage*, but the editors retain the MS. reading, though with some uncertainty about its meaning. E (II 169) hesitates between 'according to the dictates of his heart' (so M⁴, 'en suivant l'impulsion de son coeur', glossary) and (with *a* either equivalent to or in error for *an, en*) 'in his mind, to himself'. The second of these alternatives is surely preferable (cf. *En son cuer dit or croit sa feme* 287), especially as Mark's praise of Tristran (1469–72) must be intended as an aside. For scribal *a* for *en* see note on 491.

1479–81. *ja si tost n'ert deslïez Q'il ne morde, s'est enragiez, Ou autre rien ou beste ou gent.* E translates (II 169) 'No sooner will he be released than he will bite something else, man or beast . . .' The adj. *autre* here seems to have the same 'expletive' force as in 2203 and 4131–3 (see notes), i.e. 'either a mere object or a beast or a person'.

1483–4. *Li rois apele un escuier Por Husdan faire deslïer.* It is possible that *faire deslïer* here = *deslïer*; cf. note on 3221.

1485. *Sor bans, sor seles puient haut.* E glosses *sele* here 'settle', a term defined as meaning in Mod. Eng. 'a long wooden bench, usu. with arms and a high back' (S.O.E.D.); probably better 'stool', cf. 'siège de bois sans dossier', Muret and M⁴.

1500. *Qant il fu pris, qu'il dut estre ars.* See note on 856–7.

1502. *Et dit chascun de venir mes.* E translates (II 169) 'All urge him to go on', and his glossary s.v. *mais* puts this reference under 'more, further'; M⁴'s glossary cites the line both under *mais* 'au sens de *plus* quantitatif' and under *mes* 'encore, plus loin'. No indication of the fundamental obscurity of the line is given except in M⁴'s note (p. 144), which says that *chascun* is 'probably' subject, and points out that the construction *dire +de +*infin. was characterized by Vaugelas as a recent Gasconism. The presence of this construction and of an unexplained use of *mes* with the verb *venir* suggests that the line may be corrupt. Muret had evidently had some doubt about it, for he mentions in M⁰ (glossary s.v. 1. *mès*) the possibility of reading *Et dit chascun: 'De venir mes!'*; but this is hardly acceptable, for the hortative use of the infin. preceded by *de* has usually the def. art. and always the adv. *or (Or del venir mes!*, cf. T.-L. II 1225–6).

1508–9. *Ainz, puis qu'il fu fors du lïen, Ne fina, si fu au moutier.* E's glossary, corrected in II 264, translates this *si* by 'and so doing, and so' (as in, e.g., *Conbati m'en, si l'en chaçai* 142). But in the construction used here, after a negative clause containing a verb such as *finer* or *cesser*, *si* has temporal force and is correctly glossed by M⁰ 'jusqu'à ce que'; cf. *il ne cesserent, si vinrent en Coustantinoble* (R. de Clari, ed. Lauer, xx 4); *Ainz ne fina, si vint droit al mostier* (*Cour. Louis*, ed. Langlois, C.F.M.A., 1943 var.). The same usage occurs in *N'avra mais pais a l'esperon, Si ert venu a Cuerlion* 3367–8.

1540–1. *Ne demora c'un petitet Li brachet, qui la rote sut* (: *connut*). E considers (II 170) three interpretations of *sut*. He begins with the translation 'who knew the way', and he lists *sut* (II 25) as pret. of *savoir* (so also M⁰); but this assumes the existence, alongside the normal *sot* (: *ot* 3208), of an analogical pret. form which is generally assigned to the Mid. F. period (Pope §1032). As possible alternatives E mentions taking *sut* as for *siut* 'follows' (so M², glossary and p. x, and still M⁴, pp. ix–x), and finally as an analogical pret. 'followed'; this last (accepted by Pope §1022 for this passage, and confirmed by similar forms in *Rou, Eneas* etc.) is undoubtedly to be preferred.

1569–70. *Certes, ce poise moi molt fort Que je li doie doner mort.* In O. F., contrary to Mod. F. practice, the mood in the *que*-clause depending on an expression of emotion is normally the indic. (cf. *poise m'en . . . Que il la mort a ici quise* 1565–6, and note on 109–11). It is therefore possible that here the scribe's model ran

Que je li doi doner la mort (for *doner la mort a aucun*, with the def. art., cf. *Bien sai qu'il me dorroit la mort* 68, also 2588); if before writing it down he mentally converted *doner la mort* into *doner mort* (cf. *Se gel t'ensein, dorras moi mort?* 1889), he was quite capable of arbitrarily adding an *-e* to *doi* in order to make up the syllable-count. There are several lines in the poem where it is generally recognized that he did exactly this kind of thing. In 1504 all editors print *O Tristran fu traït et pris*, which is no doubt what stood in the original, but the scribe apparently read *trait* as the monosyllabic past part. of *traire* instead of the disyllabic past part. of *traïr*, and rectified the measure by changing *pris* to the meaning-less *apris* (*O Tristran fu trait et apris*); similarly with *Trop se criement, sont esfroï* 1535, written as *Trop se criement, sont en esfroi*, with *Di lui qu'il set bien un marchés* 3294 written as *Di lui que il set bien marchés*, with *Dit Evains, li filz Urïen* 3483 written as *Et dit Evains, li filz Dinan* (cf. also 1576, 3245). Errors of the same character seem to have occurred in 1265, 1653, 1655, 1992, 2698, 4314, 4318 (see the notes on these passages).

1576–8. *J'oï ja dire qu'uns seüs Avoit un forestier galois, Puis que Artus en fu fait rois.* E's note (II 171) and M⁴'s glossary explain *en* ('of Wales', implied in *galois*), but not the rather surprising *Puis que*: one expects a reference to the distant past such as *Ainz que Artus* (or *Ançois qu'Artus*) *en fust fait rois*. It is not impossible that this is in fact what stood in the scribe's model: for other instances where he has replaced a word by its opposite see note on 955–8.

1582–6. *Puis ne füst par cele trace Que li chiens ne süst le saut; Por crïer n'en tornast le faut Ne ja n'atainsist tant sa beste Ja criast ne feïst moleste.* Taking the text of this passage as it stands in the MS., E's free translation (II 171) is acceptable, but his syntactical analy-sis is at fault. He considers 'the subjunctives *süst, tornast, atainsist* as parallel and consecutive (dependent on *ne füst par cele trace*)'. In reality, as stated in M⁴ (p. 144), *tornast* and *atainsist* are not dependent on *füst* and parallel with *süst* (in which case they would have to be not negative but affirmative); they are, as implied by E's own punctuation, parallel with *füst*, and all three clauses (1582–3, 1584, 1585–6) are best considered as principal clauses rather than with M⁴ as consecutive clauses dependent on *si* 1579 (*Que il avoit si afaitié: Qant il avoit son cerf sagnié De la seete berserece, Puis ne füst . . .*). The literal construction is: '(the wounded stag) would not flee by any course so that the hound did not follow; he would not . . . through barking, nor would he get so close to his quarry that he barked'. Though E shows that the words *torner* and *le faut* can both be technical terms of hunting, 1584 remains obscure; he conjectures (II 172) 'for any barking he might do, he would not pass beyond the break in the scent', but the whole point of the story is that the hound had been trained not to bark at all. In these circumstances, the ingenious and palaeo-graphically plausible emendation of 1584 introduced in Muret's later editions and retained by M⁴, *Por crïer n'estonast le gaut*, is attractive, though highly speculative.

1593. *Puis dist itant: 'Se je pooie . . .'*. E glosses *itant* here 'then'; but there is no authority for taking *itant* as a form of *atant* (or *aïtant*) 'thereupon, then'. As is normal, it is a variant of *tant*, and the meaning here is 'this much', 'the following, what follows'; cf. note on 2364–5, and for the same use of *tant* 2411–13 and note.

1604–5. *Or vuel peine metre et entendre A beste prendre sanz crïer.* See note on 89–90.

1613–15. *Li chien a son seignor s'areste, Lait le crïer, gerpist la beste; Haut l'esgarde, ne set qu'il face.* E glosses *haut* 'high up' (as in *Se haut hurte, haut est feruz* 1758); but presumably *haut l'esgarde* means 'he looks up at him', cf. *La roïne li enclina, Amont le regarde, a la chiere* 3158–9.

1621–2. *Ainz que li premier mois pasast Fu si le chien dontez u gast Que . . .* E glosses *donter* 'tame'; better 'break in, train' (cf. Muret and M⁴ 'dresser').

1631–2. *Et s'il enmi lande l'ataint, Com il s'avient en i prent maint . . .* E translates (II 172) 'as it happens that he takes many', assuming that *en* is here the pron. adv. 'of them'. It may equally well be taken, with M⁰ (glossary s.v. *ome*) as for *on*—'as it happens that many are taken'; the form *en* (as distinct from *l'en* = *l'on*) appears in *En l'art por moi* 988 and, without a following *l*, in *Que en consent lor felonie* 2899.

1649–50. *Chascun d'eus soffre paine elgal, Qar l'un por l'autre ne sent mal*. E paraphrases (II 173) 'The sufferings of the lovers are shared equally; for neither of them feels their pangs because of the other (i.e. thanks to the company and love of the other)' (cf. M⁴, p. 144). E. Vinaver (*Studies in Medieval French presented to Alfred Ewert*, Oxford, 1961, p. 91) had judged it uncharacteristic of Beroul to say that the lovers' sufferings were equal because neither felt them, brought out the difference between *soffre paine* referring to the endurance of physical hardships and *sent mal* referring to the consciousness of these miseries (cf. *Aspre vie meinent et dure; Tant s'entraiment de bone amor, L'un por l'autre ne sent dolor* 1364–6), and proposed to interpret *Qar* as 'therefore' or as 'with the result that'. Neither of these senses, however, seems to be attested for Beroul's period and region; I have therefore suggested (*Vinaver Misc.*, p. 281) that *Qar* may be a scribal error, perhaps for *Mais* (cf. *Fu ainz maiss gent tant eüst paine? Mais l'un por l'autre ne le* (MS. *se*) *sent* 1784–5). Without such a correction of the introductory conjunction (cf. note on 1382–4), it would seem impossible to retain the *ne sent* of the MS., and Muret's emendation to *resent* (rejected by G. Paris, cf. M⁰ p. 254, and abandoned in M⁴) would impose itself.

1650–2. *l'un por l'autre ne sent mal: Grant poor a Yseut la gente Tristran por lié ne se repente*. With Muret's affirmative *resent mal*, the following lines could be understood as explanatory of 1649–50, hence the colon placed by Muret after *mal*. With the *ne sent mal* of the MS. restored, as Vinaver has shown (art. cit., p. 94), the following lines are no longer explanatory but contradictory; the colon still printed by E and M⁴ must be replaced by a full stop, and 1651–2 understood as '[Yet] Iseut is afraid that Tristran will repent for her sake' (cf. 1364–6, quoted above, where 1365 lacks the explicit *Mais* of the parallel passage 1784–5, also quoted above). E's paraphrase of 1651–2 runs 'the fear of Iseut being that Tristran should repine because of her'; the choice of the verb 'repine' instead of 'repent' may suggest an echo of the content of 1649–50 which is not in fact present in the text.

1653–5. *Et a Tristran repoise fort Que Yseut a por lui descort, Qu'el repente de la folie.* Here E translates 'while Tristran, for his part, is distressed that Iseut is embroiled because of him and lest she repent of their misconduct', and comments 'l. 1654 being virtually causal and containing a statement of fact, l. 1655 a subjective clause depending directly on *repoise*'. The construction *a Tristran repoise fort Que Yseut a por lui descort* 1653–4 is of course perfectly normal (for the indic. in clauses depending on expressions of emotion such as *(re)peser* impers. see note on 109–11). The explanation offered for 1655, however, is hardly admissible. There is no 'and' in the text; a second clause depending on *repoise* would not normally have a verb in the subjunctive, and its meaning would in any case be 'is distressed that (*or* because) she repents of their misconduct'; E's 'lest she repent' (a subordinate clause which, incidentally, could hardly depend on *repoise*) would be expressed by *Qu'el ne repente*. Finally, it must be remembered that the MS. text is *Qu'il repente* (M⁰ misread it as *Qu'el*, but Muret's later eds. print *Qu'il*, and all assume a lacuna between 1654 and 1655; *Qu'el* was introduced as a correction by E and adopted in M⁴). It is for these reasons that I have suggested (*Vinaver Misc.*, p. 282) that the original text of 1653–5 may have been *Et Tristran repoise si fort* (an alternative possibility is *Et a Tristran poise si fort*) *Que Yseut a por lui descort Qu'il se repent de la folie.* This construction, consisting of (1) principal clause containing a verb of emotion, (2) causal clause depending on this verb, (3) consecutive clause taking up a *si* or *tel* in the principal clause, would be exactly parallel to that in *Qar j'ai tel duel c'onques le roi Out mal pensé de vos vers moi Qu'il n'i a el* . . . 109–11. The copying errors by which this reconstructed text could have become that which stands in the MS. are paralleled elsewhere in the poem: in 1653 the scribe might have omitted *si* after the *-se* of *poise*, and in 1655 he might have written *repente* under the influence of *repente* 1652; he might then have restored the measure (cf. note on 1569–70) in 1653 by introducing the preposition *a* (or the prefix *re-*) and in 1655 by omitting the pronoun *se* (though *repentir* is normally reflexive in Beroul as in O. F. generally, it is used as intrans. in 1390).

For a discussion of the effects of this reconstruction on the substance of the episode see *Vinaver Misc.*, p. 282.

1661–3. *De Cornoualle du païs De Morrois ere[n]t si eschis Qu'il n'i osout un sol entrer.* E translates (II 175) 'Those of the land of Cornwall were so shy of the forest of Morrois that . . .'; M⁴ (p. 144) 'De [toutes les parties de la] Cornouaille on évitait avec tant de soin le pays de M. que . . .'. The second of these interpretations, rather than the first, is perhaps supported by the lines quoted by E, *Par Cornoualle ont a[n]tendu L'un des trois a le chief perdu* 1719–20; but both are distinctly forced, and the original may well have run, as emended by Muret, *De Cornoualle li naïf De Morrois erent si eschif . . .* (cf. *trois naïs Que par mal sont parti de cort* 3280–1).

1664. *Bien lor faisoit a redouter.* Two distinct constructions with *faire +a+*infin. come into consideration here: (1) personal *faire a* with an infin. usually to be understood in a passive sense (T.-L. III 1587–8; cf. note on 29–30); so here *bien faisoit a redoter* 'it (the forest) was much to be feared', but the construction is not normally found with an indirect obj. of the person; (2) impersonal *faire +*adj. (*+a*)*+*infin., which can have an indirect obj. of the person, e.g. *ci li fet buen demorer* (*Yvain* 1393), 'here it is pleasant for her to stay' (T.-L. III 1577–8); so here *il (le) lor faisoit bon redoter* 'it was good for them to fear it', but this has only exceptionally *a* before the infin., or an adv. (*bien*) for the adj. (*bon*). It is this second construction that is implied by the translations of E (II 175), 'They had good reason (*or* were well-advised) to fear', and M⁴ (glossary), 'c'est avec raison qu'ils devaient le redouter'; but what stands in the text appears to be a hybrid between the two (cf. Friedwagner's note to *Vengeance Raguidel* 3358).

1677–8. *Endormi erent amedoi. Governal ert en un esquoi.* The form *amedoi* is abnormal (the masc. nom. of the words 'two' and 'both' is elsewhere the normal *dui, andui*, rhyming with *lui* 87–8, 2937–8; E's suggestion (II 12, following M⁰, p. xl) that *amedoi* might represent a remodelling on the obl. *dous* is hardly tenable); and the only attested noun *esquoi, escoi* is one meaning 'boat, ship', which seems improbable in the context, though the passage is quoted under it by T.-L. (III 937). Each of the numerous interpretations or emendations that have been put forward is open to serious objections. E tentatively suggests (glossary and II 176) that *esquoi* may represent an unattested noun of Germanic origin related to Eng. *skulk* and meaning 'hiding-place', but this presents phonetic difficulties; worth reconsidering is the suggestion of W. Röttiger (*Der heutige Stand der Tristanforschung*, Hamburg, 1897) that *esquoi* may be an error for *estui*, which normally means 'container, store etc.', but is the noun from *estuier*, one of whose meanings was 'to hide'.

1687–8. *Vit cel venir que il bien set Que ses sires onques plus het.* E's gloss of *onques plus* here, 'the very most', is acceptable; a close parallel is *Ce est la gens el monde qui onques plus le heent* (*Aiol* 10654, in T.-L. VI 1146). M⁴ (glossary) explains the clause as a 'curieux amalgame de deux phrases distinctes = *que ses sires het plus que onques ne haït homme*'; but this is to confuse two distinct uses of *onques*: (1) *onc, onques* temporal, 'ever, at any time in the past', with a verb in the pret., in Beroul often replaced by *ainz* (cf. note on 498–9), and (2) *onc, onques* generalizing, 'ever', without temporal restriction, as in *qui o., qui c'o.* 'whoever' etc. What we have here is an extension from the use of generalizing *onques* in the relative clause depending on a superlative expression: thus *La plus droite voie tandra Que il onques pourra tenir* (Guil. d'Angl. 9) could give rise to *la voie tandra que il onques plus droite pourra.*

1690–2. *Des esperons a son destrier A tant doné que il escache, Sovent el col fiert o sa mache.* The word *escache* (according to M⁰ and E, II 176, the MS. has *estache*, but Muret's later eds. and M⁴ read it as *escache*) is obscure. M⁰ emended to *l'en cache* (Northern for *chace*); E and M⁴ (also M²) interpret it as a Northern dialectal form of *eschace* < EX-CAPTIAT, and *il escache* is taken by M⁴ (glossary s.v. *il*), and presumably by E, as for *il l'escache* (cf. note on 269–70) 'he drives it, urges it on' (E, glossary; cf. M⁴, glossary, 'chasser, lancer en avant'), though the attested sense of *eschacier* is rather 'drive away, expel, disperse' (T.-L. III 826–7); A. Holden (*Rom.* 89 (1968), 392) considers emending to *estanche*, but because of the rhyme decides in favour of Acher's interpretation, *escache* < EX-COACTICAT, though this verb is attested only in the sense of 'crush, destroy'. The simple verb *chacier* could mean 'drive, urge on (the horse one is riding)' (see examples in T.-L. II 155); it is therefore probable that the *il escache* of the MS. is scribal and dialectal for *il le chace* or *il l'en chace*.

1704–5. *par lui et par sa faisance Durent il estre tuit destruit.* See note on 856–7.

1729–32. *Tristran se jut a la fullie; Chau tens faisoit, si fu jonchie. Endormiz est, ne savoit mie Que cil eüst perdu la vie* . . . Although the tenses of the narration vary, sometimes unexpectedly, it is unlikely that the present *est* should stand here in isolation among the past tenses of 1724–33. The scribe has elsewhere confused *est* and *ert*, and all editors have corrected *est* 1767 to *ert* (and *ert* 2700 to *est*); here also we should no doubt read *ert*.

1733. (*cil* . . .) *Par qui il dut mort recevoir.* See note on 856–7.

1735–8. *Governal a la loge vient, La teste au mort a sa main tient; A la forche de sa ramee L'a cil par les cheveus nouee.* Muret, followed by M⁴, corrects to *la ramee*; as this *ramee* (cf. 1841) is the *loge* or *fullie* in which Tristran and Iseut sleep (and was presumably made, like their first *loge* in Morrois, by Tristran himself (1289–91) and not by Governal), the correction appears to be necessary. The *forche* was evidently (as in the case of the gallows, cf. 3332 and E's note, II 229) a forked branch or crotch fixed in the ground as the main support of the bower (cf. Muret and M⁴, glossaries), not a growing tree as suggested in E's glossary.

1763–4. *Molt a buen non l'arc, qui ne faut Riens qui l'en fire, bas ne haut.* E retains the MS. text (*quil enfire*), understanding (II 178) 'which does not miss anything which may strike (make contact with) it, high or low'. But the verb *falir, fa(i)llir* is not attested in the transitive sense of 'miss' (see T.-L. III 1607–14), and in none of the other examples of *l'arc qui ne faut* assembled by M. D. Legge in *Medium Ævum* 25 (1956), 79–83 has *faut* any possible object or complement; moreover, even if in our passage the verb could be so taken the *en* would remain unaccounted for. M⁰ printed *Mout a buen non l'arc Qui ne faut: Riens qu'il en fire, bas ne haut* . . .; here presumably *il* refers to Tristran, but the assumption of a lacuna means that the sentence beginning *Riens* is incomprehensible. If no lacuna is assumed, the text must be emended with Muret's later eds. and M⁴ to *qu'il ne fire*; but even in this form its construction is far from clear. It is possible that *Riens qu'il ne fire* should be understood as *qu'il ne fire riens*, with *que* consecutive and *riens* object of *fire*: 'which does not fail so that it does not strike anything', i.e. 'which does not fail to strike anything'; but T.-L. has no example of such a consecutive clause depending on *falir*, and the position of *riens* would be unusual. It is more probable that the correct punctuation is that of M⁰ with colon after 1763; 1764 may then constitute an independent verbless sentence, with *que* relative: '[there is] nothing that it does not strike'. Such a use of *rien* with intrinsic negative force, even in the absence of a finite verb, would be unexpected at the period, unless the line were considered as carrying on the sense and construction of *Riens ne trove qu'il n'oceïst* 1754.

1771. *Longuement fu en tel dechaz.* The word *dechaz* is translated by E (glossary and II 180) 'exile'; M⁴ glosses 'poursuite (des fugitifs), exil', but adds 'On peut aussi penser à "poursuite (du gibier)" et cela cadrerait mieux avec le sens général du passage'. It is true that most of the preceding and following lines (1765–8, 1772–3) refer to Tristran's success as a hunter; but there seems to be no evidence that *dechaz* could be used of the hunt. Neither Gdf. (II 442) nor T.-L. (II 1248) has any other example of the noun, and their examples of the verb *dechacier* all mean 'pursue, persecute' or 'drive out, expel' (apart from a single passage from Machaut in Gdf., *un chien deschace apres sa beste*); so also in Beroul, where the hermit apostrophizes Tristran and Iseut as *gent dechacie* 2295. In any case, the immediately preceding lines, *Qar falliz lor estoit li pains, N'il n'osoient issir as plains* 1769–70 lead up to the notion of expulsion and exile.

1779–80. *Tristran de la loge ou il gist, Çaint s'espee, tot sol s'en ist.*
Although it is possible that the scribe here understood *çaint* as
pres. indic., it is clearly an absolute construction with the past
part. that was intended by the author, as in *Espee çainte, sor cheval,
De la cité s'en est issuz* 966–7, . . . *Se n'i veez Tristran venir, S'espee
çainte* 4291–2, also *L'espee nue, an la loge entre* 1987. But in this construction the adj. or past part. must agree with the noun, and in
1780 neither *Çainte s'espee* nor *S'espee çainte* is metrically possible.
E tries (II 180) to justify the MS. text by explaining *çaint* as a past
part. with active force, 'having girded on his sword', and cites
as a parallel *La forest est si esfree[e] Que nus n'i ose ester dedenz*
1748–9, where *esfreé*, properly 'frightened', has the active sense
of 'fear-inspiring'. In his note on this line (II 177) he refers to the
detailed discussion in *V.B.* I 126 (= I³ 151 ff.) of past parts. used
in an active sense; but though Tobler's numerous examples
include *esfreé* 'frightening', they do not include any past part. of a
transitive verb of concrete meaning such as *ceindre*, nor any
accompanied by an object such as *s'espee* would be here (the type
est mer passez, V.B. I³ 157, is to be explained differently). The
text of 1780 is therefore in all probability corrupt; we should no
doubt read *Çaint' espee*, as in *Es chanbres entre, çaint' espee* 3153.

1783–4. *Ainz qu'il venist, fu en tel paine; Fu ainz maiss gent tant eüst
paine?* This suggests that before he returned Tristran was over-
whelmed by some catastrophe; but all that happened was that he
exhausted himself hunting (1798–1800). The content, together
with the identical rhyme *paine : paine*, suggests that 1783 may be
corrupt.

1784–5. *Fu ainz maiss gent tant eüst paine? Mais l'un por l'autre ne le
sent.* In 1785 the MS. has *ne se sent*. Although E's text (like those
of Muret and M⁴) makes the correction, he suggests (II 180–1)
that *se* is defensible; but (as is indeed implied by the line he quotes
in support, *Por celi muir qui ne s'en sent*) the reflexive construction is
soi sentir de, and the MS. reading would still have to be corrected
to *ne s'en sent*, with *en* referring to *paine*.

1786. *Bien orent lor aaisement.* For *aaisement* E's glossary gives 'comfort', M⁴'s 'aise, bien-être matériel', but E's note (II 181) translates 'they had their solace'. The context suggests 'solace' (that of their love) rather than material comfort.

1832–4. *Quar Governal, ce m'est avis, S'en ert alez o le destrier Aval el bois au forestier.* The MS. has here three lines on the same rhyme (cf. note on 697–8): *S'en ert alez o le destrier Aval el bois au forestier En ot mené le bon destrier.* Somewhat similarly in 1631–2 the scribe had repeated 1631 after 1632, but he then expuncted it; in the present instance the first line has been repeated in a different form after the second, and has not been expuncted, but a satisfactory couplet is formed by either the first and second or the second and third (the decision which line to omit is arbitrary).

1836. *Tant lor dut estre pesme et dure!* See note on 856–7.

1837–41. *Par le bois vint uns forestiers, Qui avoit trové lor fulliers Ou il erent el bois geü; Tant a par le fuellier seü Qu'il fu venuz a la ramee . . .* The word *fu(e)llier* is not otherwise known. E now (II 181–2) follows M⁰ and M⁴ in translating 'dense wood, thicket', in preference to the 'bower' of his glossary and to T.-L.'s tentative 'Eindruck' (III 1981). There can be little doubt, however, that the word is derived from FULLARE, though influenced by FOLIA, and that the meaning is in fact 'trampled grass', 'trace(s)'; cf. the Eng. hunting terms *foil* 'track of a hunted animal', *foiling* 'the treading of a deer or other animal; hence the slot or trail' (*S.O.E.D.*). The word in this sense could naturally be used in the pl. as well as in the sing.; 1840 means 'followed by means of the trace' and 1838 'had found their traces' (there is therefore no need to consider *fulliers*, with E (II 20), as a possible example of the nom. sing. form in *-s* used in obl. function).

1862. *Por ce acort (il) a tel esploit.* A better correction of the nine-syllable line in the MS. is that of Muret and M⁴, *Por c'acort il a tel esploit;* after the initial adverbial locution it is normal for the pronoun subject to be expressed after the verb, and elision of the final vowel of *Por ce* is indicated by all editors in *Rois, por c(e) est biens devant eus set . . . 3263.*

1877. *Tu senbles hom(e) qui ait besoin.* So also M⁴; better, with Muret, *Tu senbles home qu'ait besoin.* The verb *senbler* is in such contexts transitive, 'resemble, look like', rather than intransitive, 'seem'; cf. a few lines earlier *Ome senbles qui core a chiens* 1874, also *Ne senbla pas home contret* 3622. The nom. of the rel. pron. is often *que*, which is elided before vowel in *la pitié q'au cor li prist* 261.

1880–1. *A toi nus hon veé son gage Ou chacié vos de ma forest?* (All editors assume that 1879 and 1880 have been interverted by the scribe; cf. note on 65–8). The word *vos* is suspect. In the first place, it is quite abnormally attached neither to a finite verb nor to an infin., but to a past part., and is in any case superfluous (the *toi* attached to the auxiliary *a* expresses both the indirect obj. of *a veé* and the direct object of *a chacié*, in normal O. F. fashion). Secondly, although the poet is sometimes careless of the distinction between 2nd person sing. and pl., it can hardly be by chance that everywhere else the form used by the king in addressing the forester is the 2nd person sing. (the king's speeches in 1873–80, 1899, 1905–13 contain 28 instances of 2nd person pronouns and verbs in the sing.). It is therefore almost certain that *chacié vos* 1881 is corrupt; it is probably an error for *chacié fors* (an alternative possibility is *dechacié*, cf. 2295 and note on 1771).

1895–6. *Li rois l'entent, boufe et sospire, Esfreez est, forment s'aïre.* Neither E nor M⁴ comments on the sense of *esfreez* here. There is no obvious reason why Mark should be 'frightened' by the news that Tristran and Iseut have been found; it is possible that he is 'terrifying, fear-inspiring' (though the glossaries give this sense only for 1748); most probably the meaning is 'excited, worked up' (cf. T.-L. III 1052).

1909–10. *A la Croiz Roge, au chemin fors, La on enfuet sovent les cors . . .* E rather hesitantly adopts (II 183) the interpretation of *au chemin fors* put forward by J. Frappier (*Rom.* 83 (1962), 251 and 84 (1963), 77), 'au chemin fourchu, à l'endroit où le chemin bifurque', supported by instances of *forc chemin* and *forchemin*. This is undoubtedly on the right lines; the only difficulty is the use (attested by the rhyme) of the form *fors*, which Frappier and

E understand as the nom. sing. used in oblique function. The only other instances of this declensional irregularity cited by E (II 20) are *filz* 1939 and 'possibly' *fulliers* 1838 and *pensis* 139; of these *filz* is well known as a special case, and for *fulliers* and *pensis* see the notes. It is therefore more probable that the form *fors* is grammatically correct, and that the text should read *as chemins fors*, to be understood as 'crossroads' rather than 'fork in the road'. T.-L.'s examples of the verb *forchier* (III 2077) show that it was used of intersections of more than three roads; cf. the use of *carreforc* in the plural, as in *Pus l'ad fet fors sacher cum un mastin pullent Et pendre as querefurs* (*Horn* 5203–4), and in the Eng. form *carfax, carfox*.

1910. *La on enfuet sovent les cors*. The glossaries of E and M⁴ merely give *la* here as '*conj.* where', 'là où'; it should be noted that this *la* is a form (found chiefly before *on*, and probably purely graphic) of monosyllabic *lau, lo, leu, leur* etc. (cf. T.-L. V 14–16), reduced form of *la ou* (which also occurs as disyllabic in Beroul 550, 1855, 2157 etc.).

1932–4. *mandé m'a une pucele Que j'alle tost a lié parler; Bien me mande n'i moigne per*. E suggests (II 183–4) that this is 'perhaps the stock "damoisele" of romance, of uncertain status, function and identity'. In fact, her function is not in doubt; neither E nor M⁴ notes the quite specific euphemistic use in O. F. of the locution *parler a aucune* in reference to an amorous assignation (see the examples in T.-L. VII 291). It is probable that the same sense should be seen, in reference to Tristran and Iseut, in 657, 697, 4283, 4330 etc., perhaps even, by way of a play on words, in the remark of Tristran as leper about Iseut, *A lui parler point ne m'ennoie* 3927. It is possible that the same implication was sometimes attached to *parlement*, as in 471 (?), 662 (cf. some of the quotations in T.-L. VII 281–2).

1944–7. *sovent regrete A lui tot sol la cuvertise Que Tristran fist, quant il l'ot prisse Yseut la bele*. E (II 26) takes *l'* in 1946 (which M⁰ had simply deleted) as an elided form of *li*, 'when he had taken from him Iseut the fair'. It is questionable, however, whether elision of

F

li ever takes place in the text except before *en* (see note on 444). Here it is possible that we should punctuate with a comma after *prisse* and understand *l'* (for *la*) as a proleptic duplication of *Yseut la bele* (especially in view of the agreement of the past part. *prisse*, more usual with a preceding than with a following object). Other probable instances of prolepsis occur with a following noun complement in *bien s'i fie, En l'espee* 1962–3, *Au departir li redemande, La bele Yseut, anuit viande* 3957–8; with a following infin. in *n'a baron Au roi ne l'ait plevi en main, Vos rendre a lui* 1374–6 (cf. 2568–70) (see the notes on all these passages); with a following clause in *Deu en mercie Que plus n'i out fait o s'amie* 383–4 (cf. 4393). There are somewhat similar uses of proleptic *le* in 87, 791, 939 etc., *en* in 409, *ce* in 75, 271, 435 etc., *cel* in 185. The complementary construction with a redundant retrospective pron. obj. occurs chiefly with *en*, e.g. in *Qu'il ne plorast ne s'en tenist* 262, *De ce qu'il ot Deu en aoure* 2332; very similarly with the adv. *la* in *Ne laira . . . qu'en ce fu ne soit la mise* 1127–8 (cf. 2817–18).

1962–3. *Li rois le sieut, qui bien s'i fie, En l'espee que il a çainte.* Muret corrected to *bien se fie En l'espee*; M⁴ restores *s'i*, but has no comma after *fie* and perhaps understands *i* as a vague 'there' or 'in the circumstances'; with E's text *i* constitutes an anticipation of *en l'espee* (see note on 1944–7).

1969–71. *Au forestier dist li roi Mars Qu'il li dorroit d'argent vint mars, Sel menoit tost a son forfet.* M¹ and M² had emended to *a lor recet*; M⁴ follows M³ and E in restoring the MS. text, but comments (p. 145) '*Forfet* n'est pas clair'. E takes *forfet* as the abstract noun; in his glossary (though placing it under *forfaire* v.n.) he had translated 'to (the scene of) his [i.e. the forester's] misdeed', but he now thinks it more likely (II 186) that *forfet* should be taken as 'forfeit, bargain' and *a son forfet* as 'to the (place of the) fulfilment of his [i.e. the king's] bargain, or the redeeming of his pledge or promise'. There does not, however, seem to be any authority for this 'local' interpretation, and it is not really supported by *Dist que pres sont de lor besoigne* 1973, to which E refers. T.-L. quotes the passage not under *forfait* sb. but under *forfait* adjectival past part. (III 2092), 'der sich vergangen hat, schuldig, frevlerisch'; though the syntactical context is different from that of the other examples there cited, the probability that this is the right interpretation is confirmed by the O. F. use of other nouns and substantivized adjectives with a possessive adj. in the sense of an 'objective genitive'. Instances of this quoted in *V.B.* II² 80–2 include *son traïtor* 'a traitor to him', *mon laron* 'the man who has robbed me', *ses bienvoellans* 'one who wishes him well', *leur nuissans* 'those who harm them'; cf. in our text *Du roi joent si losengier* 3494 'those who deceitfully flatter him'. *Son forfet* may therefore similiarly mean 'the man who had offended against him'.

1987–90. *L'espee nue, an la loge entre. Le forestier entre soventre, Grant erre aprés le roi acort; Li ros li çoine qu'il retort.* The word *entre* 1988 is highly suspect: it is probable from 1989–90 that the forester does not actually enter the bower, and *entre* is quite likely to have been erroneously introduced by the scribe because of the rhyme-words *entre* : *soventre* (cf. note on 819–20). The adv. *so(v)entre* is often used in O. F. with the verb *aler* and particularly with *en aler*: cf. *Eurialus s'en vet soantre* (*Eneas* 5127), *Si compaignon en vont soantre* (*Partonopeus* 3449), also with *so(v)entre* prep. *Soantre lui grant gent la'n vait* (*Eneas* 59). It is therefore probable that in the original 1988 read *Li forestiers en vait soventre* 'goes along behind him'. Cf. note on 3150–2.

1991–2. *Li rois en haut le cop leva, Iré le fait, si se tresva.* E para-phrases 'Mark raised his unsheathed sword in anger, but . . . his strength fails him' (II 186, cf. II 43); but though 'his strength fails him' may fit the context, it is hardly justified as a rendering of *tresaler*, for which the glossaries give 'swoon', 'défaillir'. A. Henry (*Etudes de syntaxe expressive*, Brussels, 1960, p. 64 n. 2), finding this interpretation unsatisfactory, prefers to take *tresaler* in the alternative general sense of 'go beyond' or 'pass away', and suggests three different adaptations of this sense to the context (in which for him the line begins with the sb. *ire*, not the past part. *iré*): 'anger causes it (i.e. the king's action) (1) and then passes away'; (2) '. . . and goes too far, passes all bounds'; (3) '. . . and he (the king) loses his self-control'. Faced with this variety of interpretations (of which the last two are otherwise unattested), B. Blakey (*F.S.* 21 (1967), 100–1) suggests that the second hemistich originally ran *sis tresua*, with the pret. of *tres(s)üer* 'sweat'; this verb is used in a very similar context in *D'ire tresue sa persone* 4431 (referring to Iseut's reaction to the sight of an enemy's shadow on her window), and, unlike *tresaler*, is amply attested in O. F. in association with the notion of anger. There is no need, however, to assume with Blakey a stage with an unattested refl. form of *tressüer*: given an original *si tresüa*, the scribe, reading the verb as *tresva*, was quite capable of restoring the measure (cf. note on 1569–70) by inserting the refl. pron. which is attested with *tresaler*. E (II 187) misunderstands Blakey's hypothesis, which does not involve 'the creation of a hypermetric line'; as for the 'introduction of a stylistically inappropriate preterite', it could be argued that it is not the pret. *tresüa* but the pres. *fait* that is inappropriate, since it is a pret. *leva* that appears in the preceding line, and a pret. *vit* which continues the narration in 1995, 1998 and 2000. On the other hand, E himself points out (II 23) that the 3rd person sing. pres. indic. of *aler* is everywhere else in the text not *va* but *vait* or *vet* (some 14 examples in rhyme). All in all, there is good reason to suppose that the second hemistich of 1992 should read *si tressüa*. The proper form of the first hemistich remains in doubt. But there is perhaps more substance than E admits in Henry's observation that the adj. 'angry' elsewhere in the text always appears as *irié*, masc. nom. sing. *iriez* (1029, 1985 etc.); and though the construction *Ire le fait* is not very plausible if taken as 'anger causes it', it should probably be understood with the factitive use of *faire* mentioned in note on 89–90, i.e. taken as equivalent to *ire li fait faire* 'anger causes him to do it'.

1993–2001. *Ja decendist li cop sor eus: Ses oceïst, ce fust grant deus.* (1995) *Qant vit qu'ele avoit sa chemise Et q'entre eus deus avoit devise,* (1997) *La bouche o l'autre n'ert jostee, Et qant il vit la nue espee* (1999) *Qui entre eus deus les desevrot, Vit les braies que Tristran out:* (2001) *'Dex!' dist li rois, 'ce que puet estre?'* The disagreement between E (II 186–7 and 43) and A. Henry (*Etudes de syntaxe expressive,* pp. 62–5) about the interpretation of this passage is in part a matter of punctuation. There are two long clauses, each introduced by *qant* (1995–7, 1998–2000): E, like Muret and M⁴, takes both with what follows (i.e. subordinates them both to '*Dex! dist li rois* 2001), Henry takes both with what precedes (i.e. subordinates them both to *Ja decendist li cop sor eus* 1993). The movement of the second *qant*-clause is such that it would be very difficult to separate it from the following words of the king; but it would be almost equally difficult, in view of the similarly-structured passages assembled by Henry, to separate the first *qant*-clause from the formally hypothetical sentence which precedes. It therefore seems probable that the full stop should be placed, contrary to the opinions of both scholars, after 1997—even though this means separating the two *qant*-clauses, which are roughly parallel in content, and attaching them grammatically to two different principal clauses.

The deletion of E's (and M⁴'s) full stop after 1994 means that *Ja decendist li cop sor eus* 1993 is to be taken with Henry as an example of what he calls a 'subjonctif d'imminence contrecarrée': 'the blow would have fallen on them, was about to fall on them—when he saw . . .' (with the result that the blow did not actually fall). E attempts to explain the line as containing a 'phrase conditionnelle à condition sous-entendue', and to associate it with other uses of the impf. subjunctive in the text; but all those he lists are of quite different types (in *Ja nu pensast nul jor par lui* 87 the condition is expressed by *par lui* = 'if he had not been influenced by others'; 143, 985, 1918, 2173 contain impf. subjunctives of *devoir*, *pooir* and *mex venir* in traditional idiomatic functions corresponding to Mod. F *devrait*, *pourrait*, *vaudrait mieux*; 1253 and 3820 are exclamations with *Qui . . . veïst . . .!*). In any case, E's paraphrase 'the blow all but descended upon the lovers (= "le coup descendait déjà sur eux")' amounts to an acceptance of Henry's interpretation for this line taken by itself.

There remains the question of the force and status of *Ses oceïst, ce fust grant deus* 1994. M² and E, and apparently also M⁴ (p. 145—in spite of its punctuation with a comma instead of E's colon after *sor eus* 1993), take this as an independent hypothetical sentence with *ses* = *se les*: 'if he had killed them, it would have been a grievous thing'. Henry, on the other hand, takes *ses* as = *si les*, and (although he puts the whole line between dashes) understands the first clause as co-ordinated with 1993: 'le coup allait fondre sur eux [et] il allait les tuer, ç'aurait été grand malheur'. On the face of the text, both interpretations are possible; but granted Henry's interpretation of 1993, his version of 1994 seems more effective and equally in harmony with Beroul's manner. It may be suggested, however, that only the second hemistich should be placed between dashes or parentheses: *Ja decendist li cop sor eus, Ses oceïst (ce fust grant deus!), Qant vit qu'ele avoit sa chemise . . .*; cf. 748, 798, 2029, 2035 etc. as printed in one or more of the editions.

2020–23. *Je lor ferai tel demostranceAnçois que il s'esvelleront, Certainement savoir porront Qu'il furent endormi trové.* In the MS. 2021 begins *Queançois que*. This is one of the rare instances where E emends while M⁴ retains the MS. text (with the elision *qu'il* for *que il*); Muret had emended to *Que puis que*. E is no doubt justified in saying that the MS. reading 'hardly makes sense' (II 187): the lovers obviously cannot know about Mark's visit before they wake. On the other hand, though it would be logically possible for the text to say 'Before they wake, I will provide such proof (that) they will be able (at a time not stated) to know . . .', this is not very convincing as a speech (why should the king stress the point that his proof will be given before they wake?); and it is open to the serious grammatical objection (as is the text of the MS. and of M⁴) that it assumes the use of *ançois que* in the temporal sense of 'before', followed by the indicative *s'esvelleront*. Now *ançois que* is not used elsewhere in the text in that sense (in 1886–7 *ançois . . . que* means 'rather than that', cf. note on 1114); but in the text, as is normal in O. F., any conjunction meaning 'before' is followed by the subjunctive (so with *ainz . . . que* 309–11, with *ainz que* 692, 1021, 1598, 1621, 1783 etc.). These objections were no doubt in Muret's mind when he emended to *Que puis que il s'esvelleront*, giving the passage the sense 'I will give them such a proof that, after they wake, they will be able to know . . .'. The order of the clauses here, with the temporal clause (2021) preceding a subordinate on which it depends (2022), whose principal itself precedes the temporal clause (2020), is a common one in the text, cf. 2815–18, 3693–6, 4391–3 (also with other types of sub-subordinate clause 1846–7, 1884–7 etc.). The assumption that the scribe could have substituted *ançois que* for its converse *puis que* is supported by other cases where words of opposite meaning have been confused (all editors replace *plus* by *mains* in 3638, *tort* by *droit* in 4171; for confusion of words for 'over' and 'under' cf. note on 955–8). The conjunction *puis que*, however, is in the text used only in reference to past time and is always followed by the pret. (104, 1465, 1508, also 1578, for which see the note); the emendation should therefore be rather to *des que* 'as soon as', which gives a somewhat better sense and is used in the text in reference to future time, followed by the fut. or fut. in the past (conditional), in 2797, 3274, 4243.

2027–9. *Ge voi el doi a la reïne L'anel o pierre esmeraudine, Or li donnai, molt par est buens.* Muret had emended *Or* 2029 to *Que*; E and M⁴ restore the MS. reading, but neither makes any comment. The only attested sense of *or* which could come into consideration here is the argumentative or explanatory 'now (in fact)', more or less as in the minor premiss of a syllogism (T.-L. VI 1167); but if this were intended, *li* would stand for *le li*, and the passage should be punctuated with a semi-colon (as in M⁴) or a full stop after 2028. But even with this punctuation neither the *Or* nor the def. art. in *L'anel* is convincing, and Muret's correction seems indispensable; the scribe has often misread or miswritten advs., relatives and conjs., especially at the beginning of the line.

2043. *L'anel du doi defors parut.* Outside what? Neither E nor M⁴ comments on the meaning of this line.

2044. *Souef le traist, qu'il ne se mut.* M⁴ comments (p. 145) 'On attend plutôt *qu'el ne se mut*: le roi a parfaitement bougé (2048–50) et l'anneau est sorti aisément (2047)'. E, however, takes *il* as referring to *doi* (II 188), i.e. 'without the finger's moving'. This is no doubt just possible if one considers only 2043–4; but it is less satisfactory if these lines are taken together with those which follow, *Primes i entra il enviz; Or avoit tant les doiz gresliz Qu'il s'en issi sanz force fere* 2045–7. Here the *il* in 2045 and 2047, like the *le* in 2044, can refer only to the ring; this makes it most improbable that the intervening *il* in 2044 can be intended to refer to the finger. The correction to *el* remains plausible.

2058–61. *De plusorz parz out demandé Ou a esté et ou tant fut. Li rois lor ment, pas n'i connut Ou il ala.* E says (II 189) that as the scribe often writes *u* for *n* one might read *ont* 2058 ('they asked'), particularly in view of *lor* 2060. The impers. construction (*i*) *out demandé* (T.-L. I 770–71) 'it was asked', however, comes much more appropriately than would *ont demandé* after *De plusorz parz*; and in O. F. there would be no difficulty about its being followed by the personal but generic *lor* 2060. E mentions M⁰'s interpretation of this *lor* as being for *lors* 'then', but omits to point out that at this stage Muret read the verb as *vint*.

2080–1. *L'espee prent com home iriez, Regarde el brant, l'osche ne voit.* 2081 is so punctuated also by Muret and M⁴; but in view of the usual constructions of *regarder* (T.-L. VIII 600–1) it ought perhaps to run *Regarde, el brant l'osche ne voit*.

2112–14. *il nos veut deçoivre; Quar il ert seus, si nos trova, Poor li prist, si s'en torna.* The punctuation (so also in Muret's later eds. and M⁴; M⁰ had semi-colons after both 2112 and 2113) suggests that 2113 is to be taken as giving the cause of the fear mentioned in 2114, 'Because he was alone and found us, fear seized him . . .'; but this construction, with a *quar*-clause preceding the clause that it explains, and apparently serving as a subordinate to it, would be most unusual. It would seem more normal to attach 2113 to what precedes; but in that case *si* comes under suspicion (it could be an error induced by the *si* in the same position in 2114). It is therefore possible that we should read *il nos veut deçoivre, Quar il ert seus quant nos trova; Poor li prist, si s'en torna.*

2119–20. *Voiant le pueple, nos veut prendre, Faire ardoir et venter la cendre.* For *venter* E's glossary gives 'blow with the wind', which seems to imply that the verb is intransitive. The examples in Gdf. (VIII 176) show that it is transitive and means, as glossed by Muret and M⁴, 'jeter au vent'.

2121–2. '. . . *Fuion, n'avon que demorer.*' *N'avet en eus que demorer.*
For the construction in 2121, with personal *avoir*, negative, and
que indef. pron. +infin. see T.-L. I 759: 'we have no reason to
delay, we must not delay'. In 2122 Muret had emended *demorer* to
sejorner; E and M⁴ restore the MS. reading, in spite of the identical
rhyme. E (II 191) translates 'There was in them no (thought of)
tarrying', and this is presumably also how Muret intended his
text to be understood, *sejorner* being merely a synonym of *demorer*;
it is not, however, an acceptable interpretation of the construction, which is quite different from that in 2121. In O. F. impersonal *avoir*, negative, with *en* +personal noun or pron. and *que* +
infin. has two well-attested uses. In the first, *que* is the indef. pron.
'what(ever), anything', and the infin. is that of a transitive verb,
as in *en lui n'ot qu'enseignier* 'in him there was nothing to correct',
en Ydoine n'a que reprendre (see T.-L. I 772–3, III 518). In the second,
que is in origin the comparative conj. 'than' (*ne . . . que* 'not . . .
except, nothing but'), and the infin. is that of an intrans. or refl.
verb, as in *en lui n'ot que corrocier* 'in him there was nothing but
anger', *el charretier n'ot que doloir* (see T.-L. I 773–4). Now, neither
of these constructions makes sense in the context with the infin.
demorer or *sejorner;* and even with a different infin. the first would
be very unlikely. The original version of 2122 must have had the
second construction, but with the infin. of a verb meaning
probably 'be disturbed, alarmed, frightened'—perhaps *N'avet
en eus que esfreer.*

2151–3. *Iseut remest en sa fullie. Tristran, sachiez, une doitie A un cerf
traist, qu'il out visé.* E rightly says (II 196) that from the context
the word *doitie(e)* (otherwise unknown) would appear to mean
'shaft', and not, as suggested by G. Raynaud de Lage, 'une
piste, une coulée de gibier'. It may perhaps be conjectured that
it is an error for *boitie(e)*, a hypothetical Western form (cf. Western
voitre 3685 for *voutre* and Pope §319) corresponding to the *boutee
d'arbaleste* cited by Gdf. (I 709) from a late text. Rather than a
derivative of the verb *bouter* (as assumed by Gdf.), such a word
might be a cognate of *bouzon, boujon, boudon* '(crossbow) bolt' (cf.
T.-L. I 1100 and *F.E.W.* *bultjo), and a derivative of the Germanic
source of O. E. *bolt*, O. H. G. *bolz* 'arrow'.

2161–3. 'Ha! Dex,' fait il, 'tant ai traval! Trois anz a hui, que riens n'i fal, Onques ne me falli pus paine . . .'. E says (II 196) that que riens n'i fal means 'as I mistake not', 'without the possibility of error', but does not define the nature of the que. In his glossary (similarly in that of M⁰) it is classified as '(conditional) if', but conditional que 'provided that, granted that' would be followed by the subjunctive; the que here must be the modal conjunction ('in such circumstances that'), which when depending on an affirmative principal clause is followed by the indic. (cf. T.-L. VIII 26–7). See also note on 2303–4.

2203. En bois estes com autre serve. E's glossary correctly indicates that autre here has an 'expletive' function, but this is not brought out by his translation (II 197) 'like any other serving maid'; rather better in Muret's and M⁴'s glossaries, 'comme une autre femme qui serait de condition servile, comme une serve'. If the word autre is to be rendered in Eng., the closest equivalent might be 'mere'. For this use of autre, which T.-L. (I 692) defines as 'autre vor subst., das nicht Oberbegriff zum vorhergehenden', see V.B. III² 83. Cf. 1481, 4132 and notes.

2209–10. Lasse! si male garde en fist! El n'en pout mais, quar j'ai trop pris. The MS. reading quar j'ai trop pris is suspect, not so much because of the imperfect rhyme (which is paralleled in vis : froidis[t] 3167–8) as because of the substance: there is no question of Iseut's having 'taken too much' of the potion, and even if the quantity she drank were relevant, the tense ai pris would not be appropriate. M⁴ retains the emendation which M³ had adopted from Jeanroy, quar trop mesprist; as noted by M⁴ (p. 146) and E (II 197), this is supported by the line Ele me[s]prist estre son voil in the Folie Tristran de Berne, ed. Hoepffner, 433. The retained quar, however, does not really make sense ('she could not help it, for she acted very wrongly'—there is no justification for M⁴'s gloss of meprendre (sic) 'pécher par étourderie'). The parallelism with the Folie de Berne suggests the further correction of quar to se: El n'en pout mais se trop mesprist 'if she acted very wrongly, she could not help it (or it was not her fault)'; cf. S'il ont poor, n'en püent mais 2123, also Que püent il se color müent? 1646 (cf. note on 1382–4).

2220. *Mex ne nos pout il pas deçoivre.* One expects rather the impf. subj., *Mex ne nos peüst il deçoivre*; cf. *Or ne peüst mex avenir* 2272. The pret. indic., however, is used also in an exactly similar context in *Il ne me pout plus ahonter* 268.

2227. . . . *Et qu'il preïst nostre escondit.* For the terms *escondit*, *escondire*, *deraisne*, *deraisnier*, which occur frequently throughout the remainder of the poem, see note on 131.

2231–5. *N'a chevalier en son roiaume, Ne de Lidan tresque en Dureaume . . . Ne m'en trovast en chanp, armé.* E says (II 106, 146) that here Durham is placed in Mark's kingdom, whereas in 4264 it is, more naturally, in Arthur's. But the words of 2231–2 do not carry the implication he suggests: after declaring in 2231 that there is not a knight in Mark's kingdom whom he would not challenge, Tristran goes on to say 'Nor (is there one) from Lidan all the way to Durham', using the common hyperbolical device of the type 'from here to Jerusalem', i.e. 'in all the world'. The necessary implication is that while Lidan is near at hand in Cornwall, Durham is far away at the other end of England; the same device is used in *De Costentin entresqu'a Rome* 2386 (see note) and *de ci jusq'en Tudele* 3410.

E (II 10) considers that the rhyme of *Dureaume* here and *Durelme* 4264 with *roiaume* exemplifies the Northern differentiation of *eau* to *iau*. This is very improbable, since the original form of *roiaume* was *realme*, *reaume*, and the word is commonly rhymed with *paume* (e.g. *Erec* 1999), *Guillaume* (e.g. *Guil. d'Angl.* 29) etc.; cf. also Pope §§539–40. Nor is any evidence of *iau* for *eau* provided by the rhyme *meseaus : joiaus* 3771–2, which E also quotes: see examples of rhymes such as *joel : isnel, boel, anel* and *jo(i)els : oisels* in T.-L. IV 1687–91.

2236–9. *Et s'il avoit en volenté, Quant vos avriez deresnie, Qu'il me soufrist de sa mesnie, Gel serviroie a grant honor.* On 2237 E gives references (II 198) for the use of *avoir* as auxiliary of a refl. verb (see also T.-L. I 766–7). There is, however, no other instance in the text (apart from the special case of *Nel se voudroit avoir pensé* 213) of this usage, which is relatively rare especially in the West. In all probability *avrïez* is an error (the scribe having mistaken the pron. obj. *vos* for the subject) for *avroie*, 'when I should have cleared you of the charge'; the preceding lines refer not to Iseut's exculpation of herself by oath or ordeal but to Tristran's offer to refute the charge against her by a judicial duel (cf. note on 131).

2241–2. *N'avroit soudoier en sa terre Qui miex le soufrist de sa gerre.* E (II 198) attempts to justify the *soufrist* of the MS. (emended to *servist* by Muret and M⁴) by assuming an extension of the sense of the verb from 'bear with, abide by the will of' (cf. *De moi ferez vostre plesir, Et je sui prest de vos soufrir* 795–6) to 'serve (in respect of his war)'; but there is a very considerable semantic gap, which other instances in the text of *soufrir* with personal object (see 2311, 2855) do nothing to bridge. It is much more probable that under the influence of *me soufrist de sa mesnie* 2238 the scribe has simply miscopied *le servist de sa gerre* as *le soufrist de sa gerre*.

2243–6. *s'il estoit a son plesir Vos a prendre et moi de gerpir . . . Ge m'en iroie.* E rejects (II 198) 'the "normalizing" correction to *degerpir*' made by M⁰ (cf. *Qant degerpir volez pechiez* 2264) on the ground that the alternation between *a* and *de* after the same verb is well attested. But he gives no evidence, and I have shown (*Vinaver Misc.*, p. 266) that there is in fact no other instance in the text of a *change* of preposition before the second of two parallel infins. depending on the same verb; on the other hand, the *non-repetition* of a preposition before a second infin. occurs in 2175–6 and 2855–6, so that *Vos a prendre et moi degerpir* is more in harmony with the author's practice. In any case, it is not a 'correction' to alter the scribe's word-divisions, some of which are quite arbitrary; see note on 29–30.

2251–4. *Ne vosise la departie, S'estre peüst la conpaignie, Ne fust, bele, la grant soufraite Que vos soufrez.* There is no need to assume with M⁴ (p. 146) that (in spite of the absence of any co-ordinating conjunction) *Ne fust . . . la soufraite* is parallel with *estre peüst la conpaignie* and depends grammatically on the conjunction *se*. It is more probable that the two conditions are independent and that the hypothetical character of the second is expressed intrinsically by the impf. subj. *fust* alone; cf. *Estre peüses a anor . . ., Ne fust, dame, li vins herbez* 2257-9. It is perhaps possible that 2251 and 2252 have been interverted by the scribe and that in the original the two conditional clauses were separated by the principal clause: *S'estre peüst la conpaignie, Ne vosise la departie, Ne fust, bele, la grant soufraite.*

2253-5. *. . . . la grant soufraite Que vos soufrez et avez faite Toz dis, por moi, par desertine.* (The MS. has *soufrance*, corrected by all editors). M⁴ comments (p. 146) '*Faire une soufraite* surprend: *traite* conviendrait mieux: cf. 2644 et surtout 2683-4'. It is not, however, necessary to assume that we have here an instance of *faire une soufraite* in the sense of *traire mal* (2644), *traire une soufrete* (2683-4): more probably *faire* is used quite normally as verbum vicarium, *avez faite* standing for *avez souferte* (cf., e.g., *Gel connois bien, si fait il moi* 3463).

2270-2. *Beaus amis douz, se ja corage Vos ert venuz de repentir, Or ne peüst mex avenir.* E translates (II 202) 'If you had then repented, it could not have come more opportunely'; but this does violence to the text (replacing *or* 'now' in the principal clause by 'then' in the conditional clause), and does not fit the context—Iseut is not arguing that Tristran ought to have repented on their earlier visit to Ogrin (the subject of the preceding lines 2265-9), but that the present moment ('*Qant degerpir volez pechiez*' 2264) is most opportune for repentance. The meaning intended must be either 'If the desire to repent were ever to come to you, it could not come at a better time than now' or 'If the desire to repent has now come to you, it could never have come at a better time'. It was presumably the second of these possibilities that Muret had in mind when he emended *ert* to *est* (cf. note on 1729-32); but further correction would be required, such as the interchange of *ja* and *or*: *se or corage Vos est venuz de repentir, Ja ne peüst mex avenir.*

2283-4. *Manderon a nostre talent Par briés sanz autre mandement.* E's note (II 202) says only '*a* "according to" '; his glossary gives for *mander* here '*v.a.* send (a message)', but there is no parallel in

T.-L. (V 1034–9) for such an absolute use of the verb, without an object either of the thing or of the person. It seems indispensable to correct with Muret and M⁴ to *Mandon au roi nostre talent*.

2286–8. *Au riche roi celestïen Puison andui crïer merci, Qu'il ait de nos, Tristran, ami!* The punctuation is the same in Muret and M⁴; the movement of the O. F. construction would perhaps be better represented without the comma after *merci* (though there is nothing exactly similar in T.-L. V 1487–8).

2295–6. *Gent dechacie, a con grant paine Amors par force vos demeine!* The verb *demener* here is glossed by E 'control, dominate', by Muret and M⁴ 'mener, gouverner, traiter'; but the examples in T.-L. II 1365–6 would justify the more appropriate sense 'drive (from place to place), persecute'.

2301–2. *Si longuement l'avon menee, Itel fu nostre destinee.* Neither E nor M⁴ makes it clear (as does M⁰) that *si* here = *se*: cf. notes on 412–14 and 1382–4.

2303–4. *Trois anz a bien, si que n'i falle, Onques ne nos falli travalle.* For *si que n'i falle* E says (II 202) 'Literally: "provided that I make no mistake about it", i.e. "if I mistake not" '; but his glossary cites the line under *si que* 'as'. There is no evidence, however, of the existence in O. F. of a pure conditional conj. *si que* (with subj.) 'provided that'; in passages like *jel feroie Molt volentiers, se je pooie, Si que Yseut fust acordee O le roi Marc* 2189–92, or 2794–5, the meaning is 'in such a way that' and the subj. is final. In 2303 the force of *si que* must be modal ('in such circumstances that'), and when depending on an affirmative principal clause this would have the indic. (cf. *Trois anz a hui, que riens n'i fal . . .* 2162 and note). The rhyme-words therefore ought probably to be *fal* (pres. indic.) and *traval* (for nom. *travalz*); the rather rare fem. noun *travalle*, in any case, does not appear elsewhere in the text.

2313–18. . . . *Gel servirai si con je doi; Sire, mon oncle est riche roi* . . .

Le mellor consel nos donnez, Por Deu, sire, de ce qu'oez, Et nos feron vos volentez. Given the MS. sequence of lines (2313–20) rhyming in *oi oi ez ez ez ine ine*, Muret at first deleted the third of the lines in -*ez*, *Et nos feron vos volentez* (so M⁰), then restored it and assumed that there was a lacuna after it (so M²); E preferred to place the lacuna after 2314; M⁴'s text shows it after *Gel servirai si con je doi* 2313 (separating the two lines ending in -*oi*), but this is probably a printing error, since the note (p. 146) says '2315 Lacune (Ewert)'. E assumes (II 202) that of four successive lines on the same rhyme in his model the scribe had omitted the first; this seems unlikely, and of the three extant lines in -*ez* it would not be difficult to dispense with 2318 (with M⁰) or 2317. On the other hand, *Sire, mon oncle est riche roi* 2314 hangs in the air as it stands; but Muret here adopted the very plausible correction of G. Paris, reading *Gel servirai si con je doi, Si con mon oncle et riche roi* (cf. 2239–40). Cf. notes on 160–2, 207–10.

2321–4. *De lui proier point ne se faint Qu'il les acort au roi, si plaint: 'Qar ja corage de folie Nen avrai je jor de ma vie . . .'*. The MS. has *se saint* 2321, *se plaint* 2322 and *ja jor* 2324, corrected by all editors; the first of these corrections is essential, and for the third see note on 75–7. As regards 2322 I have argued (*Vinaver Misc.*, p. 269) that *se* ought to be retained and the passage punctuated differently: *De lui proier point ne se faint; Qu'il les acort au roi se plaint: 'Qar ja corage . . .'* 'She does not fail to implore him; she begs that he will reconcile them with the king: "For never in all the days of my life will I have a mind for folly" '. This interpretation requires *se plaint que*+subj. to be taken in the unusual sense of 'begs that', but the same sense is found in the compound *se conplaint* in 432–5 (see note), where T.-L. (II 629) glosses 'fleht' and M⁰'s glossary 'supplier avec plainte'. There is nothing unusual about the use of *proier* 2321 without a *que*-clause (cf. *Fai grant senblant de toi proier* 543) nor about the order of the clauses in 2322 (cf. *Qu'il ne plorast ne s'en tenist* 262). On the other hand, the editors' version, with *se* corrected to *si* 'and', requires Iseut's words beginning with *Qar* to be taken, very unnaturally, as object of *plaint* (presumably understood in its usual sense of 'complains, laments', though the words are not in fact a lament).

2332. *De ce qu'il ot Deu en aoure.* For the sense of *ao(u)rer Deu* 'thank God' cf. *a Deu en prist grant pitié, S'en aorames Damledé* 2583-4 and T.-L. I 413; E's glossary gives for *aorer* only 'worship'.

2340. *Buen consel averez de moi.* According to E (II 25) 'the syllable-count confirms the Northern form *averez*'; but there is no other future form in the text with svarabhaktic *e*, and it is probable that the line originally ran *Buen consel en avrez de moi* (*consel* and *con-sellier*, in the sense of 'counsel', usually have a 'respective' comple-ment, often *en* 'about it, in the matter', cf. *de lor pechiez A moi en vindrent consel prendre* 2336-7, *Conseliez m'en, gel vos requier* 631, also 1571, 2529-30 etc.).

2345-9. *Qant home et feme font pechié, S'anz se sont pris et sont quitié Et s'aus vienent a penitance Et aient bone repentance, Dex lor pardone lor mesfait.* M³, followed by M⁴, corrects the *Sanz* of the MS. in 2346, as suggested by G. Paris, to *S'aus*, assuming that in both 2346 and 2347 the scribe's model had the dialectal form *aus* for *eus*, and that in both lines this pron., properly the strong obl. form, is used as subject of the verb. But *aus* for *eus* is a Northern and Eastern form (Pope §501) of which there is no other example in the MS. Though in the 12th century strong obl. forms like *eus* had begun to be used in the function of nominatives, they were still rare except in conjunctive and disjunctive constructions like *je nes vuel noient ocire, Ne moi ne gent de mon enpire* 2025-6, *Torne a un gué lui* (MS. *lie*) *et Andrez* 3877 (see also note on 2492), or in locutions like *Toi tiers seras fet chevaliers* 3408. E is undoubtedly right in restoring *anz* 2346, understood as a spelling of *ainz* (cf. *nan* 1311 for *nain* etc.) 'first, previously'. But if the scribe's *sanz* in 2346 is not an error for *s'aus* = *s'eus*, the case for taking his *saus* in 2347 as *s'aus* = *s'eus* is very much weakened. It is more probable that it is an error, perhaps for *puis* (*pus*): 'if they have first taken each other, and have separated, and then come to penance . . .'.

2364-5. *Vos ferïez por lui itant, Vos en irïez a sa cort.* E comments (II 203) 'You would do the like for him' or 'You would do this much for him, [viz.] go to his court . . .'. The second of these alternatives is alone acceptable (cf. notes on 1593 and 2411-13), and the lines should be printed as in M⁰ with a colon after *itant*.

2365–70. *Vos en iriez a sa cort; N'i avroit fort, sage ne lort, S'il veut dire qu'e[n] vilanie Eüsiez prise drüerie, Si vos face li rois Marc pendre* . . . The apparent meaning of 2366 is either 'There would be no one, strong or wise or foolish, who . . .' or 'There would be no s trong man, either wise or foolish, who . . .'. It is hard to believe that either of these is what the author intended to say. The word *fort* has no doubt been erroneously introduced under the influence of the rhyme-words *cort* and *lort* (cf. note on 819–20). (There is another erroneous *fort* in 2604, where all editors correct to *s'or*). The minimum correction required would be to *N'i avroit lors sage ne lort* . . .; but the condit. *avroit* is not essential to the construction, and the original may have read something like *N'i a baron, sage ne lort* . . . (cf. 2578–9).

2371–3. *Tristran, por ce t'os bien loer, Que ja n'i troveras ton per Qui gage doinst encontre toi.* The sense requires a direct pron. obj. to *os loer* (what the hermit advises is what he has just said, 2357–70); read *por ce[l] t'os bien loer* (cf. note on 269–70) or correct to *por ce le t'os loer*, or, with M⁰, to *por ce l'os bien loer*.

2385–7. *Tel saut feïstes qu'il n'a home De Costentin entresqu'a Rome, Se il le voit, n'en ait hisdor.* The identification of *Costentin* with Constantine in Cornwall, favoured by E (II 32, 203–4), rather than with the Cotentin (as preferred by Muret and M⁴), is supported by the comparison with 2232 (see note on 2231–5).

2400–3. *Et se lui venoit a viaire, Qant vos serez de lui loiaus Au loement de vos vasaus, Preïst sa feme la cortoise.* E now accepts (II 204) Muret's correction of *vos vasaus* to *ses vasaus*; but the passage remains obscure. A first problem is that of the syntactical position of *Au loement de ses vasaus* 2402. E's punctuation associates it with 2401, and he translates 'when, in the judgment of his vassals, you will be his loyal subject'; but Muret and M⁴, who punctuate with a comma after *loiaus* and none after *vasaus*, are probably right in taking it with 2403, since the locution *au* (or *par le*) *loement de*

G

means 'by the advice of' or 'with the consent of' (cf. T.-L. V 560–1) rather than 'in the judgment of', and implies a choice of action and not merely of opinion. The meaning of 2402–3 therefore seems to be 'by the advice of his vassals he would take (back) his wife'. If this is correct, 2401 depends only on 2400, and the meaning of these two lines as they stand would have to be, roughly, 'if it seemed good to him, when you were loyal to him'. But in this context such a temporal clause (even if its verb were in a more appropriate tense than is *serez*) is not very convincing: would Tristran be more loyal at a later date than now? (E's 'when your loyalty is established' and Muret's and M⁴'s 'quand il sera certain de votre fidélité' (glossaries, s.v. *loial*) is hardly justified by the text.) One wonders, therefore, whether 2400–1 were not intended to mean 'if it seemed to him that you would be loyal to him'. In fact, 'seem to someone (to be the case)' is the usual sense of *estre a viaire a aucun*, with which *venir a viaire*, not registered in Gdf. VIII 224, is presumably synonymous; and for the sentence as a whole compare *quant vendra jusqu'a un an, Que tu seras aseürez Qu'Yseut te tienge loiautez* . . . 2902–4. In that case, 2401 should be corrected to something like *Que vos fussiez a lui loiaus* (perhaps with *seiez*, which might be misread as *serez*, for *fussiez*; but *loial de* does not seem to be attested).

2403–5. *Preïst sa feme la cortoise. Et, se savez que lui n'en poise, O lui serez ses soudoiers.* In O. F. one expects the subjunctive in a noun clause depending on a conditional clause. Neither M⁰ (p. lviii) nor E (II 24) lists *poise* here among the pres. subj. forms with analogical *-e*, and in fact it is probably intended as pres. indic. (so M⁰ and E, glossary). Cf. note on 1431–6.

2411–13. *Tant ait plus [mis, beau] sire Ogrin, Vostre merci, el parchemin, Que je ne m'os en lui fïer.* The meaning is not, as stated by E (glossary s.v. *tant* and II 204) 'However much is put in the letter . . .', but 'Let this much more be put in the letter, [viz.] that I dare not trust him'; for clarity the comma after 2412 should be replaced by a colon. Cf. 1593, 2364, 2713, 3487, 3496 and notes.

2449–51. *Anuit, aprés solel couchier, Qant li tens prist a espoisier,*

Tristran s'en torne avoc son mestre. The MS. has *Qanuit* (the scribe had momentarily mistaken the line for a continuation of Tristran's speech ending at 2448; he may also have been influenced by *Qant* 2450). All editors emend to *Anuit*; but this adv. means 'last night' or 'tonight', and is used only to situate an event from the point of view of the speaker (cf. 2281, 2647, 3958, 4294). What is required here is the equally modest emendation *La nuit*, meaning 'That night', from the point of view of the narrator; cf. 679, 701, 2651, 4089, 4112.

2463–4. *Li rois s'esvelle et dit aprés: 'Qui es, qui a tel eure ves?'* The use of *aprés* 'afterwards' is surprising. It is possible that it is an error, perhaps for *adés* 'immediately'; but cf. 2733–5 and note.

2479–80. *Governal dist: 'Fol, quar esploites! Alon nos en les destoletes!'* The form *esploites*, functioning as imper. but with unetymological -*s*, is taken by E (II 23) as a pres. subj. used in command; but it is not listed by him in II 24 (though it is by M⁰, p. xxii) among the pres. subj. forms with analogical -*e*. Such imper. forms in -*es*, however, are usually explained as based on the analogy of the pres. indic. (cf. Fouché, p. 209; Pope §913, where they are attributed to a rather later date); and we have an undoubted indic. form used as imper. in *Rois, quar le retiens, Plus en seras doutez et criens* 2871–2 (corrected in M¹ only to *s'or le retiens*, with pres. indic.), also in the first person pl. *dimes* in *Alon au ro et si li dimes . . .* 600.

2492. *Tresque l'ermite et el les virent.* In addition to the obvious correction of *Tresque* for *Tresqua*, all editors replace the *et eus* of the MS. (for which see note on 2345–9) by *et el*, because besides the hermit only Iseut was present.

2495–6. *Qant el le vit venir, lor prie . . . Qu(e) il i fist, ne fu pas parole.* The MS. has *ne fu pas pole*; M⁰ printed *ne fu parole*; Muret's later eds. have *Que il i fist, ne fu parole*, M⁴ *Qu'il i fist, ne fu pas parole.* All editors indicate a lacuna between 2495 and 2496; E's note (II 204) says 'Lacuna?' but does not explain the query. In fact, it seems unlikely that 2495 and 2496 could have been miscopied from a rhyming couplet; at least two lines must have been omitted, and the extant lines cannot therefore be understood. It is probable, however, that *pole* in 2496 should be corrected not to *parole* but to *fole*: for *ne fu pas fole* referring to Iseut cf. *Yseut parla, qui n'ert pas fole* 2805, also Ogrin's words to her, *Entendez, ne soiez pas fole* 2344.

2497–8. *Amis, di moi, se Dex t'anort, Fus tu donc pus a la roi cort?* M⁴'s glossary describes *anort* here (and *enort* 2832) as 'subj. pr. 3 de *honorer* (cf. 506) ou de *anorter*'. There can be no question of *anorter*; both forms are (as stated in E's glossary) from the verb (*h*)*onorer, enorer,* as is shown by the parallel formula *se Dex anor te donst* 506 (see note).

2563–4. *Rois, tu la preïs a mollier, Si que virent ti chevalier.* See note on 269–70.

2565–80. This passage is unusually involved and incoherent, even for Beroul. Apart from corrections made by all editors in 2566 and 2573, Muret introduced emendations in 2572 and in 2578–9 (see below). B. Blakey (*F.S.* 21 (1967), 101–2) suggests different and more far-reaching changes, involving, besides *ait* for *a* 2579, the interchange of the couplets 2573–4 and 2577–8; but these proposals, while removing several of the difficulties, introduce others, such as *en* in *gage en donge* 2568 referring back to the general sense of 2566–7 (in a much looser way than in 26–31 cited as an analogue), or *Lié alegier* 2570 depending on *Adonc me fai* coming three lines later and taken in the sense of 'allow me to defend her'. The reconstitution, ingenious though it is, therefore remains less than convincing.

2568–70. *Ge sui tot prest que gage en donge, Qui li voudroit blasme lever, Lié alegier contre mon per.* Although, as Blakey says, one might expect *en* to be taken up by an infin. introduced by *de*, there are in the text somewhat analogous cases, such as *en* taken up by a *que*-clause (*Qu'ele l'en croie qu'il l'a mort* 4393) and *le* taken up by a pure infin. (. . . *Au roi ne l'ait plevi en main Vos rendre a lui* 1375–6).

2575–9. *Se je ne l'en puis alegier Et en ta cort moi deraisnier, Adonc me fai devant ton ost; N'i a baron que je t'en ost, N'i a baron* . . . Muret took *fai* as the imper. of *faire*, and introduced as a dependent infin. first *Ardoir* for *Adonc* (M⁰), then *Jugier*, placed first in 2577 (M²: *Jugier me fai devant ton ost*), later in 2578 (*Adonc me fai devant ton ost Jugier: n'i a qui je t'en ost*; so still in M⁴). The last of these has the advantage of getting rid of the rather unlikely repetition of *N'i a baron* in successive lines, but all seem somewhat arbitrary. On the other hand, E's interpretation of *fai* as imper. of *faidir* raises serious difficulties: this verb is attested only in the past part. *faidi*, and the sequence 'outlaw me before your host; there is not a baron that I except' is obscure.

2579–80. *N'i a baron, por moi laisier, Ne me face ardrë, ou jugier.* E interprets the MS. text (II 206) as 'There is not a single baron who, to my hurt, may not have me burnt or condemned', taking *laisier* as the representative of a verb *LAESIARE (cf. T.-L. V 333); but no other example of this verb is known in O. F. (Mod. F. *léser* dates only from the 16th century). Muret, followed by M⁴, adopts Acher's emendation to *plaisier* (i.e. *plaissier*) 'bring down, humble' (T.-L. VII 1062–3) which is well attested. In 2580 the disjunction 'burnt or condemned' is illogical; M⁰ emended *jugier*, rather arbitrarily, to *niier* 'drown'; Muret's later eds. and M⁴ avoid this difficulty by taking *ou* as = *en+le*, i.e. 'have me burnt in the judging, at the judgment', but this is not very plausible, and does not seem to have been the interpretation of the scribe who, according to E (II 27), writes only *el* or *u* for *en+le* before consonant. It seems probable that *ou* is in fact disjunctive 'or' and that *jugier* is an error for a different infin.; this may have been *depecier*, which is used in a similar context in *Mex se laisast vif depecier* 811, also in 1019 and 1041, and would, incidentally, dispose of the hiatus in *ardrë ou* (which Muret corrected to *ardoir ou*).

2581–2. *Vos savez bien, beaus oncles, sire, Nos vosistes ardoir en ire.* In the MS. the first word of 2582 is *Vos*, which as subject-pron. can begin the clause. All editors have adopted Muret's correction to *Nos*; but this placing of the weak pron. obj. would be most unusual in O. F. The line should perhaps run *Vos nos vosistes ardre en ire.*

2591–3. *Lors fu donnee la roïne As malades en decepline; Ge l'en portai,*
si li toli. G. Paris suggested correcting *li* to *lor* = *la lor* 'her from
them'; if *li* is retained it must be understood as = *la li* 'her from
him' (i.e. from Ivain, who is not separately mentioned but will
be remembered as the person to whom she was handed over, 1223).
It cannot be taken as the strong fem. pron. (E's first suggestion,
II 206): there is no emphasis on the notion of the direct obj. 'her',
and in the context the expression of the indirect obj. 'from him' is
indispensable.

2596. *Qant a tort dut por moi morir.* See note on 856–7.

2604–5. *Mais, s'or estoit vostre plesir A prendre Yseut* . . . (The MS.
has *fort,* corrected to *s'or* by all editors). E says (II 207; cf. 19 n. 5)
that '*estoit* is to be taken as impersonal, followed by oblique
vostre plesir used as an indirect object; cf. *soit vostre gré* 2802'. But
the obl. case without preposition, commonly used as indirect obj.
when it designates a person, is very rarely so used with other
nouns (cf. Foulet, §§37–43), and never with an abstract noun
such as *plesir* or *gré.* These nouns must therefore be taken as in
function predicative nominatives, in spite of their form (attested
by rhyme with *fuïr* and *loiauté* respectively).

2610–12. *Ge m'en irai au roi de Frise; Jamais n'oras de moi parler,*
Passerai m'en outre la mer. In view of the number of occasions on
which the scribe has interverted the lines of the couplet (cf. note
on 65–8), it is probable that the original had the more logical
order 2612–2611.

2631. *Au riche roi aut, en Gavoie.* The *Gavoie* referred to here and
perhaps in an emended form of 2925 (see note on 2925–6) is
now definitely identified by E (II 198–9, 207), as by Muret and
M⁴, with Galloway. There is, however, nothing in the text of
Beroul to support the description of Galloway as a land of evil
omen, 'the bourne from which no knight returns', as suggested
by M. D. Legge, *Anglo-Norman Literature and its Background*
(Oxford, 1963), p. 59, and 'Gautier Espec et Ailred', *Mélanges*
Frappier (Paris, 1970), p. 622.

2633–5. Si se porra la contenir, Et tant porrez de lui oïr, Vos manderez por lui, qu'il vienge. In E's note (II 207) 2633 is not translated, but his glossary gives for *soi contenir* here 'remain'; Muret and M⁴ also include 'rester' among the glosses for *soi contenir* 1069 and 2633. No such meaning, however, is recognized by Gdf. (II 263, IX 174) or T.-L. (II 766–7); the sense is clearly 'comport oneself, behave', and *si* is the adv. of manner 'in such a way': 'there he may so acquit himself, and you may hear so much about him, that you will send for him'.

2636. Ne savon el qel voie tienge. E translates (II 207) 'otherwise we shall not know whither he goes'; but the subjunctive *tienge* shows that the indirect question is deliberative, and the meaning is therefore 'we do not know where else he is to go'. Other instances of the same construction in the text are *De duel ne set con se contienge* 1069 'how (he is) to contain himself'; *Ne set qu'il die* 612, *ne set qu'il face* 1615, *je ne sai que doie faire* 2003, *ne sai pas Comment isse de cest Mal Pas* 3785–6.

2658–61. Lut les letres, vit la franchise Du roi, qui pardonne a Yseut Son mautalent, et que il veut Repenre la tant bonement. All editors print *Repenre* for the *Repenra* of the MS.; but since the normal expression of 'he is willing to take her back' would be *il la veut repenre*, not *il veut repenre la* (or *la repenre*), it is possible that the MS. reading should be retained: 'he saw the nobility of the king, and what he wishes—he will most graciously take her back'. For the co-ordination of a noun and a clause as objects of the same verb cf. *Or sevent tuit par la contree Le terme asis de l'asenblee, Et que la ert li rois Artus* 3283–5.

2677–9. Devant le Gué Aventuros Est li plez mis de vos et d'eus; La li rendroiz, iluec ert prise. The rhyme of *aventuros* with *eus* implies a diphthongal pronunciation of the product of closed *o* tonic free, contrary to the evidence of many other rhymes; Muret therefore corrected *de vos et d'eus* to *d'eus et de vos* (cf. *de vos : Aventuros* 1319–20, and similarly 2747–8, 3109–10 etc.). E and M⁴ restore the MS. reading without comment (though the statement that closed *o* tonic free does not diphthongize remains in M⁴, p. ix, and E,

II 11). In 2679 *La* is not only probably (M⁴, p. 147) but undoubtedly (E, II 207) the adv. 'there' (the weak pers. pron. *la* could not
begin the sentence); but the opposition seen by M⁴ between
la indicating motion and *iluec* indicating rest is surely illusory.
On the other hand, M⁴ is certainly right in taking *li* as the weak
dative pron., standing here for *la li*; the strong fem. pron., which
E considers a possibility, could hardly be used in this context
(cf. note on 2591–3).

2682. *Molt est dolenz qui pert s'amie!* This appears to be a proverbial
expression; cf. *Grant duel a qui son ami pert* (*Thebes* 6403), *Quar qui
sa bone amie pert Molt a perdu, ce m'est avis* (*Mantel mautaillié* 794–5,
Montaiglon et Raynaud III 28), also *Dolenz est qui pert* (Morawski
593).

2689–90. *Ja ne serai en cele terre Que ja me tienge pais ne gerre* . . . For
the repetition of *ja* see note on 75–7.

2697–9. *Ainz berseret a veneor N'ert gardé e a tel honor Con cist sera.*
The MS. has *Nert gardee a*; M⁰ corrected to *Nen ert gardé*, but all
later editions interpret the reading as *gardé* followed by *e* for *et*.
This is unsatisfactory in several respects: there is no place in the
sense for the conj. 'and'; in any case, the conj. is nowhere else
written *e* in the interior of the line (initial *E* for *Et* appears once
only, in 3185); *ainz* in the sense of *onc* 'ever' is elsewhere (as is
normal in O. F.) used only with the preterite, cf. *Ainz, puis que
la loi fu jugie, Ne fu beste si herbergie* 2704–5, also 498, 561, 582,
1161, 1167, 1545, 1787, 1928 etc. (cf. note on 1033–4). The line
must originally have read *Ne fu gardé* (for *gardez*) *a tel honor*; the
scribe erroneously wrote *N'ert* (intending *ert* as a fut., under the
influence of the futs. *sera* 2699, *verrai* 2700 etc.; he also wrote a
fut. in *ce m'ert avis* 2700, corrected by all editors to *ce m'est avis*);
he then made up the measure of the line by simply giving the past
part. the fem. form *gardee* (for other arbitrary modifications made
for metrical purposes see note on 1569–70).

2702–6. *Ja n'avrai si le cuer dolent, Se je le voi, ne soie lie. Ainz, puis
que la loi fu jugie, Ne fu beste si herbergie Ne en si riche lit couchie.* This

is a second case (cf. 725–8 and note) where the MS. text shows two successive couplets on the same rhyme. Here again it is quite possible that in the original the second couplet had a different rhyme; it may well have read *Ne fu brachez si herbergiez Ne en si riche lit couchiez*, for *brachet* is (after *chien*) the term most commonly applied in the text to Husdent (1440, 1457, 1501, 1539, 1541, 1608, 2696, 2728; cf. also the use of the specific term *berseret* in the parallel couplet 2697–8, above). For the scribe's tendency to carry on with the same rhyme cf. 2505–8, where following a couplet with the rhyme-words *rent* and *briment* he has ended the next two lines with the meaningless *romenz* (for *roi Marc*) and *ent* (for *arc*).

2707–8. *Amis Tristran, j'ai un anel, Un jaspe vert a u seel.* The MS. has *et .i. seel*; Muret (M⁰–M²) and E correct to *a u seel* 'there is in the seal' (for *u = el < en + le* cf. 917 etc.). M³ and M⁴ substitute *a un seel* (presumably understood as 'with a seal'), which assumes a rather less extensive scribal error but is contextually much less satisfactory.

2711–12. *Et s'il vos vient, sire, a corage Que me mandez rien par mesage* . . . The locution *venir a corage* is glossed by M⁰ 'venir à l'esprit' and by E 'come to mind, occur to'; but in the context the meaning must be 'seem good to', and *mandez* must be pres. subj.: 'if you wish to send any message to me . . .'.

2713–14. *Tant vos dirai, ce saciez bien, Certes, je n'en croiroie rien* . . . So punctuated also by Muret and M⁴, but better with a colon after *bien*; cf. note on 2411–13.

2717–20. *Se voi l'anel, ne lairai mie* . . . *Ne face con que il dira, Qui cest anel m'aportera.* E and M⁴ retain the MS. reading in 2719 *con que*, which E glosses 'as' (neither has any note on it). There is, however, no evidence of the existence in O. F. of a pure generalizing use of *con que* in the sense of 'however, in every way that', with indic. (parallel to *ou que* with indic. 'wherever, in every place where'); the only example of *con que* in T.-L. (II 600, 45) is with subj. in the concessive sense of 'however, no matter how (much)':

com qu'il seient e lonc e gros. It therefore seems essential to correct with Muret to *çou que* 'that which', or rather (since the spelling *çou* does not occur elsewhere in the text either for *ce* or for *cel* neuter) to *ce que.* It is not, however, necessary also to correct *il* to *cil*, as tentatively suggested by G. Paris (though M⁴ is mistaken in thinking (p. 147) that the retention of *il* is supported by *Rien qu'il deïst ge ne croiroie* 2796, where no *qui*-clause follows).

2722. *Je vos pramet par fine amor.* See note on 269–70.

2733–5. *Li hermites en vet au Mont, Por les richeces qui la sont; Aprés achate ver et gris . . .* Muret, followed by M⁴, corrects *Aprés* to *Assés*, which would indeed be much more natural in the context (cf. *Asez orras d'Iseut novele* 995). E restores the MS. reading, assuming that *aprés* here expresses a 'weakened notion of sequence or succession' (II 210). Even when one takes into consideration 2463 (see note), which he cites as a parallel, this does not seem very probable; and *aprés* may well be an error, perhaps for *assez*, but possibly for *adés* or for *senpres* (cf. 2160).

2761–2. *Perinis . . . L'ocist puis d'un gibet el bois.* E (glossary and II 211) translates *gibet* by 'sling' and Muret, followed by M⁴, glosses 'bâton muni à l'une de ses extrémités d'une fronde'. The authority for this interpretation is a fourteenth-century glossary cited by Gdf. (IV 274) and T.-L. (IV 304): 'Fundibula sunt quaedam parvae machinae cum funda in baculo dependente, gallice *gibet*'; but none of the O. F. examples of *gibet* as the name of a weapon makes any reference to its use as a sling, and many imply that it is simply a club or cudgel.

2778–80. *Dame, vos retenez Hudent. Pri vos, por Deu, que le gardez; S'onques l'amastes, donc l'amez.* Muret corrected to *m'amastes* (which is supported by the text of Eilhart, quoted by E, II 214); E and M⁴ restore the MS. reading, which E attempts to justify by translating 'If ever you bore him affection, show that affection now'. But this forces the sense of both *donc* (see T.-L. II 2006) and *amez*; and the correction seems indispensable: 'if ever you loved me, then love him'.

2801–2. . . . *Solonc m'enor et loiauté Et je sace soit vostre gré.* E translates (II 214) 'According to my honour and loyalty and what I
know to be your wish'; but this would be *et (solonc) que je sai qu'est
vostre gré* (cf. *cel . . . que il bien set Que ses sires onques plus het* 1687–8).
The subjunctive *sace* (with its dependent subjunctive *soit*) must
have intrinsic conditional force (cf. 906 and note): 'and provided
that I know it is your wish'.

   To explain the obl. case of *vostre gré* after the verb *estre* M⁰ took
it as adverbial, in the sense of *a* (or *de*) *vostre gré*; but this adverbial
or rather absolute use seems to be confined to *mon gré* etc. equivalent to *mon vueil* etc., 'if I had my way'. E takes *vostre gré* as equivalent to an indirect object, but see note on 2604–5.

2812–14. . . . *ne partez de cest païs Tant qos saciez conment li rois Sera
vers moi, iriez ou lois.* Muret emended *lois* first to *cois* 'quiet', then
to *voirs* (retained by M⁴), understood as 'véridique, sincère, fidèle
à ses engagements'. E restores the MS. reading, suggesting that
lois, attested in O. F. only in the literal sense of 'squinting', could
figuratively mean 'ambiguous, uncertain' (glossary), 'equivocal in
attitude' (II 215). A. Holden (*Rom.* 89 (1968) 393) objects that
this does not form an antithesis with *iriez*, and proposes to return
to Muret's earlier correction (though in the declensionally
irregular form *coi* : *le roi*). E, however, rightly points out that the
antithesis would be only very partial even with *cois* or *voirs*, and
that in any case no antithesis may have been intended; and it may
be added that neither *cois* nor *voirs* seems particularly appropriate
in the context. For the implications of the rhyme *rois* : *lois* see
M.L.R. 60 (1965), 355–6.

2820–1. *Nos i geümes mainte nuit, En nostre lit que nos fist faire.*
Iseut is speaking to Tristran of the *bel celier* (3319; *buen celier* 2828)
at the home of Orri the forester, which in this part of the romance
is referred to as having been the refuge of the lovers. On the face
of the text, the subject of *fist* could only be Orri. But in 3350–2
Tristran, in the *celier*, says to Perinis *A la roïne puez retraire Ce
que t'ai dit el sozterrin Que fist fere si bel, perrin*, and here there has
been no mention of Orri. It would therefore appear that it was
Iseut who had the underground refuge made, and that *fist* 2821

is an error for *fis* (for another probable instance of the same error see 4205–6 and note).

2822–7. Muret at first placed these lines after 2836 (so in M[0]) but afterwards reverted to the MS. order; M[4] (p. 147) and E (II 215) are both inclined to follow M[0] (though they have not done so in their printed texts). This would indeed give a rather more coherent sequence; but it would not reduce the number of lacunas assumed by the editors, for in the 17 lines from 2821 to 2837 there would be no fewer than three (after the present lines 2821, 2827 and 2836), as against the two in the printed texts of E and M[4]. (E's comments in his note, II 215, do not seem to be reconcilable with his suggestion in II 6 that *faire* 2821 and *moleste* 2822 may form an assonance.) The notes below on 2821–3 and 2833–7 assume that the MS. order in 2822–36 is to be retained, though minor corrections are needed; the abruptness of the transitions in the text as it stands is in fact hardly more marked than at other points in the narrative.

2821–3. . . . *En nostre lit que nos fist faire . . . Li trois qui er[en]t de moleste Mal troveront en la parfin.* All editors assume a lacuna of at least two lines between 2821 and 2822, not only because of the sudden change of theme but because the two lines do not rhyme (though E, II 6, now considers it possible that the assonance *faire* : *moleste* was in the original). But the wording of 2822 is in any case suspect. The MS. has *Li trois qui ert de moleste*, which is both ungrammatical and hypometric. Muret, followed by M[4], corrected to *qui nos quierent moleste*, presumably taken to mean 'who seek our harm'; E makes the more modest emendation *qui erent de moleste*, presumably 'who were troublesome' ('*moleste*, sf. trouble', glossary). Now the noun *moleste* appears in 1586 in the well-attested locution *faire moleste* 'do harm'; but among the numerous examples in Gdf. (V 373) and T.-L. (VI 178–9) there is not one that contains either the locution *querre moleste* or the locution *estre de moleste*. It therefore seems possible that the word *moleste* itself may be a corruption; and if so it may be an error for a word rhyming with *faire* 2821. Accepting E's emendation *er[ent]*, I would suggest that *de moleste* may be miscopied for *demalaire* 'of evil birth or origin', hence 'ill-disposed, wicked'; the very similar formation *deputaire* occurs in 3092 and the antonym *debonere* in 3914, 4106, 4150 (both these always in rhyme with (*a*)*faire*). The scribe was certainly capable of direct errors as gross as this; but it is also conceivable that there was, either in his model or in his mind as he copied, an intermediate stage *de mal estre* 'of evil nature' (cf. *de bon estre, de put estre,* T.-L. III 1463). If 2822 originally ended in *demalaire,* rhyming with *faire* 2821 (or indeed if *de moleste* was considered as forming an acceptable assonance with *faire*), it is extremely unlikely that there is a lacuna between the two lines. But what seems at first sight an abrupt transition, from the theme of the underground refuge to that of the hostile barons, is perhaps less so when considered in relation to Iseut's associations of ideas.

2824–7. *Li cors giront el bois, sovin; Beaus chiers amis, et g'en ai dote; Enfer ovre, qui les tranglote! Ges dot, quar il sont molt felon.* (All editors correct *gisent* of the MS. to *giront*). Muret (M⁰–M²) interverted 2825 and 2826, and in *Vinaver Misc.,* p. 276, I suggested that he might have been right in doing so. E and M⁴ restore the MS. order, perhaps justifiably: the curse in 2826 can be taken as one of the parentheses characteristic of the manner of the poem.

2832–3. *Li miens amis, que Dex t'enort! Ne t'ennuit pas la herbergier!* Correct to *se Dex t'enort* (without exclamation mark); cf. note on 506–7.

2833–7. '*Ne t'ennuit pas la herbergier! Sovent verrez mon mesagier; Manderai toi de ci mon estre Par mon vaslet et a ton mestre . . .*' '*Non fera il, ma chiere amie*'. All editors assume a lacuna between 2836 and 2837; but this is quite unnecessary. The words *Non fera il* are Tristran's reply to Iseut's request *Ne t'ennuit pas la herbergier!*: 'Let it not incommode you to take lodging there! . . .' 'Nor will it, dear love!' The formula with *Non,* the appropriate tense of *faire* as verbum vicarium, and the subject-pron. (here *il* impersonal) is normal in O. F. in a reply assenting to a negative request (cf. '*Ne porte ire a la roïne N'a moi, qui sui de vostre orine.*' '*Non ferai je,*

beaus niés' 565-7, and *Pope Studies*, p. 309). It is true that three
lines intervene between the request and the reply; but these lines
merely explain the reasonableness of the request, which in any
case would remain all the more clearly in the mind of Tristran
(and of the audience) because it had already been expressed
earlier in Iseut's speech: *Por moi sejorner ne t'ennuit!* 2819.

2843-4. *Tant sont alé et cil venu Qu'il s'entredïent lor salu.* These lines
are not commented on by E or M⁴. The subject of *sont alé* is
presumably Tristran and Iseut, while *cil* appears to refer to Mark
and his party, last mentioned in 2765-76, and the *salu* comes in
2850.

2861-3. *Onques ne firent jugement, Conbatre a pié ou autrement,
Dedenz ta cort, se ge t'en sueffre.* E retains the MS. reading in this
obscure passage. Muret, followed by M⁴, punctuates with a full
stop after *jugement* and without a comma after *autrement*, and
emends *se ge t'en sueffre* to *sire, m'en soffre*, thus understanding
2862-3 as 'Allow me at your court, Sire, to fight on foot or
otherwise'. So far as can be judged by E's punctuation and his
note (II 215-16), he takes 2862 as depending on 2861 '(Your
vassals) never pronounced any judgment (about my) fighting on
foot or otherwise', which assumes a very loose use of the dependent infinitive. For *se ge t'en sueffre* his first suggestion is, attaching
this to what precedes, 'if I suffer your bidding' (which is hardly
convincing), or perhaps 'as I suffer your bidding' (apparently
implying that *se*, which the glossary gives as here standing for *si*
'hortative', is used in asseveration; but the word-order and the
nature of the content exclude this interpretation, cf. note on
506-7). His alternative suggestion is to put a heavy stop after
cort (or after *autrement*) and to attach *se ge t'en sueffre* (deleting the
semi-colon after *sueffre*) as a further conditional clause to the
following line, *Se sui dannez, si m'art en soffre* 2864, 'if I submit to
your pleasure (and in token of it), then burn me in sulphur if I am
condemned'. But such a sequence of two *se*-clauses is rather
unlikely; the *en* is unaccounted for; and the sense attributed to
soufrir is questionable (cf. note on 2241-2). It seems necessary to
adopt Muret's punctuation and some such emendation as his.

2865–7. *Et se je m'en pus faire saus, Qu'il n'i ait chevelu ne chaus* . . .
Si me retien ovocques toi. E wonders (II 216) whether instead of
assuming a lacuna it is possible to 'interpret this as an elliptical
exclamation, the sentence remaining uncompleted'. It is clearly
not a normal case of aposiopesis, for the conclusion (no doubt
in the form of a relative clause depending on *chevelu ne chaus*)
cannot be deduced from the context; there is little doubt that the
editors have been right in indicating a lacuna between 2866 and
2867.

2869–71. *Li rois a son nevo parole. Andrez, qui fu nez de Nicole, Li a
dit* . . . (According to Muret and M⁴ (Index of Proper Names) the
name in 2870 is in the MS. *Andrez* or *Audrez*, according to E
(II 217) it is *Audrez*). It is very probable that, as E suggests,
Beroul had created from the Andret or Audret of his source two
separate personages, one friendly and one hostile to the lovers;
but it also seems likely that for Beroul (as for Eilhart and the
Prose Romance) the Andret mentioned here was like Tristran a
nephew of Mark. According to E, it is reasonable to suppose that
the nephew referred to in 2869 is Tristran, who has just been
appealing to Mark to allow him to clear himself and Iseut by
battle; but there has been no indication that Mark replies, and the
text does not exclude the possibility that the reference is to Andret.
A few lines later we are told that *A une part li rois le trait; La roïne
ovoc Dinas let* 2875–6: the *le* here cannot refer to Tristran, because
in 2892 the hostile barons come to the king and recommend the
dismissal of Tristran (who is evidently not now present); Mark
agrees, and it is the barons who carry the king's message to
Tristran (2909–10). The *le* in 2875 could, however, refer to
Andret 'of Lincoln', especially if he is identified with the Andret
who later accompanies Dinas and the queen (3783 as emended,
3877). Indeed, if *le* 2875 is not to be taken as referring to Andret,
it seems necessary to adopt Muret's emendation (M¹ and M²
only) to *se* (cf. *Li roi se traient une part* 4137).

2873. *Molt en faut poi que ne l'otroie.* The verb *otroie* is not in the pres.
subj. as stated in E's glossary (it is not, however, listed among the
pres. subj. forms with analogical *-e* in II 24). In this construction

the indic. is normal; cf. *petit falli Que de l'arbre jus ne chaï* 481–2, and T.-L. III 1614.

2882–3. *Ele out vestu une tunique Desus un grant bliaut de soie.* E says (II 218) that 'as indicated in this line, the *bliaut* was a sort of over-tunic'; but the lines, as punctuated by all editors, say that the *tunique* was worn over the *bliaut* (with a comma after *tunique* it might be possible to take *desus* as an adv.: 'she had a tunic on, (and) on top (i.e. over it) a *bliaut*'). The fem. noun *tunique* is very rare in O. F. proper; the commoner form is *tonicle, turnicle* etc., usually masc. and applied to a garment worn by men (Gdf. VIII 108, X 818). This form is used in *Eneas* 6402, where the *tonicle* or *tunicle* is put on the body of Pallas over his *blialt*.

2911. *Quant Tristran oit n'i a porloigne* . . . E's gloss for *porloigne* is 'surcease'; the meaning is rather 'delay' (cf. M⁰ and M⁴ 'retard, délai', T.-L. 'Aufschub').

2912. *Que li rois veut qu'il s'en esloigne.* The pres. subj. form *esloigne* should no doubt be listed among those forms with analogical *-e* (E II 24); the phonetic form would presumably be *esloint*, cf. pres. indic. 1 *ensein* 1889 and subjunctives such as *acompaint, deint, ressoint* (Fouché p. 197).

2919. *Li rois demande ou tornera.* The form *tornera* is described as an analogical replacement of phonetic *torra* (3461) by E (II 25) and Pope (§970 (i)). According to Fouché, however, the early fall of intertonic *e* after *n* in fut. stems was confined to those in -*n*-post-vocalic (*donra, dorra, menra, merra* etc., p. 381), and the reduction of those with stems in -*rn*- dates only from the thirteenth century (p. 382).

2924. *Ja n'en prendrai mie maalle.* It is very probable that *mie* is an error for *une* (from which it is palaeographically difficult to distinguish; Muret did in fact at first read *une*). In locutions of the type 'not a farthing' complements of negation like *mie* (themselves of similar origin) are not normally inserted in O. F., but the indef. art. is often used; cf. *n'en portera qui valle Un sol ferlinc n'une maalle* 3979–80 and T.-L. V 751 (also with *denier* II 1394 and *ferlin* III 1738). In any case, a complement like *mie* is not normally used in a negative clause containing emphatic *Ja*.

2925–6. *A qant que puis vois a grant joie, Au roi riche que l'en gerroie.* So all recent editions (except that M⁴ has no comma after *joie*). E (II 219) takes *A qant que puis* with *a grant joie* and understands 'I go with the greatest possible joy'; as far as the actual words are concerned this is perhaps supported by *A qant qu'il puet s'escrie en haut* 1246 if this means 'he cries as loudly as he can' (elsewhere, however, (*a*) *quant que puis* normally modifies not an adverbial locution but a verb expressing effort and means 'with all my might', cf. *Ogrins prioit Au roi celestre quant qu'il pot Tristran defende* 2483–5, also *Rol.* 1175, 1198 etc. cited in M⁴'s glossary, and other examples in T.-L. II 32–3). But there is no obvious reason why Tristran should depart from Cornwall 'with great joy' or 'the greatest possible joy'. It is generally agreed that the *roi riche* referred to in 2926 is the king of Galloway to whom the barons recommended Tristran to go in 2631–2 (*Au riche roi aut, en Gavoie, A qui li rois* [*escoz*] *gerroie*); there is therefore much to be said for Muret's early emendation (M⁰, M¹) of *a grant joie* to *en Gavoie* (cf. A. Holden, *Rom.* 89 (1968), 393). But this throws the meaning of *A qant que puis* into uncertainty again; the interpretation of M⁰ and M⁴, 'aussi vite que je puis', is not supported by evidence, and it is perhaps just possible that if we accept the emendation we should understand 'with whatever (resources) I can (command)', referring to Tristran's immediately preceding refusal to accept any gifts from Mark.

2945–50. *Dinas li prie ja nel dot, Die son buen; il fera tot. Dit molt a bele desevree. Mais, sor sa foi aseüree, La retendra ensenble o soi; Non feroit, certes, por le roi.* (All editors correct *vos foi* 2948 to *sa foi*). This obscure passage needs more discussion than it receives in E's notes (II 219), where the only comment is the rendering of 2947 as 'He declares that this is a noble leave-taking'. This does not seem an appropriate remark for Dinas, and taking the line by itself one might suspect that the comment is that of the narrator and should read *D'eus a molt bele desevree* (referring to the parting

H

of Tristran and Dinas). In 2949, however, *La* appears to refer to Iseut, who in the extant text has not been mentioned since 2930–2. The explanation may be that Muret and M⁴ are right in assuming a lacuna between 2947 and 2948, and that Iseut was named in the intervening lines. Alternatively, however, the corruption of 2947 may be more extensive: *a bele* may be an error for *la bele*, referring to Iseut (as in 3513, 3525, 3604 etc.), and the line may have stated that she would not be parted from Dinas. There is also some obscurity about 2950; the formula *Non feroit certes* expresses the contradiction of a preceding assertion (cf. *Pope Studies*, pp. 306–8), and should therefore mean here 'he would certainly not do so (for the king)', which is not clear.

3011–12. *Tristran s'en part . . . Let le chemin, prent une sente.* The MS. has *Lez le chemin lez une sente*, corrected by all editors in accordance with a suggestion of G. Paris. Though it is quite conceivable that the scribe might have written *lez* in error once (e.g. for *let*, as he did in 1424), it is hardly likely that he would do so twice in one line; the original reading may have been *Lez le chemin prent* (or *vet*) *une sente*.

3020–1. *Senglers, lehes prenet o pans, En ses hai[e]s grans cers et biches.* For *haie* E gives 'enclosure', Muret and M⁴ 'clôture, garenne', T.-L. 'Hecke, Gehegen'; but it seems probable that the word is used here in the technical sense attested in *Modus*, 'artificial hedge constructed to direct game into a net or snare', T.-L. IV 821.

3026–7. *Par Perinis . . . Soit Tristran noves de s'amie.* According to E (glossary and II 220) *soit* is here 'a scribal variant of *sait* as in 3441, 4458; cf. *soiz* 1873'. While in the context of 1873 and 3441 the pres. of *savoir* is clearly required, it is the pret. that would be expected here and probably in *Tristran s'estut, si pensa pose, Bien soit q'el voit aucune chose Qui li desplaist; garda en haut . . .* 4457–9; and in these lines *soit* is no doubt scribal for *sot* (cf. M⁰, glossary), since the impf. ending *-ot* is several times written as *-oit* (*prioit* 2483 : *pot, gardoit* 4345 : *tripot*, perhaps *estoit* 2200 : *dementot*; cf. conversely spellings such as *avot* 751 for *avoit, faisot* 585 for *faisoit*).

3028–30. *Oiez des trois, que Dex maudie: Par eus fu molt li rois malez, Qui a Tristran estoit meslez.* In 3029–30 the MS. has *Qui o Tristran avoit alez Par eus fu molt li rois malez*; Muret, followed by M⁴, corrects 3029 to *Par qui Tristran an est alez.* This correction, supported in part by the fact that the scribe has elsewhere written *avoit* for *an est* (1403; cf. *avoit* for *an ot* 2380, 3731, for *an ait* 3696) gives an acceptable sense, and there seems to be no need for E's bolder emendation, involving not only corrections in 3029 but also interversion of 3029 and 3030.

3044. *S'a vilanie vos est dit.* E takes *dire* here as impers. (glossary) and says (II 221) that *S'* = *se* for *si* (< SIC), which he translates 'and so'; but the word-order makes this impossible (the line would have to be *Si vos est a vilanie dit*). Unless Muret was right in assuming a lacuna between 3043 and 3044 (in which case *S'* might be for *Se* 'if', cf. M⁰, glossary), *S'* here must be for *Ç'* = *Ce* 'This'; cf. *sil* 4143 written for *cil*, and conversely *ceseroit* 846 for *si seroiz, cele* 996 for *sele* (see also notes on 4131–3, 4180).

3045–7. *li baron de ton païs T'en ont par mainte foiz requis, Qu'il vuelent bien s'en escondie . . .* (The MS. has *son escondire*, corrected by all editors). As the text stands, *Qu'il* 3047 must mean 'For they'; it is possible, however, that *Qu'il* is here a spelling for *Qui* (cf. note on 269–70).

3048. *Qu(e) on Tristran n'ot sa drüerie.* Muret read *ou Tristran* (so M²); M⁴ reads like E *on*, but corrects to *o* 'with'. The construction *avoir sa drüerie o* is not, however, justified by M⁴'s comparison with *prendre drüerie o* in 130; and E is surely right in seeing *on* as a spelling for *onc* 'ever'.

3049. *Escondire se doit c'on ment.* So all editions except M⁰ (which has *se doit. Coument?*); but while the verb *escondire* (trans. or refl.), like *alegier* and the noun *escondit*, is not infrequently followed by a *que*-clause containing a negation of the accusation that has been made (as in the immediately preceding lines 3047–8, cf. 2227–9, 2570–3, Gdf. III 419, T.-L. III 955–7), there seems to be no evidence of its use with a following affirmative clause such as *c'on ment.* It is probable that *Escondire* here is an error for some other verb of more positive meaning, and has been introduced under the influence of elements in the context such as *escondit* 3043, *s'en escondie* (MS. *son escondire*) 3047, *escondire* 3053.

3067. *Lui ai chacié; or chaz ma feme?* E correctly translates (II 221) 'and am I now to drive forth my wife?'; *chaz* is pres. subj., not as stated in his glossary and that of M⁰ pres. indic.

3073. *S'il se mesfist, il est en fort.* (The MS. has *et il est fort*, corrected by M⁰ to *et il ait tort*, by later editors, in accordance with Acher's suggestion, to *il est en fort*.) For the construction see note on 1382–4.

3084. *Por noient, certes, ne vos monte.* E glosses *monter* 'be of conse-quence, matter', but in the context the sense is clearly 'avail' (cf. Muret and M⁴, 'valoir, profiter'). The construction with *por noient* is abnormal; in this use of *monter* the complement is most com-monly *noient* or *rien* without preposition, 'avail nothing, be of no avail' (cf. *rien ne li monte* 901), sometimes with *a* (cf. T.-L. VI 235), and it seems likely that here an original *A noient ne vos monte* has been miscopied under the influence of the common locution *por noient* 'in vain' (as in 987). Whether in the form with *por* or with *a*, the meaning here cannot be 'en aucune façon' (M⁰, glossary), 'in no wise' (E, glossary).

3087–9. *Qant il voient le roi marri, En la lande, sor un larri, Sont decendu tuit troi a pié.* M⁴, following M⁰, retains the MS. reading *soz un larri*, interpreting *larri* as 'terrain inculte au flanc d'une colline'; but in the application of the word *larri(z)* the nature of the vegetation seems to be more essential than the altitude, and none of the numerous examples in Gdf. (IV 728) and T.-L. (V 194–6) shows it governed by the preposition *soz*. M², M³ and E adopt Acher's correction to *sor* (the scribe has elsewhere confused words for 'on' and 'under', cf. note on 955–8); but *sor un larri* seems redundant after *en la lande*, and in any case the word *larriz* or *larris* is normally indeclinable (though an obl. *larri* does occur). On the whole, it seems most likely that the original had the reading which Muret at first thought of introducing, *soz un jarri* 'under a holm-oak' (M⁰, p. lvi, n. 3); the word *jarri* (rhyming with *cri*) occurs in 1260 in the sense of 'cudgel (of holm-oak)', and the scribe has confused initial *i* and *l* in *Ia* 4033 for *La* and *lonc* 4082 for *jonc*.

3093. *Bien tost mandera son neveu.* In the context (the return of Tristran is considered hypothetical by the speakers, cf. *S'il ça revient* 3095) the sense of *bien tost* is more likely to be 'perhaps', 'probably' (cf. note on 515–16) than 'soon', which is preferred in E's note (II 221) and given without alternative in his and M⁰'s glossaries (s.v. *tost*).

3112–3. *L'en devroit par droit son seignor Consellier.* All editors substitute *consellier* for the *consentir* of the MS. (for the verb *consellier* in references to the vassal's duty to counsel his lord cf. 631–2, 2529–30 etc.); but E now thinks (II 222) that *consentir* might well have been retained, understood as 'bear with', 'humour'. But the examples in T.-L. (II 734), to which he refers, hardly support this extension of sense: *consentir* with a personal direct obj. is attested only as meaning 'admit, allow to stay (in a country etc.)', 'tolerate'.

3114–18. *Mal ait quant qu'a soz son baudré—Ja mar o tois'en marrira—Cil qui te het! Cil s'en ira; Mais nos, qui somes ti feel, Te donions loial consel.* Muret had interverted 3115 and 3116, but E and M⁴ restore the MS. text. The first obscurity is 3114, literally 'Cursed be whatever he has under his (sword-)belt'; no other instance of this apparently fig. use is known. E (II 222) understands *quant qu'a soz son baudré* to mean 'whatever or whoever he be', apparently taken as in apposition with *Cil*; but the literal construction is 'Cursed be whatever he who hates you has under his belt', i.e. more probably 'cursed be the heart of him who hates you'. Secondly, 3115 is translated by E 'woe to him if he is resentful towards you'; but *Ja mar* with the fut. normally expresses a prohibition (T.-L. V 1109–11), 'Let him not . . ., He must not . . ., He need not . . .'. In addition, while 'be angry with', 'be resentful towards' could be expressed by *soi marrir a* or *de* (cf. 3183 and

T.-L. V 1197), this sense is not attested with *o* (hence Tanquerey's proposed emendations mentioned by E); as it stands, and taking into consideration *Cil s'en ira* 3116, the line may mean 'He need not (*or* must not) be resentful in your company'. Finally, in spite of the frequency of parenthetical remarks elsewhere in the text, it is hard to believe that the sentence *Mal ait quant qu'a soz son baudré cil qui te het* is really intended to be cut in two by the inter-polated exclamation *Ja mar o toi s'en marrira*. The only reason-ably satisfactory solution is therefore to adopt Muret's inter-version of 3115 and 3116 (cf. note on 65–8) and to understand 'Cursed be the heart of him who hates you. He will go away; he need not stay with you in his resentment. But we, who are your faithful barons, we were giving you loyal counsel'. The reference in 3114–16 is probably, as E tentatively suggests, to Tristran.

3128. *Ne vosistes escu ballier*. E translates (II 222) 'You were un-willing to present your shield (to fight)'; but *ballier* here means 'take' (with E's glossary) or 'take up, take in hand' (cf. 3530, of taking up knightly equipment, and T.-L. I 804). Cf., referring to the same episode, *Ainz nus . . . Ne vout armes saisir ne prendre* 3422–3.

3129. *Querant alez a terre pié*. This evidently contains an idiomatic expression, of which no other example is known. E explains (II 222) 'you wish to remain on foot (and not to mount your charger)', Muret and M⁴ (glossary s.v. *pié*) 'vous cherchez à mettre pied à terre (comme pour esquiver un combat)', which gives more accurately the literal meaning and implies a figurative application; T.-L. (VII 895) hesitates between the literal and the figurative, 'sich dem Kampfe entziehen wollen? Ausflüchte suchen?' In spite of the immediately preceding references to the barons' failure to take up Tristran's challenge, the figurative sense 'make excuses, prevaricate' seems more likely in the general context.

3140–1. *Li troi [l']ont aresnié entr'eus, Mais n'i porent plai encontrer*. For the MS. reading *Li troi ont* M⁴ prints the ungrammatical

Li roi ont; but if it is assumed that *Li troi* is a scribal error (which is rather more probable than E's interpretation), it seems reasonable to correct with Muret to *Le roi*. For *plai encontrer* E (II 223) gives 'obtain satisfaction': better 'reach agreement, understanding' (cf. glossary s.v. *plait*).

3150–2. *A Tintajol, devant sa tor, Est decendu, dedenz s'en entre— Nus ne set ne ne voit son estre.* E and M⁴ retain the MS. text, on which E makes no comment except to list *entre : estre* among the 'imperfect rhymes' attributable to the author (II 31). But even apart from the faulty rhyme, the implied meaning 'no one knows nor sees his mind *or* condition' (glossary s.v. *estre*) is not very appropriate in the context; and there can be little doubt that the original text was that proposed by G. Paris and adopted by Muret, *Nus nel siut ne ne vait soentre* (M⁰), or *Nus ne sut ne ne voit soventre* (M²), or perhaps rather *Nus ne[l] se[u]t ne n'e[n] voit soventre*, 'No one follows him or goes along behind him'. For *ne[l]* cf. note on 269–70; for *seut* 'follows' cf. *sieut* 1962, *porseut* 2156; for *voit* 'goes' cf. 1271, 1511, 1606; for omission of the titulus on *e[n]* and substitution of *n* for *u* in *soventre* cf. Ewert, *Pope Studies*, p. 91; for the locution *en aler soventre* cf. note on 1987–90.

3157. *Prist l'a la main.* See note on 1220.

3177–8. *Qant ele l'ot qui l'aseüre, Sa color vient, si aseüre.* In 3177 the MS. has *si l'aseüre*, corrected by all editors. In 3178 E's text footnote had tentatively suggested correcting to *si est seüre*; but he now considers the MS. rhyme legitimate on the ground that *aseüre* has two different grammatical functions (II 5), and refers to T.-L. for its intransitive use (II 225). It is true that T.-L. has three examples of *aseürer* intrans. (I 592), but they are all in the sense, inappropriate here, of 'sich ruhig halten, anhalten', used negatively. A suitable sense would be given by *aseürer* or *raseürer* reflexive (*s'i aseüre* 'she trusts in him', cf. T.-L. I 591; *se raseüre* 'she takes heart again', cf. T.-L. VIII 320), but neither of these would admit of the conj. *si*, which seems indispensable. As M⁰'s emendation *si rest seüre* is a little unlikely with *li rest asouagié* in 3179, we are left with E's original conjecture *si est seüre*.

3188–90. Mais se encor nes en desment, Que nes enchaz fors de ma terre, Li fel ne criement mais ma gerre. Muret's assumption of a lacuna between 3188 and 3189 (with full stop after 3189) has rightly been abandoned by E and M⁴. The form *enchaz* is described by E (glossary) as pres. indic., but in the clause depending on a conditional clause it is more probably pres. subj. (see, however, 2404 and note). For 3190 E gives (II 226) 'the felons will nevermore fear my hostility' and M⁴ (pp. 147–8) 'ces félons ne craignent plus (ne craindront plus désormais) ma guerre (la guerre que je peux leur faire'; perhaps more exactly 'have no longer any need to fear my hostility' (cf. T.-L. II 1054).

3210–12. Sire, quel mal ont dit de moi? Chascun puet dire ce qu'il pense. Fors vos, ge n'ai nule defense. Neither E nor M⁴ makes any comment on 3211, which has presumably been taken as meaning 'Everyone is entitled to express his opinion'. In the context, it is probably not a simple expression of tolerance, but equivalent to proverbial locutions like *Tuit dit se laissent dire* (Morawski 2433), *Toute parole se lait dire* (Rutebeuf, *Testament de l'asne* 108; *Fabliaux*, ed. Johnston and Owen, p. 41), i.e. meaning 'It is easy to make accusations', 'I can't prevent them from saying what they like', with the implication that what they say is untrue; cf. also *vos diroiz vostre pleisir, Mes po m'est de quanque vos dites* (*Lancelot* 3290–1). For other proverbs in the text see note on 40.

3221. Blasmer te font. As recognized by Muret and M⁴ (glossary s.v. *faire*), this is an instance of the use of *faire*+infin. to form a periphrasis for the simple verb. E notes this usage (II 233) in *Plorer en font* 3448 'they weep'; Muret and M⁴ include in the same group instances of *faire* with *amanantir* 4312, *brandir* 4476, *pendre* 1666, 3470, 3492, but in all these cases it is possible to take the infin. as intrans. and give *faire* its normal value. The periphrastic usage may, however, be present in 835–6 and 1483–4 (see notes).

3223–7. 'N'as fait de Tristran escondit.' 'Se je l'en faz?' 'Et il m'ont dit . . . Qu'il le m'ont dit.' 'Ge prest' en sui.' 'Qant le feras? Ancor ancui?' 'Brif terme i met.' 'Asez est loncs.' The text of this stichomythic (or hemistichomythic) dialogue, as of that in 4295–4305 (see notes), is obscure even where not obviously corrupt. E (II 255) sees in these passages a possible sign of the influence of romances such as those of Chrétien de Troyes on the latter part of Beroul's narrative (cf. G. Whitteridge, *Vinaver Misc.*, p. 342). Their absence from the first part may be an indication of difference of authorship, but cannot be taken as evidence of difference of date; for similar passages are common already in the romances of antiquity (see, e.g., *Eneas* 645–52, 1273–6, 1677–86 etc.). The *Tristran* poet does not, however, seem to have mastered the technique, and even allowing for some scribal corruption his dialogues are not very effective. In 3223–7 the emendations and the distribution of the speeches vary from edition to edition. E and M⁴ assume, like Muret, that there is a lacuna between 3224 and 3225, but in other respects preserve the MS. text. Unless, however, another lacuna is allowed for after 3223 or between the two hemistichs of 3224, the earlier part of the passage remains obscure; and *Brif terme i met* 3227 can hardly be understood as 'I shall fix an early date for it' (E says 'Iseut proposes some delay'), and should no doubt be emended to *Brif terme i mez* 'You are setting an early date, demanding a very brief delay, for it' (the correction was made by Muret, though in M⁰ the words were assigned to Mark, not Iseut).

3233–8. E's notes on these lines and 3248–64 (II 226–7) rightly stress the importance for Iseut of the presence of Arthur and his court at her *escondit*. It is not merely, or even mainly, that their participation 'adds a certain solemnity to the exculpation of Iseut and glamour to the jousting and entertainment' (II 106): they play an essential part in the proceedings as sureties and guarantors (see note on 4223–5).

3242. *Mais de ce me seret molt bel.* E translates (II 227) 'yet this would please me well', apparently implying that Iseut would be happy if she had kinsmen in Cornwall who would stir up strife on her behalf. It is possible, however, that *estre molt bel* has here an attenuated sense, 'yet I should not mind about that' (i.e. the fact that she has *no* kinsmen at hand). This interpretation is perhaps supported by the following line *De lor rebeche n'ai mes cure*

'I no longer care about (*or* take any notice of) their chatter' (i.e. that of her enemies).

3255. *Por ce m'est bel que cil i soient*. In the clause depending on *estre bel a* 'be pleasing' the indic. is normal, cf. note on 109–11 and *mout m'est bel que vos Estes li plus cortois de nos* (*Yvain* 74); but here Iseut is expressing not her feeling about what is but her desire about what is to be, hence the (optative) subjunctive.

3261–2. *N'en mentiront por rien qu'il oient, Por les seurdiz se conbatroient*. Muret had at first corrected *oient* to *voient* on the assumption that this was the only rhyme in the text joining *oi* from Early O. F. *oi* to *oi* from Early O. F. *ei*. Other examples of such rhymes are now recognized (cf. *M.L.R.* 60 (1965), 355–6, *Rom.* 90 (1969), 386–7), and Muret's later eds., E and M⁴ retain *oient*.

3300–2. *Un henap port o soi de madre—Une botele ait dedesoz—O coroie atachié par noz*. (So also M³ and M⁴; Muret had earlier printed in 3302 *atachie*, and corrected *par* to *a*). The description of the leper's equipment worn by Tristran (apart from the crutch and rattle) is rather obscure; it is referred to again in *O sa botele el henap fiert* 3691 and *Qant li ladres le henap loche, O la coroie fiert la boche Et o l'autre des mains flavele* 3821–3. I have suggested (*M.L.R.* 60 (1965), 355 n. 1) that *botele* 3301 and 3691 may be, not a spelling of *boteille* (the scribe hardly ever uses a single *l* to represent palatal *l*), but an error for *bocele* (which is how Muret first read it in the MS.); that *boche* 3822 is the Northern form (probably the same word as the *boches* of *Robin et Marion*, ed. Langlois, 657) of a Central *boce*; and that both *bocele* and *boce*, like the corresponding masc. forms *bocel* and *boz*, mean '(small) keg or leather bottle'. In 3822 *boche* rhymes with *loche*, which has open *o*; this is prima facie evidence that it is not to be identified with *boche* 'mouth', which has closed *o* > *u* and is in fact written *bouche* in the MS. (1823, 1997).

3313–14. *Dist Perinis: 'Dame, par soi Bien li dirai si le secroi'*. E retains *par soi*, which he understands (II 229) as ' "by himself", i.e. in confidence'. He does not, however, produce any evidence to suggest that *dire a aucun par soi* (with *soi* not referring to the subject) could ever mean 'tell someone in confidence'; and the position of *par soi* here, followed by *Bien* before *li dirai*, makes it certain that it is an error for exclamatory *par foi*, to which it is corrected by Muret and M⁴ (cf. *soi* for *foi* 1318, and see note on 1325–6).

3329–30. *Et jure quant que puet ataindre: Mar l'ont pensé.* E translates (II 229) 'He swears by whatever is within his reach (power): woe to them that they ever had this thought'; M⁴ (p. 148) suggests that *quant que puet ataindre* may be part of the oath: 'Tout ce qu'il peut atteindre, c.-à-d. tous ceux qu'il pourra atteindre, c'est pour leur malheur qu'ils ont eu cette pensée'. Although *quant que* can in certain contexts mean 'all those who(m)' (cf. T.-L. II 31), it seems unlikely that Tristran would here consider the possibility of not getting hold of all his enemies, and that, even if he did, it would be expressed by the pres. *puet* rather than the future. The punctuation of Muret and E is supported by the fact that *jurer* is often followed by a direct object of the person or thing sworn by (cf. *Deu te jur et la loi de Rome* 660, also 2339, 3104 and T.-L. IV 1879–82). Comparison with passages such as *Si jure quanqu'il puet veoir Que mar le fist el gué cheoir* (*Lancelot* 895–6) and *Li amiralz en juret quanqu'il poet De Mahumet les vertuz e le cors* (*Rol.* 3232–3, translated by Bédier 'L'amiral jure par tous les serments qu'il peut, par les miracles de Mahomet et par son corps') suggests that the meaning is rather 'swears by all (the saints) he can think of'.

3340–1. *Di li que tot ai bien trové A sauver soi du soirement.* E translates (II 229) 'Tell her that I have contrived everything to save her from [the predicament of] the oath'. But this would surely have *A sauver lié* (or *A lié sauver*): the pron. *soi* would not be used in reference to a person other than the subject of the clause (cf. note on 1325–6; E cites as a parallel *Li terme aprime De soi alegier la roïne* 3564–5, but here *soi* refers to *la roïne* as subject of the infin. phrase, cf. note). In any case, Tristran cannot say that he has contrived everything, or indeed anything, for this is his immediate reply to Iseut's instructions. It is necessary to adopt Muret's correction (abandoned in M⁴) of *ai* to *ait*: 'Tell her (that she is) to have everything contrived to save herself from [the implications of] the oath'.

3349. *S'aumosne avrai, se l'en pus traire.* E (II 229): 'I will have his alms, if I can get any out of him'; more exactly, 'if I can get them out of him'.

3353-4. *De moi li porte plus saluz Qu'il n'a sor moi botons menuz.* The MS. has not *botons* but *boces*, and if it were not for the masc. adj. *menuz*, editors would no doubt have adopted the obvious interpretation 'more greetings than there are tumours on my person', with reference to the marks of leprosy that Iseut had instructed him to simulate (*Ja set assez bociez son vis* 3306; cf. his own words later, *Por lié ai je ces boces lees* 3763). In fact, E thinks (II 229-30) that the scribe may have thus understood the line in his model; but all editions after M⁰ assume that the word he copied as *boces* was really *botons*, and that *moi* is a spelling for *mai*: 'more greetings than there are buds on a may-tree or branch of hawthorn'. This is not very convincing either as a correction of the MS. text or intrinsically; *mai* in O. F. means primarily 'verdure, spring foliage and flowers (used for decoration, garlands etc.)', cf. T.-L. V 788-9, and *boton* (apart from its use for 'rosebud' in the *Roman de la Rose*) seems to mean primarily 'haw or hip', cf. T.-L. I 1095. The possibility should therefore be considered that the line does in fact refer to tumours on Tristran's face. The adj. *menu* was often used adverbially (with or without agreement) in the sense of 'closely, tightly, in close formation' (cf. *d'un fil d'or menu cosue* 1148, *Ovrez fu en bestes, menuz* 4127), but apparently only with past parts. (T.-L. V 1460-2). It is perhaps just possible, however, that the scribe's *boces* represents *bocés* as the obl. pl. of either *bocet* or *bocel*, unattested diminutives of *boce* (cf. the attested *bocete* 'pimple' and the participial adjs. in the text meaning 'covered with tumours', *bocelé* 3626, *bocié* 3306, 3716, *boçu* 3922 and probably 1162, see E's note II 151-2); it is true that in the text the obl. pl. of *bocet* would normally appear as *bocez* and that of *bocel* as *boceaus*.

3373. *Isneldone.* To E's note (II 231) it should be added that the Arthurian city of Senaudon is identified with the Roman fort of Segontium near Caernarvon.

3382. *Dist Perinis: Ja en iron.* Although the text contains a number of examples of the comparatively unusual construction of *aler* with *en* but without refl. pron. (T.-L. III 156), this is usually followed by a precise indication of the destination (*Li hermites en vet au Mont* 2733, cf. 595, 2365, 3357); the present instance is paralleled by *Sire, g'en vois* 596, but the exact force of both remains obscure.

3390. *Va, dont viens tu?* See note on 389.

3395-6. *vint a l'estage Ou s[e]oient tuit li barnage.* Muret (from M⁰, p. 254) had emended *tuit* to *toz*; E and M⁴ restore *tuit*. E suggests (II 232) that *barnage* may have been intended as a nom. pl., which would justify *tuit*; but this is not supported by the passage he quotes, *E li barnages de la terre firent lur rei de Joaz* (*Quatre Livre des Reis* p. 224), where *li barnages* is clearly a collective noun in the nom. sing. Our scribe may have written *tuit* as appropriate to the subject of *seoient*, thinking momentarily of *tuit li baron* (for the regularity with which he writes *tuit* as masc. nom. pl. see note on 955-8); but the correction to *toz* seems necessary.

3428-9. *Ge oi dire que souef nage Cil qui on sostient le menton.* As E says (II 232), the present tense is normal in this use of *oïr dire*, the sense of which ('they say', often citing a proverb as here) is well brought out in *Qui contre aguillon eschaucire Dous foiz se point, toz jors l'oi dire* (*Eneas* 8651-2). E mentions as an 'alternative interpretation' (i.e. to the non-elision of *Ge*) *G'oï ja dire*; but this (which would in fact be an emendation) is metrically impossible here, and in any case has a different implication in the lines cited as a parallel, *J'oï ja dire qu'uns seüs Avoit un forestier galois* 1576-7.

3434-5. *La bele Yseut respondu l'a Qu(e) ele en fera droit devant vos.* E lists (II 26) *l'a* 3434 as one of the instances of the elision of the dat. pron. *li* before a word other than the pron. adv. *en* (see note on 444). M⁴, however, (glossary s.v. *respondre*) takes it as an example of the O. F. use of *respondre* with a direct obj. of the person; and it is also conceivable that *l'* is a proleptic duplication of the object-clause *Qu'ele en fera droit*, cf. note on 1944-7.

3440–3. *Cent i aiez de vos amis. Vostre cort soit atant loial, Vostre mesnie natural; Dedevant vos iert alegiee.* E translates 3441–3 (II 233) 'She knows your court to be so loyal and your household sincere; before you she will be cleared of the charge'. He adds that M⁴ 'adopts a somewhat different interpretation and punctuation'; in fact M⁴ has, like Muret, a full stop after *natural* 3442, and yet translates (p. 148) 'Elle sait votre cour si loyale . . . que devant vous elle sera disculpée (qu'elle se tient sûre d'etre disculpée)'. M⁴ is certainly right in understanding 3443 as a consecutive clause depending on 3441; the semi-colon or full stop after 3442 must therefore be replaced by a comma. But *atant* cannot mean 'so'; it must be read (as in M⁰, and tentatively suggested in M⁴'s glossary) as *a tant*, in which *a* is the preposition commonly used in O. F. before the predicative complement of *savoir*, as in *a mesfeite se savoit* (*Yvain* 1789; cf. T.-L. I 17). This still leaves 3442 unaccounted for; it can hardly stand for [*Et*] *vostre mesnie* [*a tant*] *natural* (with *natural* taken as 'sincere', as proposed by Muret, E and T.-L. VI 527), for this would demand a really excessive degree of ellipsis. I have therefore suggested (*Vinaver Misc.*, p. 276) that this is another case where the scribe has interverted the lines of the couplet (cf. note on 65–8), the more easily because both begin *Vostre*, and that the original text must have run *Cent i aiez de vos amis, Vostre mesnie natural; Vostre cort set a tant loial, Dedevant vos iert alegiee* (with *natural* in the sense of 'bound by feudal ties', cf. M⁴'s glossary): 'Have there a hundred of your friends, your own liegemen; she knows your court to be so honourable that she will be exculpated before you'.

3445–6. *Que pus li seriez garant, N'en faudriez ne tant ne quant.* The punctuation with comma after *Que* is common to Muret's later eds. and M⁴, but is appropriate only to M⁴, which takes *pus* as a conjunction 'après que', a function unattested in Continental O. F. except in *S. Léger* 96 (Gdf. VI 461, T.-L. VII 1641). E translates (II 233) 'Because henceforth you would be her protector and would not fail her in any way whatsoever'; but *n'en faudriez* (as distinct from *ne li faudriez*) no doubt means 'you would not fail, be found wanting, in the matter' (as in *falir de covenant, de covent* etc., cf. T.-L. III 1609).

3448. *Plorer en font.* See note on 3221.

3454–6. *Ja ne voist il s'anz paradis, Se li rois veut, qui la n'ira Et qui par droit ne l'aidera!* (The MS. has in 3455 *quil larara,* corrected by all editors). E translates (II 233) 'May that man never enter Paradise who does not go there (i.e. to the Gué Aventuros) and help her as it is meet, if such be the king's wish'; similarly M⁴. But this involves taking *anz* (*enz*) as a prep., a use which is rare except in Northern and Anglo-Norman texts, and of which there is no other instance in the text; and it leaves *s'* unaccounted for. Muret (M⁰–M²) had emended to *voist il en paradis,* which is irreproachable in itself but could hardly have given rise, through misreading or miscopying, to the version in the MS. Restoring the MS. text, M⁴ (p. 148) explains *s'* as 'un *soi* élidé' and adds that 'la construction normale serait *Ja ne voist se il*'; but in fact neither *Ja ne voist il soi* nor *Ja ne voist se il* is conceivable in O. F., for (granted that *aler* is here reflexive without *en,* a usage almost unknown except in certain impersonal locutions) the only normal construction would be *Ja ne se voist il.* E takes *s'* as 'the elided form of *se* for *si* (< sic), which is frequently used to reinforce an optative or jussive subjunctive'; but it is difficult to see what function such a *si* could fulfil here, and in any case it could appear only in initial position (*Si ne voist il ja*). I have therefore suggested (*Vinaver Misc.,* p. 283) that the line is indeed corrupt, as Muret saw, but that the original reading was probably *Ja ne voie il saint paradis . . .* 'May that man never see holy Paradise who . . .'. For the use of *veoir* in a similar formula cf. *Ja ne voie Deu en la face, Qui trovera le nain en place, Qi nu ferra d'un glaive el cors!* 841–3 (also 58–9, see note); for *saint paradis* cf. *Rol.* 1522 and other examples in T.-L. VII 190–1. If this stood in the scribe's model, he might easily have made the two alterations shown by his copy. He could have confused the verb-forms *voi(e)* and *voist,* since he has conversely dropped a final *-st* in *tenti[st]* 1530 (: *s'esbaudist*; alternatively, it is possible that both verbs should be in the pret., and that *-st* has been added to *s'esbaudi*) and in *Fu[st]* 1726 (also perhaps in *porpensa[st]* 647 and probaly in *fu[st]* 4112, see the notes). He could also have written *sanz* for *saint* (for *-an-* cf. *nan* 1311 for *nain, son* 634 etc. for *soin, am* 1401 for *aim,* cf. also note on 2345–9; for *-nz* cf. *genz* 1227 for *gent*).

3469–70. *Ge li feroie asez ennui Et lui pendrë a[n] un haut pui*. E says (II 234) that the infin. is here 'used loosely as the equivalent of a second finite clause' (i.e. = *ge le pendroie*), and then goes on 'it might be partly explained as dependent on *feroie*' (i.e. = *ge le feroie pendre*). These explanations cannot both be right, and neither is very satisfactory. T.-L. quotes the line s.v. *pui* (VII 2052) with *pendré* (i.e. fut. 1 sing.); but though the fut. might be used thus co-ordinated with the condit. *feroie*, it would not be preceded by the strong pron. obj. *lui*. It is possible that *Et lui pendrë* is a scribal corruption for *Com de lui pendre* (for *com de* + infin. see T.-L. II 595).

It is not explained why Gauvain should want to hang Guenelon *an un haut pui*; the *pui* may have been suggested by the rhyme-word *ennui*, but there may also have been a vague notion of a lord's stronghold like those referred to in *Forz chasteaus* . . . *Soiant sor roche, sor haut pui* 3144–5.

3478–9. *de ma grant lance fresnine Ne pasent outre li coutel*. For *coutel* E's glossary and note (II 234) give 'blades'; more exactly 'edges'.

3480–1. *Ja n'en enbraz soz le mantel Bele dame desoz cortine*. The MS. reading *Jannenbraz* is corrected by E and M⁴ to *Ja n'en enbraz*, but no explanation is offered for the *en*. Unless a more substantial correction is to be made, e.g. to *Ja mais n'enbraz* (M⁰), or better to *Ne ja n'enbraz* (co-ordinated with *Ja ne me tienge Dex en sens* 3476), it seems necessary to print with Muret's later eds. *Ja nen enbraz* (for *nen* cf. note on 76 and E II 26).

The word *mantel* is glossed by Muret and M⁴ 'couverture de lit', by E 'bedcover'. No such sense is recognized by Gdf. (V 155, X 119) or T.-L. (V 1094–9); on the other hand, the normal literal sense of 'cloak' is hardly consistent with *desoz cortine*. It is perhaps possible that the locution *soz le mantel* had already acquired (as had *soz (la) chape*, cf. T.-L. II 236) the figurative sense of 'in secret'.

3483. *Dit Evains, li filz Urïen*. The MS has *Et dit Evains li filz Dinan*, corrected by all editors; for scribal restoration of the measure, destroyed by an error, see note on 1569–70.

3486–90. *Bien set faire le roi muser; Tant li dirai que il me croie. Se je l'encontre enmié ma voie, Con je fis ja une autre foiz, Ja ne m'en tienge lois ne fois* . . . Muret, followed by M⁴, corrects *dirai* and *me* 3487 to *dira* and *le* :'Guenelon will say so much to the king that he will believe him'. E restores the MS. reading and makes 3487 an independent sentence, but does not translate it. As it stands, with the full stop at the end, it would appear to mean 'I will say so much to him that he will believe me' (the subjunctive *croie* presumably implying purpose, as in Muret's version). It is more probable, however, that the line is intended to introduce the following threats against Denoalen (3488–92), and that it should be punctuated *Tant li dirai (que il me croie!): Se je l'encontre* . . . 'This much I will say to him (and let him believe me!): if ever I meet him . . .'. For the construction with *tant, itant* in apposition with a following statement or clause cf. notes on 1593 and 2411–13; for the subjunctive of command in an independent sentence introduced by *que* (still rare at this period) cf. *mon cheval Enreigneȝ, mestre Governal; Se mestier m'est, que vos soieȝ Au pasage, preȝ, enbuschieȝ* 3587–90, and perhaps '*Ha! Dex,' fait il, 'regarde moi, Que cil qui vient ne m'aperçoive* . . .' 4360–1, also T.-L. VIII 34.

3493. *Molt doit on felon chastïer.* This line has the appearance of a proverb, but does not seem to be attested as such.

3494. *Du roi joent si losengier.* See note on 1969–71.

3496–7. *Sire, je sui de tant seür Que li felon prendront colee.* Punctuate with a colon after 3496; cf. note on 2411–13.

3502–3. *Au partir en remestrent grief Tuit cil qui l'ourent deservi.* In E's note (II 234) *au partir* is translated 'in the settlement of it' (sc. of the affair indicated in 3499–501); the meaning is rather 'in the end, finally' (cf. T.-L. VII 393–4).

3525–9. *Tuit li conte sont de la bele, Qu'il metra lance par astele. Ainȝ que parte de parlemenȝ, Li rois offre les garnemenȝ Perinis d'estre chevalier.* The editors disagree about the status of 3527: M⁰ and M⁴ attach the line to what precedes (taking *parlemenȝ* to refer to

I

Iseut's approaching *escondit*), Muret's later eds. and E rather more plausibly attach it to what follows (taking *parlemenz* to refer to the conversation at present going on between Perinis and Arthur).

In 3525–6 Muret, followed by M⁴, corrects *Qu'il* to *Qui* (cf. note on 269–70), understanding (M⁴, p. 148) 'La belle fera rompre plus d'une lance pour l'amour d'elle'. E (II 234–5) finds the use of *metra* = 'fera mettre' rather unconvincing (see, however, note on 89–90); he suggests that if the correction is made *Qui* might be taken as 'generic': 'All their talk is of the fair one [and of] whoever will splinter a lance [sc. in her honour]'; he prefers, however, to retain *Qu'il*, taking *il* to refer to Arthur (presumably 'about the fair one [and about the fact] that he will splinter a lance'). But both E's alternatives are syntactically very awkward, and the best version of the lines remains that of Muret.

In 3527 E retains the MS. text and understands 'before he (Arthur) breaks off their exchanges'; but *parlement* is not used in the plural in reference to a single meeting or interview (cf. T.-L. VII 281–3), and again it seems desirable to correct with Muret and M⁴ to *li parlemenz*: 'before the interview breaks up' (for *partir* in this sense cf. T.-L. VII 391).

3544–5. *Por lié serai entalentez; El me porra molt avancier.* The MS. reads *Por uc* (or *ue*) *serai des alentez*; all editors adopt Muret's correction, understood as 'For her I will be full of zeal' (E II 235), but as *entalenté* elsewhere normally means 'desirous' and is followed by a complement (*de* + noun or infin., or a *que*-clause, cf. T.-L. III 553), the rather radical correction hardly carries conviction. It seems more probable that the original had a sentence negative in force such as *Poroc ne serai alentez* (cf. Gdf. I 217, T.-L. I 285) or *Poi en serai destalentez* (cf. T.-L. II 1758–9).

For 3545 E gives 'she will have cause to favour me greatly'; but though *pooir* can certainly mean 'have reason to', this is not exactly the kind of context in which it occurs in that sense (see T.-L. VII 1419–20), and we should probably adopt the correction suggested by G. Paris, *El me pot ja . . .*, i.e. 'She was able, on an earlier occasion, to help me' (with reference to the mysterious incident alluded to in the following lines).

3559–60. *Reconté a sa chevauchie A celi qui molt en fu lie.* It is not clear why E here follows Muret in correcting *celui* as fem. demonstr. pron. to *celi*, since he elsewhere retains scribal *lui* for the strong fem. pers. pron. *li* (cf. his II 22 and 59 n. 1); M⁴, more consistently, restores the MS. reading *celui.*

3564–5. *Li terme aprime De soi alegier la roïne.* E refers (II 238) for what he calls 'this rare use of the infinitive with pronoun subject' to his note on 891 (II 136). The construction with preposition, infin. and strong pers. pron. as subject of the infin. occurs in 891 (*Por estre moi desherité*) and 1927, but here the subject of the infin. is the noun *la roïne*, and the strong pers. pron. *soi* is the refl. object.

3566–7. *Tristran, li suens amis, ne fine, Vestu se fu de mainte guise.* For 3566 E gives (II 238) 'he does not desist', 'he is not laggardly'; the sense is rather 'he does not rest, does not delay', cf. T.-L. III 1875.

3581–2. *Prenez garde de la roïne, Qu'el n'en fera senblant et signe.* In 3582 the MS. has *Quil*; Muret corrected to *Qu'el ne fera senblant ne signe*; E and M⁴ retain only the correction *Qu'el* (it would be at least equally possible to take *Quil* as = *qui*, cf. note on 269–70). E translates (II 238) 'for she will give no sign or token [of being aware of your identity?].' G. Paris had tentatively suggested reading *Qu'el vos fera senblant et signe*, which is grammatically preferable to the version of E and M⁴ (*ne . . . et* is abnormal), involves no more emendation than that of Muret, and is contextually better than either of these.

3601–2. *Et, por l'amor Yseut m'amie, I ferai tost une esbaudie.* It is very doubtful whether the phrase *por l'amor Yseut m'amie* is sufficiently closely connected to the rest of the sentence to support a weak pron. obj. *i* before the verb, and there is no other instance in the text of *i* initial of the line; we should no doubt correct to *G'i ferai* (cf. 3796, 3819 etc.).

On *esbaudie* E comments (II 238–9) that no other example is given by Gdf. or T.-L., and that the usual form of the word is *esbaudise*: in fact, Gdf. and T.-L. cite *esbaudie* also from the *Roman de la Rose*, but have only one example of *esbaudise* (from Thibaut de Champagne). M⁰ does not gloss *esbaudie*, Muret's later eds. and M⁴ gloss 'joute?', but the only sense justified by the examples and the etymology is 'bold or reckless act' (E, glossary and II 239).

3615–16. *Sor la mote . . . S'asist Tristran sanz autre afaire.* (The MS. has *Safist*, corrected by all editors.) Muret glosses *sanz autre afaire* 'simplement, sans s'embarrasser de rien', M⁴ adds '(en homme qui est habitué a agir ainsi)'; better with E (II 239, 263) 'without more ado'.

3621. *Sor la mote forment se tret.* M⁴ translates (glossary s.v. *traire*) 'il se dirige vers la motte, ou plutôt: (assis) sur la motte il se redresse'; E has no note, and his glossary gives only for *traire* refl. 'betake oneself, make one's way out.' Perhaps 'he makes his way well up on to the mound'.

3628. *En plaignant disoit: 'Mar i fui!'* There is no justification for the correction in Muret's later eds. to *Mar i sui*. E translates 'In an evil hour did I come to this'; but it appears from numerous examples in T.-L. (V 1106–8) that in this locution *i* has no specific force, and the meaning is simply 'Woe is me!, Alas (for me)!'

3632–4. *Tristran lor fait des borses trere, Que il fait tant, chascun li done; Il les reçoit, que nus n'en sone.* In 3634 *les* presumably refers, as E suggests (II 239), to 'alms' or 'coins', implied by *li done*; cf. *Ferlin ou maalle esterline Li ont doné: il les reçoit* 3654–5. The clause *que nus n'en sone*, translated by E 'without anyone saying anything (i.e. without making any observation indicating suspicion)', does not correspond to any attested use of *soner*, and Muret, followed by M⁴, emends to *que mot ne sone* 'without uttering a word'; E objects that this is contradicted by the context, but the same locution occurs in a similar context in *Escoute Tristran, mot ne sone; Por Deu, ce dit, le lor pardone* 3645–6. The meaning in both passages is no doubt 'without comment' rather than 'without opening his mouth'.

3654. *Ferlin ou maalle esterline.* E says (II 240) that '20 *sous* made a *livre esterline*': more correctly, a *livre d'esterlins* (also a *livre de tournois, de parisis* etc.), cf. *cinc soz d'esterlins* 3972. The adjectives *esterlin, tournois, parisi(s)* etc. were applied only to actual coins such as the *denier, maaille* or *ferlin*, not to moneys of account like the *livre* or *marc.*

3663–5. *Pensent vaslet et escuier Qu'il se hastent de soi logier Et des tres tendre lor seignors.* In 3664 the MS. has *Quil se hast de nus alegier*; the quite substantial emendations proposed by G. Paris and adopted by all editors require us to believe that the servants and squires hasten first to set up dwellings for themselves. In any case, the construction *Pensent . . . Qu'il se hast[ent]* is abnormal: the meaning clearly cannot be 'think that they are hastening', and if it were 'bethink themselves to make haste' (E, II 240) or 'think that they will hasten' the dependent verb would be in the fut. indic. (T.-L. VII 673–5 has no example of *penser que* + subjunctive in this sense). I have therefore suggested (*Vinaver Misc.*, p. 284) that *Pensent* is probably corrupt and that the introduction of *soi logier* is unjustified; and I proposed to correct to *Passent vaslet et escuier Qui se hastent d'eus alegier Et des tres tendre . . .* 'Past him go servants and squires who hasten to unburden themselves [sc. of their loads of material] and to pitch the tents' (for *eus* in a refl. sense cf. Foulet §179 and T.-L. IV 1304). I noted that the scribe had elsewhere misread forms of the verb *passer* (he writes *parler* 3694 for *passer*, *port* 3975 for *past*) and confused *Qui* and *Qu'il* before consonant (see note on 269–70); and if he misunderstood the first hemistich of 3664 as *Qu'il se hast* (perhaps taken as subj. depending on *penser* 'think (mistakenly)'; cf. also, two lines above, *Qu'il ne soit ladres*), he might well have restored the measure (cf. note on 1569–70) by arbitrarily writing *denus* for *deus*. E (II 240) describes my proposal as a 'bold emendation'; but it actually changes fewer letters of the MS. text than that of G. Paris, and is palaeographically no less plausible.

3684. *Li ladres a sa main fors traite.* It is not clear whence or why the 'leper' draws out his hand; but no comment is made by Muret, E or M⁴.

3691. *O sa botele el henap fiert.* See note on 3300–2.

3701. *Cil qui la passe n'est seürs* (: *Artus*). The MS. has *Cil qui les passe n'est seuez*, and Muret's correction, retained by E and M⁴, is not obviously right. His *la* presumably refers to *la paluz* 3700, or it may be the adverb, 'He who crosses it (*or* there) is not safe', a comment which has no marked relevance. If the *les* of the MS. were retained, *Cil qui les passe* 'he who sets them across' might refer to Tristran, who has been directing people how to cross the mire; and it is perhaps possible that *seuez* is for *seüz* (for the rhyme cf. *Artus* : *druz* 4109–10), to be taken here in the sense of 'known, recognized' which it sometimes had in O. F. (cf. Gdf. X 635).

3702–4. *Atant es vos le roi Artus; Esgarder vient le passeor, O lui de ses barons plusor.* All editors take *passeor* here in the attested sense of 'passage, crossing'. In *Li passeor sollent lor dras* 3698, however, what is formally the same word is understood by all editors as 'those who cross' (see E II 240); and it seems probable that Muret was right in expecting the same sense in 3703 and tentatively suggesting (M⁰, glossary) the correction of *le passeor* to *les passeors* and the consequent correction of *plusor* 3704 to *plusors*. In the construction 'he comes . . ., with him several of his barons' the correct case-form would of course be the nom. *plusor*; it is possible that 3703 and 3704 have been interverted by the scribe (cf. note on 65–8), and that the original text ran *Atant es vos le roi Artus, O lui de ses barons plusors; Esgarder vient les passeors* (in which the obl. *plusors*, like *le roi*, is normal after *es vos*, cf. 570, 2101). Whether in this reconstruction *Artus* is taken as nom. (rhyming correctly with *seürs* or *seüz* 3701) or as a scribal error for *Artur* (with incorrect rhyme) is of little importance: there are parallels in the text for both.

3711. *Maint drap de soie i ot levé.* Both M⁰ and E take *lever* here as meaning 'wear'; but no such sense of the verb is registered by Gdf. or T.-L. Although equipment and armour have just been described (3708–10), and *dras de soie* may elsewhere refer to clothes (e.g. 2736, 3903), the reference here must be either to banners and pennons or to the hangings of the tents and pavilions (cf. *beles chanbres . . . Portendues de dras de soie* 2182–3). The verb *lever* is therefore to be taken in the sense of 'raise' (cf., of banners, tents, pavilions etc., T.-L. V 359–61).

3738–9. (*Li ladres . . .*) *Fins dras en a a grant plenté Et les sorchauz Artus le roi.* The MS. has *Fait dras*, which all editors have with reason assumed to be corrupt; M⁰ corrected to *Mais*, Muret's later eds., E and M⁴ correct to *Fins*, while Acher suggested *Frois* and Tanquerey *Faiz* taken as meaning 'convenables'. E now wonders (II 241) whether it is possible to retain *Fait*, understood as *Fait que . . .*, 'He contrives to obtain raiment in great quantity . . .'; but the paratactic noun-clause without *que* is not attested as obj. of *faire* in the sense of 'bring it about (that . . .)' (cf. T.-L. III 1564).

3755–6. *Desoz la chape a mis l'aumuce, Qant qu'il puet la trestorne et muce.* It is not clear why Tristran hides Mark's hood; but none of the editors comments.

3773–6. '*Cist maus me prist de la comune; Mais plus bele ne fu que une.*' '*Qui est ele?*' '*La bele Yseut; Einsi se vest con cele seut*'. (The correction *comune* for *covine* is made by all editors.) The glossaries of E and M⁴ place *Mais* 3774 under the temporal adv., and E glosses it 'ever'; but as temporal adv. *mais* means 'henceforth, (any) longer, again' (the sense of 'ever' arises only in conjunction with *ja, ainz* etc.), and the word is here the conj. 'but'.

E (II 237) summarizes Tristran's speech (3771–6) 'Through her I had this malady, her husband being leprous; the fair Iseut she is called'. What Tristran and Mark actually say in the text is: 'This malady laid hold on me through the intercourse; but only one [lady] was more beautiful [than my mistress].' 'Who is that one?' 'The fair Iseut; she [sc. Iseut] dresses just as she [sc. my mistress] used to do'. For the pres. indic. of *soloir* used with past sense cf., e.g., *la janz . . . n'aimment mes si come il suelent* (*Yvain* 5395). There is no suggestion that the supposed mistress of the leper was herself called Iseut.

3794. *Vez la cel torbe aprés cel fanc.* In their glossaries the editors give *torbe* as masc. (E) or masc. and fem. (Muret, M⁴); but it is registered only as fem. in Gdf. (X 784) and Littré. Hence (together with the repetition of *cel*) the correction suggested by G. Paris to *Vez la grant torbe*. An alternative correction would be *Veez la torbe aprés cel fanc?*, with the normal pres. indic. form *vëez* (cf. 4333), used here in a question, instead of the shortened imper. form *vez* used chiefly with *ci* or *la* like Mod. F. *voici, voilà*.

3795. *La est li droiz asseneors*. The glossaries of Muret, E and M⁴ give for *asseneor* 'direction'. The word is not in Gdf., and T.-L. has only one example (from Gilles li Muisis), in which it is clearly (as its origin would imply) the agent-noun 'director', 'guide'. The meaning here is therefore no doubt 'landmark'.

3805-6. *Alez, seignor! Par saint apostre, Si me done chascun du vostre!* E (II 24, 241-2), following M⁰, glossary, thinks *done* is most probably intended as 3 sing. pres. subj.; but in the text this form of *doner* appears in rhyme only as *donge* 292, 430 (MS. *doige*) and *don(s)t* 506, 2186, internally also *doinst* 2373, 2542, 4450. It is perhaps more likely to be imper., the sing. (whether original or scribal) being induced by *chascun*; the situation is somewhat similar in *Mais li lion, destroiz de faim, Chascun la prenoit par la main* 2071-2.

3821-2. *Qant li ladres le henap loche, O la coroie fiert la boche*. For the suggestion that *boche* may here be a Northern form of *boce*, referring to the object elsewhere called *botele*, see note on 3300-2.

3868-9. *cel siglaton Estera ja forment laidiz*. The form *estera* is assigned by E (glossary) to the verb *ester*; but the use of *ester* with a predicative complement in the sense of *estre* is extremely rare. T.-L. (III 1382-3) has a few alleged examples, but apart from one of *estommes* (for which there is a variant with *somes*) they are all, as here, futures. Future forms *estera, esterons* are similarly used in *Eneas* 4265, 5035, 5970 etc.; note particularly *quarz estera* 2943 parallel to *sera rois* 2941, *ert setmes* 2951 etc. All these forms should therefore be taken as analogical forms of the fut. of *estre* (Fouché, p. 416), or more accurately, with M⁰, glossary, as forms borrowed, like the past part. *esté*, by *estre* from *ester*.

3870–2. *Cist garez est plain de rouïz. Marriz en sui, forment m'en poise, Se a vos dras poi en adoise.* The MS. has in 3872 *posen adoise*; Muret printed (M⁰) *pose n'adoise*, understood as 'if it (the mud) rests on or touches your clothes', but afterwards adopted Tobler's correction *point en adoise*, retained by M⁴. E says (II 244) that *posen* may be the scribe's misreading of *poi en* or of *poĩ* (= *poin* for *point*) *en*. In the context, *poi* is hardly possible; in O. F., as in Mod. F., it could mean only 'little', 'a small quantity, not a great deal'. The correction to *point* is therefore indispensable (scribal *pos* is probably due to the influence of the rhyme-words *poise*, *adoise*, cf. note on 819–20).

3879. *De l'autre part fu Yseut sole.* E comments (II 244) 'i.e. apart from Tristran (and Dinas?)'. Dinas had been with Iseut earlier (3853–66), but had just crossed, with Andret, by a ford lower down the stream (3876–8); Iseut was now alone on one bank (apart from the 'leper' Tristran), and Mark and Arthur and all their retinues were beyond the stream (3880–4, 3899–902).

3899–900. *La roïne out molt grant esgart De ceus qui sont de l'autre part.* Though the noun *esgart* is common in O. F. (cf. 4138, 4272), no example of the locution *avoir esgart de* is cited by Gdf. (III 466–7, IX 529) or T.-L. (III 1067–9) from the O. F. period proper. M⁴'s glossary gives ' "fut regardée attentivement par ceux . . ." ou peut-être "regarda attentivement ceux . . .", "ne perdit pas de vue un instant ceux . . ." '. To the first of these alternatives corresponds Muret's gloss 'regard', to the second E's 'care, caution'. Neither of these interpretations can be excluded, but the first is perhaps the more probable in view of the context and 3883–4 (*Yseut . . . Bien savoit que cil l'esgardoient Qui outre le Mal Pas estoient*; cf. also note on 3933–4).

3909–10. *Un cercle d'or out sor son chief, Qui empare de chief en chief.* For *emparer* (of which no other instance in O. F. proper is cited by Gdf., III 52–3, or T.-L., III 89) Muret and M⁴ give 'entourer' and E 'encircle'. M⁰ (glossary) and E (II 244) take *Qui* as the direct object of *empare*; but the use as direct object of a verb of *qui* (*cui*) referring to a concrete object would be very unusual at this period (cf. T.-L. II 1125–6), and *Qui empare* is perhaps an error for *Qui l'empare* 'which (sc. the circlet) encircles it (sc. her head)'.

3913. *Ge vuel avoir a toi afere.* These words of Iseut are deliberately ambiguous; *avoir a faire a* can mean 'have sexual relations with' (cf. T.-L. III 1572). For the use made of this theme cf. *A lui parler point ne m'ennoie* 3927 and note on 1932–4.

3928. *O le puiot sovent s'apoie.* E cites (II 244) J. Frappier's interpretation of *sovent* as 'beaucoup, fortement, longuement', but no doubt rightly prefers here the more normal sense of 'often, repeatedly'. For less usual senses of *sovent* see notes on 612 and 4473.

3930. *Tor la ton vis et ça ton dos.* Muret in his later eds. emended the first hemistich to *Ton vis la torne*, but E and M⁴ restore the MS. reading. E takes *Tor* as imper. of *tordre*; so presumably also M⁴, whose glossary does not include this line among the 11 listed under *torner*. However, no similar use of *tordre* appears in Gdf. (X 779), and the verb one would expect is undoubtedly *torner*, under which M⁰ cites the line (cf. *Torne le dos* 3933, and T.-L. II 2037). It is possible that there existed a shortened form of the imper. 2 sing. of *torner*, comparable to *gar, agar, esgar* from *garder* etc. (for which see T.-L. s.vv.), *don* from *doner* (*Raoul de Cambrai* 4269, T.-L. IV 97), *lai* from *laier* (other such forms seem to be confined to Anglo-Norman, cf. Fouché, pp. 207–8); a formation of this kind might have been encouraged by the existence of fut. forms like *torra* 3461 (see note on 2919).

3933–4. *Torne le dos, et ele monte; Tuit les gardent, et roi et conte.* Muret's later eds. and M⁴ also follow the MS. exactly and print *les gardent*; M⁰, however, printed *l'esgardent*, and E now (II 244) admits the possibility that 'the scribe made a wrong word-division and the poet intended *l'esgardent*'. For the legitimacy of editorial intervention in such a case see note on 29–30. In fact, the trans. use of *garder* in the sense of 'look at, watch' is very rare in O. F. (cf. T.-L. IV 143) and does not occur elsewhere in the text, whereas *esgarder* is common and appears in the same context in 3703, 3831 etc. The pron. obj. in *l'esgardent* refers to Iseut alone, as in *Bien savoit que cil l'esgardoient Qui outre le Mal Pas estoient* 3883–4.

3936. *L'un pié sorlieve et l'autre clot.* The verb *clore* is glossed by Muret and M⁴ 'poser', by E 'plant (one's foot)'; no further information is given. Neither Gdf. nor T.-L. gives any similar sense for the verb *clore* 'close etc.'; and neither they nor *F.E.W.* include any verb representing Lat. CLAUDĒRE (CLAUDĔRE) v.n. 'limp, be lame'.

3943–4. *Vez la roïne chevauchier Un malade qui set clochier.* E takes *set* (II 245) to be an 'attenuated use of *savoir* "know how to" '; he says this use is well attested, but gives no evidence, and there seems to be nothing similar in Gdf. Muret's emendation to *seut* 'is in the habit of' is retained by M⁴ and should be adopted; E points out that the 3 sing. pres. indic. of *soloir* appears in rhyme as *seut* 3776, but this does not mean that the scribe could not have miswritten it here as *set*.

3947–50. '*Alon encontre cel mesel A l'issue de cest gacel.*' *La coururent li damoisel* . . . The MS. has here three successive lines rhyming in -*el*. Muret originally (M⁰) suppressed the third line (3949); but he later restored it and assumed, as do E and M⁴ in their texts, that a fourth line in -*el* (3950) had dropped out. In II 4 E admits both possibilities, that the scribe has omitted one of four lines on the same rhyme (but see note on 160–2) or that one of the three is a variant wrongly incorporated (see note on 207–10). Though 3949 is not obviously a variant of either of the preceding lines, it could certainly be dispensed with.

3957–8. *Au departir li redemande, La bele Yseut, anuit viande.* Muret emended *li* to *il* (punctuating *il redemande La bele Yseut anuit viande*), retained by M⁴; but after the adverbial complement *au departir* the pers. pron. subject would normally follow the verb instead of preceding it; cf. *Au partir en remestrent grief Tuit cil* . . . 3502–3, where the influence of the initial adverbial phrase is

shown by the position before the verb of the weak pron. obj. *en.*
For the *li* of the MS. version see note on 1944–7.

3973–5. *Et de l'aumuce mon seignor Achat bien lit, si soit pastor, Ou un asne qui past le tai.* (In 3974 Muret read *bun lit,* but M⁴ accepts E's reading with *bien*; in 3975 the MS. has *port le tai,* corrected by all editors.) The passage is obscure and probably corrupt. M⁰ emended the second hemistich of 3974 to *ci soit en tor,* presumably understanding 'Let him buy a good litter and be hereabouts with an ass to cross the mire'; Acher, on the same lines, proposed *si soit passor* (or *soit passeor*), understanding 'qu'il achète . . . une bonne litière ou un âne qui lui permettra de s'établir passeur au marais'. There seems, however, to be no authority for taking *lit* in the sense of 'litter'; and Muret in his later eds. changed the emendation to *et covertor,* 'let him buy a good bed and a blanket', apparently abandoning any connection of sense between 3974 and 3975. E and M⁴ restore the MS. version of 3974, but do not explain how they understand it. 'Let him buy a bed (the sense of *bien* is not clear) and be a shepherd, or an ass to cross the mire' is not a very natural sequence; I have therefore suggested (*Vinaver Misc.,* p. 285) that the *bñ lit* of the MS. may be an error for *brebiz* (*berbiz*): 'let him buy sheep and be a shepherd . . .'. For the use of imparisyllabic obl. forms like *pastor* in nom. function see E II 21.

3976. *Il est herlot, si que jel sai.* E glosses *si que* here 'as'; but this would normally be *si com,* and in fact Muret's later eds. corrected to *si con jel sai* (M⁴ restores the MS. reading). With *si com,* however, one would expect *je sai,* without the pron. obj.; it is probable that *si que* should be retained and understood as modal (cf. notes on 2161–3, 2303–4), 'in such circumstances that I know it', i.e. 'and well I know it'.

3984. *Qui ont armes, lor bohorderent.* E (II 264) corrects his glossary entry under *lores,* adv. 'then', to add '*lor* 2495, 3984'; but the MS. reading in 3984 is *lors,* cf. his text correction, II 263, also Muret and M⁴. For *lor* 2495 see note.

4014–17. '*Ges connois bien,*' *Girflet respont,* '*Noir cheval a et noire* *enseigne, Ce est li Noirs de la Montaigne. L'autre connois as armes vaires . . .'.* It seems possible that 4015 and 4016 have been interverted by the scribe; cf. note on 65–8.

4020–1. *Icil vindrent fors de la rote, Les escus pres, lances levees.* M⁴'s glossary cites 4020 both under *rote* (1) 'route, chemin' (where it was placed by M⁰) and under *rote* (2) 'bande, compagnie'; E's gives it correctly as 'crowd' (cf. 3625). Neither glossary includes *pres* 4021; E (II 248) is inclined to reject the interpretations of it as (with M⁰) the adv. (meaning here 'held close to their bodies'), or as scribal for *prez* (obl. pl. of *prest* 'ready'), and, no doubt rightly, now takes it as an error for *pris*, citing as a parallel *Lance levee, l'escu pris* 4037 (: *le vis*).

4038. *A Tristran saut en mié le vis.* M⁴ offers no explanation of this line, and E gives only the gloss (s.v. *mié*) '*en mié* in the middle of 4038'. It is presumably a locution, analogous to Mod. F. *sauter au visage* (or *aux yeux*) *de quelqu'un* 'make a sudden attack on'; but it does not seem to be attested elsewhere.

4051–2. *Le fer trenchant li mist el cors, O l'acier bote le cuir fors.* For *cuir* the glossaries of Muret, E and M⁴ give 'peau humaine', 'skin'; T.-L. (II 1133) also quotes the lines under 'Haut', but with a query. The query is justified: if the lance-blade, piercing the victim's body, carried some of his skin with it, this would surely not be sufficiently surprising to merit mention. In similar descriptions of exploits with the lance it was traditional to say that the blade carried with it, right through the body of the enemy, the ensign or pennon attached to it (examples in T.-L. s.v. *outre*, VI 1420–2), or that both blade and shaft passed through him (examples in T.-L. s.v. *fust*, III 2365). It therefore seems possible that *cuir* here refers to a part of the lance below the blade, perhaps the *camois* or *chamois* (T.-L. II 195) covering the butt; alternatively, the word may be an error for *fust*.

4071. *En pais remestrent, tuit estroit.* Muret adopted the correction of G. Paris to *destroit*, which is retained by M⁴. E interprets the MS. form *estroit* as the past part. of *estreindre*, taken in the sense

of 'grip (with fear)'; the same past part. is seen by all the editors
in a concrete sense in *il li out si les poinz estroiz* 1053 and by Muret
(M⁰ to M²) in *Dorment estroit et enbrachiez* 1901 (where E, II 182,
now seems inclined to follow M³ and M⁴ in accepting Jeanroy's
reading *estroitet*, adj. used adverbially). Although *estroit* <
STRICTUM is etymologically the past part. of *estreindre*, it was very
early replaced in that function by *estreint* <*STRINCTUM, and it is
not registered under the verb by Fouché (p. 356) or Pope (§1055); but
T.-L. (III 1469) has examples from *Prise d'Orange* 686 and Garnier,
S. Thomas 462. There is therefore no need to correct here to *destroit*.

4088. *De maint grant cerf ot la menee.* For *menee* E's glossary gives
'pursuit', which he now (II 249) modifies to 'the sounding of the
pursuit or of the mort'. In the context, it perhaps means rather
the sounding of the horn to signify the return from a successful
hunt (T.-L. V 1405-6).

4096-100. *La ot petit de dras de laine, Tuit li plusor furent de soie;
Des vesteüres que diroie? De laine i out, ce fu en graine, Escarlate cel
drap de laine.* (F. Michel's correction of *voteures* to *vesteüres* is
adopted by all editors). Extensive but varying emendations were
introduced by Muret; E and M⁴ revert (apart from *vesteüres*) to the
MS. text, while noting that it 'seems corrupt' (E II 249), 'semble
peu assuré' (M⁴ p. 149). It is hardly possible to make sense of
4099 as it stands, and it should no doubt be emended as in M⁰ by
the substitution of *Se* for *De* (for the construction *Se laine i out,
ce fu en graine* cf. note on 1382-4). According to M⁴ (p. 149) 4098
contradicts 4096-7, but this seems exaggerated: *dras* 4096 need
not mean only 'clothes', but may include the hangings of the
pavilions (cf. note on 3711). With the correction mentioned the
passage, though a little repetitive, is quite comprehensible: 'There
were few woollen fabrics there; most were of silk. What should
I say about the garments? If there was any wool, it was dyed in
grain (i.e. with kermes); scarlet (i.e. a fine wool fabric) [was] that
woollen cloth' (*cel drap* obl. for *cil dras* nom.). For *escarlate* (*teinte*)
en graine see examples in T.-L. IV 521-2.

4103. *Mestier nen est dont la nen ait.* (The MS. has *Maistre*, corrected by all editors). E translates freely (II 250) 'There is no need of anything but it is found there'; but this would normally be expressed as *Mestier n'est de rien dont la n'ait*. The only attested construction of *estre mestier* that is possible here is *mestier(s) est de* (T.-L. V 1702–3); it would therefore seem that the line must be read as *Mestier n'en est dont la nen* (or *n'en*) *ait*, literally 'There is no need of that of which there is not (some) there', in which the first *en* is antecedent of *dont*. For *nen* and *n'en* see note on 76.

4111–13. *Maint calemel, mainte troïne, Qui fu la nuit en la gaudine Oïst an pavellon soner.* Grammatically the mood in the *qui*-clause must correspond to that in the principal clause: emend either to *Oï* 4113 (cf. *Cil qui la fu enz en la pree De maint grant cerf ot la menee* 4087–8), or more probably with Muret and M⁴ to *Qui fust* 4112, 'Whoever had been that night in the woods would have heard . . .' (for scribal dropping of final *-st* see note on 646–8).

4114–15. *Devant le jor prist a toner A fermeté, fu de chalor.* E translates (II 250) 'Before daylight it began to thunder, decidedly'; Muret and M⁴ punctuate with a colon after *toner*, but they too have a comma after *A fermeté*, which they gloss 'assurément, sans doute'. There is no authority for attributing this sense to the locution *a fermeté*; T.-L. (III 1751) has no other example and cites these lines under the gloss 'sicherlich' only with a query, and G. Paris evidently did not find Muret's reading convincing, since he tentatively proposed emending to *A ferm esté* (M⁰, p. 254). I have therefore suggested (*Vinaver Misc.*, p. 265) that the lines should be punctuated with a colon or semi-colon after *toner*, but without comma after *fermeté*, and that *A fermeté fu de chalor* should be understood as 'It was by way of a guarantee of (later) heat'. As regards content, this agrees with the context: cf., after the sun and the assembled company had risen, *Li soleuz fu chauz sor la prime, Choiete fu et nielle et frime.* For *fermeté* 'guarantee' cf. Gdf. III 762; for *estre*+*a*+predicative noun cf. *c'est a grant sens* 4184; for administrative formulas of the type *a fermeté* cf. *a plus grant seurtei* (1252, Gdf. X 671), *a plus grant fermeté et segurté des devant dites chouses* (1276, Gdf. VII 409) etc.

4130–5. *En Cornoualle n'ot reliques . . . Sor le paile(s) les orent mises*. E
(II 250) correctly notes that logically 4135 is dependent on the
negative statement in 4130, but that 'the construction is loose
and the clause takes the form of an independent, positive statement of fact'; M⁴ (p. 150) says 'Accord avec l'idée; plus gram-
maticalement on attendrait *nes orent mises*', but in fact what one
would expect is *nes eüssent mises* (or, taking 4135 not as a modal
but as a relative clause, *n'eüssent mises*), with the subjunctive as
in the parallel cited by M⁴, *Il n'ira ja en cel païs, Dex ne li soit verais
amis* 457–8. For the construction in 4130–5 cf. *Iseuz la blonde N'ot
tant les crins sors ne luisanz Que a cesti ne fu neanz* (*Erec* 424–6;
logically *Que a cesti fust neanz*), and *V.B.* II² 108 n.

4131–3. *En tresor ne en filatieres, En aumaires n'en autres bieres, En
fiertres n'en escrinz n'en chases* . . . The MS. has *autres ceres* 4132;
Muret's correction to *bieres* is retained by E and M⁴. The only
attested meaning of *biere*, however, is 'bier, litter' (or by extension
'coffin', or 'corpse'); there is no authority for the glosses 'châsse'
(Muret and M⁴), 'reliquary' (E). It therefore seems possible that
ceres may be an error or a misspelling for some word other than
bieres—perhaps for *serres* 'lock-ups, safe places' (cf. *Dame! vos an
portez la clef, Et la serre et l'escrin avez, Ou ma joie est* (*Yvain* 4632–4)).
The spelling would present no obstacle (for the initial *c*- cf. *cele*
996 for *sele* and note on 3044; for the single -*r*- cf. spellings such as
seure, arire, dura, oras beside *seurre, arrire, durra, orras* etc.). With
serres, autres would have its normal sense of 'other' (with *bieres*
it would have to be taken in the 'expletive' function, cf. note on
2203). It is true that *serres* does not appear to form a correct
rhyme with *filatieres*; but as regards the stressed vowel, apart
from the fact that the text contains other rhymes joining -*er* and
-*ier* (cf. E II 9–10), the word *filatiere* often appears in the form
filatere, and T.-L. (III 1846–7) has examples in rhyme with *batistere*,
frere, mere. The only difficulty would be the rhyme between -*r*-
and -*rr*-, which is abnormal in O. F. and does not occur elsewhere
in the text (it is no doubt mere coincidence that the source of
serre is Lat. SERA); but in view of the number of rhymes of the
type *fiers* : *niés* (see E II 15–16) this does not constitute a very
serious objection.

4141–3. '*Rois Marc*', *fait il*, '*qui te conselle Tel outrage si fait mervelle; Certes*', *fait il*, '*sil se desloie*.' So punctuated also by Muret and M⁴; but T.-L. (V 1539) prints *qui te conselle Tel outrage, sifait mervelle?*, with a co-ordination of affective terms which is very much in the style of the poem (cf. *Si grant desroi, tel felonie* 559, also 643–4 etc.), but as the line stands would require *merveille* to be taken as masc., a usage of which there is very little evidence (T.-L. V 1535–46 has no example, Gdf. V 263 and X 143–4 only one from Palsgrave). It is possible that the scribe has interverted *tel* and *sifait*, and that the original version of 4142 was *Sifait outrage, tel mervelle*; alternatively, *fait* may be an error (under the influence of *fait* in 4141 and 4143) for *grant* (for *grant* with *mervelle* in the sense of 'misdeed, crime' cf. *Qui son droit seignor mesconselle Ne puet faire greignor mervelle* 2543–4). In any event, the content of 4142 is less likely to have been a question than a relative clause taken up by *sil* (= *cil*) 4143: '*qui te conselle Tel outrage, si grant mervelle, Certes*', *fait il*, '*cil se desloie*'. For the construction *qui . . ., cil . . .* cf., e.g., *Qui plus tost cort, cil s'en fuit plus* 1716.

4148–9. *Molt li devroit du cors coster Et ennuier, qui voloit faire.* E translates (II 250) 'it should cost him dear in his own person and distress him, whoever [it was that] desired to do this'; but *qui* with the indic. cannot be the generalizing pron. used concessively that is implied by 'whoever it was that' (this would be *qui quel vosist faire*), and the construction is more accurately represented by M⁴ (p. 150), 'il devrait lui en coûter cher et lui valoir bien des ennuis pour avoir voulu cela (littéralement: à lui qui voulait cela)', in which *qui* is the ordinary relative pron. with the weak pers. pron. obj. *li* as antecedent. Cf. *ges ferai encore pendre Qui la reteront de folie* 4154–5, in which the antecedent of *Qui* is the *les* in *ges*.

E explains *qui voloit faire* as containing *faire* used without a pron. obj. in the sense of 'complete an act'; but the situation is not the same as in 728 and 2431, which he cites as parallels, and the text must be understood as, or corrected to, *qui[l] voloit faire*. Cf. note on 269–70.

4158–9. *Or oiez, roi: qui ara tort, La roïne vendra avant . . .* The function and meaning of *qui ara tort* is obscure. E's first tentative

K

suggestion is (II 250–1) 'whoever may be at fault', referring to the preceding lines containing Arthur's threats against Iseut's accusers; but such an adverbial concessive clause would take the form *qui qui* (or *qu'*) *ait tort* (cf. note on 4148–9). E's alternative explanation, 'Whoever shall have a wrong' (i.e. 'if anyone has a grievance [against her]'), 'the queen will come forward . . .', is grammatically possible, but requires *tort* to be taken in the unattested sense of 'ground for complaint, cause of action', which is not really paralleled, as E suggests, by 4470 or Eng. *tort*.

4163–5. (*La roïne . . . jurra . . .*) *Qu'el onques n'ot amor conmune A ton nevo, ne deus ne une, Que l'en tornast a vilanie.* The expression *ne deus ne une* is not explained by the editors, nor does it appear in the dictionaries. The context suggests that the meaning is 'at all', 'in any degree'.

In 4165 E's glossary entry under *torner* v.a., '*t.a* interpret as, impute 4165', and his translation (II 251), 'upon which an evil interpretation might be put', imply that *que* is object and *l'en* = *l'on*. It would also be possible to take *que* as subject and *l'en* as = *li*+*en*, with *torner* v.n., 'which might turn out (*or* result) in dishonour to her'. This construction occurs several times in the text, cf. especially, in very similar contexts to this, *N'ai corage de drüerie Qui tort a nule vilanie* 33–4, *onques . . . N'oi o vos point de drüerie Qui li* (sc. to Mark) *tornast a vilanie* 2228–30; the only objection to taking 4165 in the same way is the presence of *en*, which would have to be understood in the vague sense of 'consequently'.

4180. *C'a esté fait, c'est sor mon pois.* E mentions (II 251) but does not adopt the suggestion of M⁴ (p. 150) that the *Ca* of the MS. (printed as *C'a* = *Qu'a* in all editions) should be read as *Ç'a* (= *S'a*; cf. note on 3044); for this interpretation, which is undoubtedly correct, see note on 1382–4, and cf. *S'il m'en poise et ge m'en plaing, C'est a bon droit* (*Eneas* 10008–9).

For 'suggested explanations of the expression *sor mon pois*' E refers to the glossary of M⁰; the material in T.-L. VII 1337–8 (numbered 2137–8) makes it certain that of the two explanations there indicated that of Ebeling is correct. In the expression *sor mon pois* of Beroul 4180, 'against my will', *pois* is a noun derived from the verb *peser* in its impers. use (*il me poise* 'it distresses me', 'I regret it'), and is not to be identified with the noun *pois* 'weight' (< PENSUM) which appears in the Mid. F. expression *sor mon pois* 'at my expense, on my account'.

4184. *c'est a grant sens*. No comment is made by the editors on this sentence: it presumably means 'this is [by way of] great wisdom', i.e. 'this is a wise arrangement.' Cf. note on 4114–15.

4185. *Yseut fu entre deus as mains*. E's glossary gives for *as mains* 'holding their hands' (i.e. those of Arthur and Mark); similarly M⁰, 'leur donnant la main', adopted by T.-L. V 812. It may be questioned, however, whether the words mean anything more than 'close to them'; cf. the locutions of this sense *avoir a main*, *estre a main*, *estre sor mains* (T.-L. V 815–16), and the reference a few lines later to Arthur *Qui fu d'Iseut le plus prochain* 4190.

4192–4. *Oiez de qoi on vos apele: Que Tristran n'ot vers vos amor De puteé* . . . E, following M⁰, glosses *apeler de* 'accuse of', but this does not fit the context. What it appears to mean here is the 'exiger une déclaration formelle' of Muret's later eds. and M⁴, or T.-L.'s 'zu einer Erklärung vor Gericht auffördern' (I 437; this is the only example cited); 'Hear what you are called upon for' (i.e. 'called upon to swear').

4193–6. . . . *Que Tristran n'ot vers vos amor De puteé ne de folor Fors cele que devoit porter Envers son oncle et vers sa per*. E provides a revised glossary entry *fors* (II 263), but neither this nor the glossary of Muret or of M⁴ registers the word with the sense it has here, 'but only' (cf. T.-L. III 2142–3). See also note on 4223–5.

4199. *Or escoutez que je ci jure*. E notes (II 252) that P. Jonin has identified the words *Or escoutez* as a recognized 'formule propitiatoire', the equivalent of *Hoc audias*, used in oaths of this kind. It should not be overlooked that the same words are also used frequently in the text in contexts where there is no question of an oath or other consecrated formula, e.g. 728, 1332, 2300, 2351, 2552 etc.

4199–205. *Or escoute*ʒ *que je ci jure, De quoi le roi ci aseüre: Si m'aït Dex et saint Ylaire, Ces reliques, cest saintuaire, Totes celes qui ci ne sont Et tuit icil de par le mont, Q'* . . . The MS. has in 4204 *tuit celes de par le m.*; M⁰ corrected to *totes celes par le m.*, Muret's later eds. and M⁴, like E, to *tuit icil de par le m.*; Muret also corrected *cest* 4202 to *cist*. It is not clear how the nouns and pronouns in 4202–4 are to be taken: Muret, with *cist saintuaire*, evidently understood them as subjects of *aït* in co-ordination with *Dex et saint Ylaire*, and this is perhaps implied also by E and M⁴ with *tuit icil* 4204 (in spite of their retention of *cest* 4202); presumably, then, *totes celes* 4203 refers to *reliques* and *tuit icil* 4204 to *saintuaire*. Alternatively, 4201 might be taken as parenthetical and complete in itself (as formulas with *Si m'aït* usually are), and the following nouns and pronouns as constituting a second object of *jure*, 'Hear now what I here swear . . . by these relics, this reliquary . . .' (cf. note on 3329–30); but in this case *tuit celes* would require correction not to the nom. *tuit icil* but to an oblique form, *to*ʒ *iceus* if referring to *saintuaire*, perhaps *iceles* if referring to *reliques*.

4205. . . . *Q'entre mes cuises n'entra home.* If in the preceding lines *reliques, saintuaire* etc. are taken as part of the subject of *Si m'aït* . . ., the *Q'* of 4205 could still be interpreted in three different ways (cf. F. S. 8 (1954), 204–5): it could be *que* replacing *com* (cf. note on 3976) in the construction *Si m'aït Dex com* . . . 'as surely may God help me as . . .'; it could be the same *que* as is found in O. F. *certes que, par ma foi que* etc.; or it could be *que* introducing a noun-clause depending on *jure* 4199. This last is no doubt the most probable interpretation, and it is of course the only one if *reliques, saintuaire* etc. are objects of *jure*.

4205–6. . . . *entre mes cuises n'entra home, Fors le ladre qui fist soi some* . . . The *fist sor some* of the MS. was corrected in M⁰ to *fist que some*, in all later editions, following Mussafia, to *fist soi some*. But this involves an abnormal use of the strong refl. pron.; normal O. F. usage would require *qui se fist some*, and though the text as transmitted contains some striking uses of the strong forms of the pers. and refl. prons., these are found after a finite verb which is immediately preceded by its subject only in certain specific conditions: in the impers. expression *ce poise moi* 307, 1569, *ce poise nos* 1938; for emphasis in disjunctive locutions, *se . . . il m'ocit ou j'oci lui* 2018; exceptionally for the sake of rhyme in *je l'afi toi* 1913 (: *roi*). The correction also requires *some* to be taken in the sense of 'beast (of burden)', of which Gdf. (VII 466, X 685) has no medieval example (in Guiot de Provins, *Bible* 1248, it means 'load', cf. ed. Orr). The MS. text *qui fist sor some* should probably be corrected to *qui* (= *cui*) *fis sorsome* 'for whom I made a very heavy load'. For scribal *fist* for *fis* cf. note on 2820–1. For *so(u)rsome* 'charge excessive, surcharge' see Gdf. VII 541; it is found most frequently in the proverb *La sorsome abat l'arne* (Morawski 1037). The 'heavy load' refers to Tristran's feigned difficulty in carrying Iseut (*Sovent fait senblant de choier, Grant chiere fait de soi doloir* 3937–8); there may perhaps be a reminiscence of a version in which the leper or beggar actually fell with her (cf. E II 243–5).

4219–20. *'Dex!' fait chascuns, 'si fiere en jure! Tant en a fait aprés droiture!'* All editors correct the *chascune* of the MS. to *chascuns*; Muret also emended *en* 4219 to *a*, understanding *jure* as the noun 'oath' (as in 3244); E and M⁴ restore *en*, but whereas M⁴ still takes *jure* as the noun, E (II 253) understands it as the verb. This means taking *fiere* as 'standing virtually in apposition to the subject (Iseut) and having adverbial force', a usage which he considers typical of Beroul's style but of which he cites no other example (he is presumably thinking of, e.g., *hardi l'atent* 1701). Thus interpreted, however, the line does not lead satisfactorily up to 4220, in which both the *en* and the *aprés* remain unaccounted for (*aprés* here can hardly mean, with M⁰ and E, 'according to'). I have therefore suggested (*Vinaver Misc.*, pp. 266–7) that the *en jure* of the MS. should be understood (cf. note on 29–30) as the noun *enjure* (*injure*) 'wrong, injustice': 'so cruel a wrong! So well has she afterwards justified herself against it' (i.e. 'disposed of the unjust accusation'). For the sense of *fiere* cf. *Molt la vit* (sc. Mark's face) *et cruel et fiere* 3160, also 1186; for *faire droiture de* cf. *faire droit de* in *ele en fera droit devant vos* 3435 ('s'en justifier', Muret and M⁴). For the exclamatory construction without verb I compared *Si grant desroi, tel felonie!* 559, which (*pace* Ewert) would be an exact parallel if punctuated as I suggest (see note on 557–9).

4223–5. *Ne li covient plus escondit Q'avez oï, grant et petit, Fors du roi et de son nevo.* Muret punctuated with a full stop after *escondit*, and a question mark after 4225, which he emended to read *Du roi Marc et de son nevo*; but the question 'What have you all heard about king Mark and his nephew?' is far from plausible. E, followed by M⁴, restores the MS. text and punctuates as above. In this form the passage has been much discussed, the controversy centring (in my view misleadingly) on the sense to be attributed to *fors de* 4225. M⁴ (p. 150) tentatively suggests 'Elle n'est tenue à aucun autre serment que celui que vous venez d'entendre, qui met hors de cause la question du roi et de son neveu', but admits that this would imply an unprecedented extension of the sense of *fors*. E (II 253) translates 'Iseut has no need of further exculpation than you, great and small, have heard, other than that in respect of the king (i.e. Mark) and his nephew (i.e. Tristran)'; H. H. Christmann (*Rom.* 80 (1959) 85–7) had given a similar explanation, but took *fors* in the sense of 'but only' (cf. 4193–6 and note). All these interpretations, assuming that the persons referred to are Mark and Tristran, are vitiated ab initio by the simple fact that Iseut is required to exculpate herself by oath—to make her *escondit* or *deraisne*—in respect of Tristran alone (the complaint of the barons, reported to her by Mark, is *N'as fait de Tristran escondit* 3223), and that it would be obvious nonsense for her to swear that she had never had sexual relations with Mark (she had in fact explicitly excluded him, together with the 'leper', from the scope of her oath: *De deus ne me pus escondire: Du ladre, du roi Marc, mon sire* 4211–12). I have therefore suggested (*Rom.* 85 (1964), 366–7) that the words *du roi et de son nevo* refer not to Mark and Tristran but to Arthur and his nephew Gauvain, and that the lines mean, taking *fors* and *de* in their most usual senses, 'she needs no further *escondit* than you have all heard except that of the king [Arthur] and his nephew'. This requires the noun *escondit* to be taken as applying not only to Iseut's declaration on oath of her innocence, but also to the guaranteeing of that declaration by the sponsors in whose presence it is made

(*Artus . . . Ensenble o lui chevaliers cent, Qui puis garant li porteroient* 3357–61; cf. 3440–6); but this double sense of the word is attested in *aprés les escondiz* 4176, where the plural covers both Iseut's declaration itself and the guarantee of it by Arthur and his knights, while the second sense corresponds to the use of the verb *escondire* by Iseut in *Cil me voudroient escondire, Qui avront veü ma deraisne* 3252–3, and similarly of the verb *deraisnier* in 4246. After Iseut's oath and the chorus of the spectators, the declaration of the sponsors' guarantee follows immediately in 4235–46 (see note on 4232–3).

The role of Arthur's nephew is stressed all through this episode: he is the first member of the household to speak after the king himself (3457); he had been specifically named by Iseut when she informed Mark of her terms for making the *escondit* (3258), and by Perinis when he transmitted her appeal to Arthur (*Oiez por qoi sui venu ci; Et si entendent cil baron, Et mes sires Gauvain par non* 3412–14), and at the oath-taking he is stated to be with Iseut and the two kings near the relics (4186). If editors and critics have taken the words *du roi et de son nevo* to refer to Mark and Tristran, it is perhaps in part because the last 'king' named had been Mark (in Iseut's declaration, 4208 and 4212); but a few lines earlier, in *Or escoutez que je ci jure, De quoi le roi ci aseüre* 4199–200, the reference is clearly to Arthur, who has just administered the oath (4191–6). In any case, there are other passages where the identity of the 'king' referred to has to be deduced from the general context, notably the words spoken by Arthur's barons, *Li rois fait ce que il conmandent, Tristran s'en vet fors du païs. Ja ne voist il s'anz paradis, Se li rois veut, qui la n'ira* 3452–5 (text of E and M⁴, see note), where the first *li rois* means Mark and the second Arthur.

To the above explanation H. H. Christmann (*Zeitschrift für französische Sprache und Literatur* 76 (1966), 243–5) objects inter alia that *escondit* would have to be understood in 4224 in the first of the senses I attach to it (the declaration of innocence) and in 4225 in the second (the guaranteeing of the declaration by the sponsors); but it seems to me that this analytical distinction is shown to be irrelevant by the phrase *aprés les escondiz* 4176 (cf. above). For Christmann's other main objection, that Iseut's *escondit* is not guaranteed by Gauvain, see note on 4232–3 below.

4232–3. *Li rois Artus en piez leva, Li roi Marc a mis a raison.* In the
MS. the beginning of 4232 reads *Lunes* or *Limes* or *Liuies* (M²,
M⁴), *Li mes* or *Lunes* or *Linies* (E II 253). M⁰, however, had read
it as *Li rois*; and this is perhaps why all later editors have introduced *Li rois* as a correction. It is obvious, however, that what
the scribe intended was *Li niés*; and what stood in the original
must surely have been *Li niés Artus*, i.e. Gauvain (cf. *Gauvains,
li niés Artus* 4010). The speech which follows (4235–46), with its
threat of warlike action against the three hostile barons, is in
fact more characteristic of the combative Gauvain than of the
benevolent but more judicial Arthur, whose threat against any
accusers of Iseut had been to have them hanged (4152–7). It
should also be noted that Iseut, having thanked the speaker of
the warning to the hostile barons (*'Sire', fait el, 'vostre merci!'*
4247), is afterwards represented as thanking king Arthur (*Yseut . . .
Mercie molt le roi Artur* 4250–1). Acceptance of the MS. reading
Li niés Artus in 4232 (which I had overlooked when writing the
note in *Rom.* 85) seems to me to strengthen the already strong
case for taking 4225 to refer to Arthur and Gauvain.

4241–6. *Ja ne seront en cele terre Que m'en tenist ne pais ne gerre, Des
que j'orroie la novele De la roïne Yseut la bele, Que n'i allons a esperon,
Lui deraisnier par grant raison.* (The MS. has in 4242 *Quil maintenist,*
corrected by all editors). There is no question of the hostile
barons being in a distant land (where their hostility would be of no
significance); it is clearly the speaker who might be far away (and
this, incidentally, is more likely to be the case with Gauvain than
with Arthur), but would nevertheless return to defend Iseut (cf.
the similarly-constructed promise of Tristran to Iseut, *Ja ne
serai en cele terre Que ja me tienge pais ne gerre Que mesage ne vos envoi*
2689–91). We must therefore conclude that *seront* 4241 is an error
(induced by the 3 pl. verbs in 4237–40) for *seroie,* the conditional
being in any case the form required by the grammatical con-
text (*tenist, orroie*); cf. scribal *porroit* 2783 for *porron.* It is possible
also that *allons* 4245 is an error (induced by the rhyme-words
esperon : raison, cf. note on 819–20) for *allasse,* since the impf.
subj. and the 1 sing. are what the construction would normally
require.

4246. *par grant raison* (not explained by E or M⁴), 'with ample justification, with good reason' (cf. T.-L. VIII 218).

4252. *je vos asur*. The MS. reading, retained by E and M⁴, should be corrected with Muret to *jos aseür* (cf. E II 22). The verb is glossed by E 'reassure', by Muret and M⁴ 'garantir, protéger'; the meaning is 'I guarantee your safety (from slander)'.

4253–5. *Ne troverez mais qui vos die . . . Nis une rien se amor non.* E glosses *nis* (s.v. *neis*) 'not even'; better with M⁰, glossary (s.v. *nis*), *nis une rien* 'quoi que ce soit, rien', preferably printed *nisune rien* (cf. T.-L. VI 614, s.v. *nesun*).

4264. *Li rois Artus vient a Durelme*. See note on 2231–5.

4277. *Li rois vos sout l'autrier malgré*. Better with M⁰ and M⁴ *mal gré* in two words; cf. T.-L. IV 601.

4282–3. *son aise atent De parler o sa chiere drue*. See note on 1932–4.

4285–7. *Tristran set molt de Malpertis; Qant li rois vait a ses deduis, En la chanbre vet congié prendre*. In the MS. 4286 (which has *son deduis*) precedes 4285; M⁰ keeps the MS. text; Muret's later eds. assume a lacuna between 4286 and 4285, and correct to *ses deduiz*; E interverts the lines and deletes the lacuna; M⁴ restores the MS. order, but without the lacuna. Neither the lacuna nor the interversion seems indispensable: *Tristran set molt de Malpertis* can be understood as parenthetical (it was printed in parentheses by Muret).

Grammatically, the subject of *vet congié prendre* could be either *li rois* or *Tristran*. On the assumption that it is Tristran who *en la chanbre vet*, M⁴ tentatively suggests (p. 150) correcting *congié* to *son gré*; but *prendre son gré* 'take one's pleasure' is not registered by Gdf. (IV 342, IX 721) or T.-L. (IV 583–602). It is conceivable, however, that *congié* may be an error for *son sez* (or even for *ses sez*: cf. *Laisiez moi faire auques mes sez* 1942); Gdf. (VII 403) cites in a similar context *cil, qui cuide avoir son sez De la dame* (*Estormi* 236,

Montaiglon et Raynaud I 206), and though the verb in this locution is most commonly *faire* or *avoir* Gdf. has one example of *prendre son sez*.

4294. *Enuit verrez venir, par main.* M⁴ (p. 150) translates 'Ce soir . . . ou demain de grand matin', because of *Encor enuit ou le matin* 2281; but the insertion of *ou* in the translation is unjustified, and E rightly prefers (II 255) 'This very night you will see him come, towards morning' (cf. the time references *hui main* 4297, *matin* 4319). Both, however, assume an abnormal omission of the pron. obj. *le* (cf. note on 269–70), and Muret corrected plausibly enough to *Enuit l'i verrez ou par main* (the scribe may have introduced *venir* under the influence of *Se n'i veez Tristran venir* 4291).

4295–305. See note on 3223–7.

4304. *Ou verro[n] nos?* See note on 269–70.

4306–7. *Se gel vos mostre, grant avoir En doi avoir, quant l'en ratent.* The MS. has *quant leuratin*. Muret first corrected to *quant en ratent*, understood as 'autant que je suis en droit d'en attendre en échange du service que je vous rends' (M⁰, glossary); but he added 'On pourrait aussi lire: *quant le* (ou *l'en*) *ratent*, "puisque j'y compte" ', and it is *quant l'en ratent* that is printed in his later eds. and in M⁴. Neither emendation is satisfactory. In the first, *quant* appears to be the pron., but the sense attributed to it by Muret does not correspond to any attested usage (see Gdf. VI 478–80, T.-L. II 29–33); 'as much as (*or* all that) I expect of it' would be *quant qu'en (r)atent*, but even this would be almost meaningless in the context. In the alternative emendation *quant* was evidently intended by Muret as the conj. 'when, since'; yet E, though adopting this text, translates (II 255) 'in such quantity as I expect it', which is open to the same objection as in the previous case and in addition fails to account for the prons. *le* and *en*. The original probably had the conj. *quant* 'when' but with a verb other than *(r)atendre*—perhaps *quant ert (r)ataint* 'when he is caught'; for the rhyme *-aint* : *argent* cf. E II 14–15 and for the declensional irregularity *-aint* for *-ainz* ib. 19–20.

4308–12. *'Nomez l'avoir.' 'Un marc d'argent.' 'Et plus assez que la pramesse, Si vos aït iglise et messe; Se tu mostres, n'i puez fallir Ne te façon amanantir.'* The punctuation and attribution of speeches is the same in Muret's later editions, in E and in M⁴. M⁰, however, made 4309–10 part of the speech of the spy: *Barons:* 'Name the reward.' *Spy:* 'A mark of silver, and much more than the promise, so help you Church and Mass.' *Barons:* 'If you show [him (cf. note on 269–70)], you cannot fail to be made rich by us'. This is not very satisfactory: is the spy asking for a mark of silver as his price, or for more? and what is the 'promise' he refers to? Later Muret transferred 4309–10 to the barons, and in M³ he emended *vos* 4310 to *nos*, so that their reply now ran, much more plausibly, 'And much more than the promise, so help us Church and Mass; if you show him . . .'. This text is retained by M⁴, with a note in justification of the change to *nos* (p. 150): 'C'est en général celui qui promet, menace, ou annonce une intention qui demande à Dieu de ne pas l'aider dans le cas où il serait défaillant', of which the last part is obscurely expressed. E has the same distribution, but by restoring the *vos* of the MS. in 4310 he makes nonsense of the speech of the barons; they cannot say in solemn confirmation of their promise 'so help *you* Church and Mass' (and it is also unlikely that they would address the spy in the 2nd person pl. in 4310 and in the 2nd person sing. in 4311–12). If *vos* is to be retained, it seems necessary to assume that 4309 and 4310 have been interverted by the scribe (cf. note on 65–8) and to re-punctuate, understanding: *Barons:* 'Name the reward.' *Spy:* 'A mark of silver, so help you Church and Mass.' *Barons:* 'And much more than the promise, if you show him; you cannot fail to be made rich by us.' In the text thus reconstructed (which is perhaps slightly preferable to that of M⁴), *Si vos aït . . .* becomes a formula of adjuration, used to emphasize the spy's demand (cf. note on 506–7 and the article there cited).

4313–15. *'Or m'entendez', fait li cuvert, . . . 'Et un petit pertus overt Endroit la chanbre la roïne'.* The MS. has *.i. petit fenestre*; Muret's correction to *pertus* (cf. *pertus* 4321, *pertuset* 4328) is retained by E and M⁴; Muret and E assume a lacuna between 4313 and 4314, but the rhyme between *cuvert* and *overt* makes this rather improbable. M⁴, rejecting it, tentatively suggests correcting *Et* to *Est* (which had in fact been printed by F. Michel), but admits that the word-order would be abnormal. The original version of 4314 was probably something like *Un petit pertus a overt* (for the scribe's tendency to make good an omitted syllable elsewhere in the line cf. note on 1569–70), or possibly, if 4313 ended with the grammatically correct nom. form *cuverz*, *Uns petiz pertus est overz*. It is not impossible that the *fenestre* of the MS. is authentic, for the word is given as sometimes masc. by T.-L. (III 1714), though the evidence cited is very slight.

4317–18. *Triés la chanbrë est grant la doiz Et bien espesse li jagloiz.* (The MS. has *clanbre*, corrected by all editors.) On 4317 E comments (II 256) that the *doiz* 'can hardly be the stream down which Tristran sent the chips'. We do not know what account Beroul gave of the message sent by the chips, and there is some ambiguity about the place at which the present episode is located; but if, as E concludes (II 254), it is at Mark's palace, it is surely unlikely that the poet envisaged two different streams flowing through or close to the royal residence.

In 4318 M⁰ and E interpret *espesse* as pres. indic. 3 of the verb *espessier* (the same verb—though they do not say so—as *espoisier* in 2450, where it means 'grow dark'); it is not glossed by M⁴. But this verb is attested only in that sense and in those of 'become thick (of mud)', 'become frequent, strong, numerous', 'increase' (Gdf. III 527, T.-L. III 1235–7); and even if it could be used in the sense of 'be thick, dense (of vegetation)', it is most unlikely that such a verb could be intercalated between the adv. *bien* and its subject. The structure and movement of the couplet clearly imply the same construction, predicative adj. +noun subject, in 4317 (*grant la doiz*) and 4318 (*espesse li jagloiz*). In any case, as I have shown (*Vinaver Misc.*, p. 278), *jagloiz* cannot, either in form or in sense, represent the nom. sing. of the noun *jaglol, jagluel, glaiol* (Gdf. IV 627, T.-L. IV 353–4), from GLADIOLUM, the name applied to various plants with long sword-shaped leaves (such as the Yellow Flag, Iris Pseudacorus, and the Sweet Sedge, Acorus calamus, used for strewing floors, cf. 4082–3), with which it is identified by E ('sword-grass') and Muret-M⁴ ('glaïeul'). In our text this word would not appear as *jagloil*, nom. sing. *jagloiz* (so M² and M⁴, glossary), but as *jaglel*, nom. sing. *jagleus* (cf. *chevrel* 1286, 1629, acc. pl. *chevreus* 1426, 3022); and neither the tonic vowel nor the final consonant of its nom. sing. would rhyme with those of *doiz* (the rhyme *doiz* : *jagloiz* is indeed noted as abnormal by M², p. x = M⁴, p. ix and E II 12, but only as regards the quality of the *o*). Moreover, the representative of GLADIOLUM is inappropriate in sense, for it is not the individual plant that is thick or dense, but the whole plantation. The form *jagloi* given by Gdf. (IV 627) with the translation 'roseau', and attested only by the present passage and one in a manuscript of *Partonopeus* (where it is probably an error for *argroi*, *agroi*, Gdf. I 169), is more correctly glossed by T.-L. (IV 352, with only the present example) as 'Bestand, Anpflanzung von Schwertlilien'. But this *jagloi* is merely a haplological form of the well-attested *jagloloi*, *glaioloi* (Gdf. IV 286, T.-L. IV 352-3), a derivative in *-oi* < *-ETUM* of *jaglol*, meaning 'bed, plantation of irises, flags, sedges' (the last example cited by T.-L., with the spelling *jaglolai*, is probably to be identified with *glaiolé*, *jaglolé* '(material) dyed black with the rootstock of the Yellow Flag', not as Gdf. and T.-L. say 'of the colour of an iris'). The original version of Beroul 4318 must have run *Et bien espés li jagloloiz* (rhyming normally with *doiz*) 'and very dense the bed of iris or sedge'; the scribe, having read the noun as *jagloiz*, has restored the measure by giving the adj. the feminine ending (cf. note on 1569-70 and particularly 2698 and note). For the significance of the rhyme *doiz* : *jagloloiz* for dialect, date and authorship see *M.L.R.* 60 (1965), 356-7.

4322. *Fors la fenestre n'i aut nus.* Muret corrected to *n'i a plus* (the sense of which is not clear), but E and M⁴ restore the MS. text. M⁴ offers no explanation. E (II 256) translates 'Let no one pass by outside the window'; but this requires *fors* to be taken in a sense which does not appear to be attested elsewhere (see Gdf. IV 95, 498; T.-L. III 2139-44, IV 1176-80). It seems probable that *la fenestre* is corrupt; it is perhaps an error for *a senestre* (cf. *senestrier* 2468 corrected by all editors to *fenestrier*; for other cases of scribal confusion of initial *f* and *s* cf. note on 1325-6), 'Let no one go except to the left', with reference to the spy's earlier words *Se vos alez a la fenestre De la chanbre, derier' a destre* 4289–90—the window is on the right, the watcher is to go to the left to avoid being seen.

4323–4. *Faites une longue brochete, A un coutel, bien agucete.* Muret, followed by M⁴, corrects to *agüete.* There is no other evidence of the existence of a diminutive adj. *agucet,* and its formation from *agu* would be difficult to account for, whereas *agüet* is normally formed (cf. the noun *agüece*), and another example is cited by Gdf. (I 170) and T.-L. (I 216).

4327–8. *La cortine souavet sache Au pertuset, c'on ne l'estache.* E translates (II 256) 'since it is not fastened', taking *estache* as pres. indic. 3 of *estachier = atachier,* and this is also the interpretation of Muret and presumably of M⁴ (who put the words in parentheses). If *estache* is for *atache* (and Gdf. I 460, III 587–8, VIII Compt. 223–4, T.-L. I 615–16, III 1332 have few if any examples of the form in *est-* in an appropriate sense), the meaning is not so much 'since it is not fastened' (E II 256) but more precisely 'for they do not attach it', which is not particularly plausible. It is conceivable that the text should read *c'on ne le sache* 'in such a way that they do not know it, without anyone's knowing'. The use here of the form *sache* < SAPIAT (: *sache* < SACCAT) would not necessarily preclude the use of the alternative (Western) form *sace* in 2803 (: *enbrace*), though it would make it a little more probable that the rhyme in 2803–4 was *sache : enbrache* (cf. *M.L.R.* 60 (1965), 354).

4330. *Qant il venra a lui parler.* See note on 1932–4.

4356–8. *(Tristran . . .) Garda, vit venir Gondoïne, Et s'en venoit de son recet. Tristran li a fet un aget.* E says (II 257) that Tristran is the subject of *s'en venoit.* It is true that Tristran's refuge in Orri's cellar has been called his *recet* (3318; cf. *sa mue* 4284); but the natural assumption in the context would be that the subject is Godoïne (one might indeed expect *Qui* rather than *Et*), and Godoïne and the other hostile barons are presumably still residing away from court in their *forz chasteaus . . . bien clos de pal, Soiant*

sor roche, sor haut pui (3144–5), which might well merit the description of *recez*. On the other interpretation the passage is, as E says,
disjointed and repetitive.

4360. '*Ha! Dex,*' *fait il,* '*regarde moi*'. The verb *regarder* here is not
glossed or commented on by E or M⁴; the sense is 'look after,
protect' (cf. M⁰, glossary, and T.-L. VIII 598–9).

4363. *En sus l'atent, s'espee tient.* E (s.v. *sus*) glosses *en sus* 'afar',
Muret and M⁴ 'au loin, à distance'. With the exception of *Passion*
509, where the text is doubtful, all the examples of *ensus* adv.
(without *de*) in Gdf. (III 244–5) and T.-L. (III 542–3) are with
verbs expressing motion, usually *soi traire*; it is possible that here
the text should read *En sus se trait* 'he moves aside (from the
path)'.

4367–8. *cil s'esloigne, Qui en fel leu a mis sa poine.* The word *poine*
here was glossed by Muret 'force du poignet, effort', implying
that it was to be identified with Mod. F. *poigne*; the entry is
omitted from the glossary of M⁴. E in his glossary placed it under
peine ('*metre p.* take trouble 525, 4368'), and I argued in favour of
this identification in *M.L.R.* 60 (1965), 356 and n. 4. In II 257,
however, E says that '*poine* is scribal for *poigne* (< PUGNA) "grip,
force, effort" '. T.-L. now has an article *poigne* s.f. (VII 1278,
numbered 2078), stating that this word is not from PUGNA (which
gave the very rare O. F. *pugne*) but from the verb *poignier* <
PUGNARE, and citing under the gloss 'Anstrengung, Mühe'
examples containing *orent sauve lor p.* and *par nostre (sa) p.*, but not
metre sa poigne (*en* or *a*). Under *peine* and *metre*, on the other hand
(besides numerous examples of *metre peine* (*a* or *en*), cf. Beroul 525,
1588, 1604), T.-L. (V 1731–2, VII 557–8) cites *metre sa peine* (*en* or
a) from *Yvain* 4819, *Perceval* 6197, Marie de France, *Chaitivel* 46
and the present passage; note particularly in Beroul *Et a ce metrai
je ma paine* 1597 (: *semaine*) and in Marie de France, in exactly the
same context as in Beroul 4368, *Mettent lur peine en malveis liu*
(*Equitan* 158/154, *Lais*, ed. Ewert, p. 30). No difficulty is presented either by the spelling with *-oi-* (cf. *poine* 3369, 3658) or by
the rhyme between *-gn-* and *-n-* (cf. *feme* = *fene* : *reigne* 287–8,

4123–4 etc., *roïne* : *signe* 3581–2); for the implications of the rhyme between the tonic vowels see the article mentioned above.

4369–71. *Tristran garda au luien, si vit—Ne demora que un petit—Denoalan venir anblant.* Following Muret (glossary), E says (II 257) that the subject of *demora* is Denoalen. Much more probably *demora* is impersonal, cf. M⁴, glossary ('litt. "la chose ne tarda guère" ') and examples of *demorer* impers. 'auf sich warten lassen' in T.-L. II 1384–5, including several of *Ne demora que un petit*, *Ne demora gaires après* etc.

4371–2. (*si vit . . .*) *Denoalan venir anblant O deus levriers, mervelles grant.* E says (II 257) that *grant* refers to Denoalen, and this is presumably also the interpretation of Muret (M⁰, M², M³) and M⁴; but there is no other suggestion that Denoalen was of exceptional stature, and the opposite is implied by the fact that he was riding *un petit palefroi noir* 4375. M¹ had corrected to *granz*, referring to the hounds, which is much more plausible (it is precisely the sort of picturesque but irrelevant detail that is especially characteristic of the second part of the romance). The only objection is the rhyme *anblant* : *granz*; but there are other such rhymes which appear to be attributable to the author, e.g. *decent* : *dedanz* 3383–4, *garnement* : *dedenz* 4023–4 (cf. E II 18).

4390–3. *O l'espee trencha les treces, En sa chauce les a boutees, Qant les avra Yseut mostrees, Qu'ele l'en croie qu'il l'a mort.* The temporal clause in 4392 is subordinate to the final clause in 4393 although it precedes the *Qu'* which introduces the latter; for this characteristic order of clauses cf. *il le fait par lecherie, Qant or verra passer s'amie . . ., Que ele an ait en son cuer joie* 3693–6 (other examples are cited in note to 2020–3).

E (II 258) naturally translates *qu'il l'a mort* 'that he has killed him'; but this hardly justifies glossing *morir* as '*v.a.* kill' (so also M⁰, glossary). The usage in question occurs only in compound tenses; *morir* is always an intrans. or refl. verb, but *avoir mort* can mean 'have killed, have caused the death of' (cf. T.-L. VI 279–82).

4395–8. '*Ha! las,*' *fait il, '*qu(e) est devenuz Goudouïnë—or s'est toluz—*

Que vi venir orainz si tost? Est il passez? Ala tantost?' These lines, thus punctuated (so also in M⁴) appear repetitive (both *orainz* and *tantost* are glossed 'but now' by E) and may be corrupt. Muret corrected 4398 to *Est il passez par la tantost?*, which taken by itself would make better sense provided that *tantost* were understood as *tant tost* 'so quickly', but would then repeat the meaning of *si tost* 4397. The normal sense of *tantost*, however, is neither 'but now' ('tantôt, tout à l'heure', M⁰) nor 'so quickly' but 'thereupon, immediately', which seems unlikely in the context of the question.

4400–1. *Ja mellor gerredon n'eüst Que Do[n]alan, le fel, en porte.* In order to introduce the four-syllable form *Donoalan* (various spellings) which is generally used elsewhere, Muret emended 4401 to *Donoalan, le fel, n'en porte.* As the poet has used variant forms of other proper names for the sake of rhyme (cf. E II 8), it is quite likely that he is responsible for the form *Donalan*, and *Que* need not be omitted; but in any case *n'* should not be introduced before *en porte*, for in O. F. the negation was not used in a comparative clause depending on a negative principal, cf. *Ne puet plus corre que il cort* 964, also 2606–7, 4223–4 (but with affirmative principal, e.g., *Plus i a mis que ne disoient* 4221).

4407. *Le chaperon el chief sei met.* The MS. reading is, according to E (II 258), *seimet* or *sennet* (M⁰ had read *se met*, M² *sennet*, M⁴ *soi met*). In view of the indistinctness of the text it seems more reasonable to print, with Muret and M⁴, the normal *se met*. In either form, however, the refl. pron. is a little unexpected.

4408. *Sor le cors un grant fust atret.* So also Muret's later eds. and M⁴; E (II 258) tentatively suggests reading *a tret* (which was in fact printed by M⁰), but although *traire* would perhaps seem more natural in the context than *atraire* (and the compound perf. would be as acceptable as the pres.), it is *atraire* that is used in rather similar conditions in *De leus en leus ot fuelle atraite* 1802.

4413–14. *La cortine ot dedenz percie; Vit la chanbre, qui fu jonchie.* So also Muret and M⁴. In the MS. the word after *cortine* is, according to M⁰, *ot*; according to M² (p. 148), *et*; according to E

L

(II 259), *ot* or *et* or *er*; according to M⁴ (p. 150), *et* or *er*. All editors print *percie*, but E points out that as abbreviated in the MS. this could also be read *partie*. Intrinsically, the reading *partie* (with either *ot* or *er*[*t*]) gives a much better sense (cf. Ewert, *Pope Studies*, p. 93); what the spy had instructed Godoïne to do with his pointed thorn stick (4323–9) was not to pierce the curtain but to part it or draw it aside. I have therefore suggested (*M.L.R.* 60 (1965) 355) that *partie* is probably what the author wrote, even though it involves a Northern or 'literary Franco-Picard' rhyme with *jonchie* (for *jonchiee*) of which there is no other instance in the text.

4433. '*Se Dex me gart*', *fait il*, '*au suen . . .*'. E translates (II 259) 'So may God keep me with his [elect]', cf. M⁰, glossary, s.v. 2 *suen* 'Ainsi Dieu puisse-t-il me garder parmi les siens!'; rather more accurately, 'keep me for his own', cf. M⁴, glossary, s.v. *suen* (2) '. . . me garder comme l'un des siens!' E adds '*se* for *si* (< sic)'; but in this form of the asseverative construction, with the verb at the end, *se* is normal (though it may ultimately derive from sic), and in the form with *si* the verb precedes the subject (*Si m'aït Dex* 628, 4201). Cf. *F.S.* 8 (1954), 199–203.

4436–7. *Jamais par lui escu ne lance N'iert achatez ne mis en pris.* For *metre en pris* the glossaries give 'faire valoir' (M⁰), 'mettre en valeur' (M², M⁴), 'enhance the value of, exploit' (E), glosses perhaps based on *Escoufle* 32, 6855, but here the object is personal; in the examples cited by T.-L. (V 1744, VII 1883) the sense is 'value' (either 'appraise' or 'esteem'). In the context, the meaning of *achatez ne mis en pris* is perhaps 'bought or bargained for'.

4439–41. '. . . *Mes prié vos que cest arc tendez, Et verron com il est bendez.' Tristran l'estent, si s'apensa.* In 4441 the MS. is read by Muret and M⁴ as *sesteut*, interpreted as equivalent to *s'estut*, by E as *sestent* corrected to *l'estent* (sc. the bow). Against *s'esteut* E points out (II 259) that the form *esteut* does not occur elsewhere; but the fact that the spelling *aperceut* 975 is found alongside *apercut* 367 suggests that in both cases -*eut* is scribal for -*ut* (M⁰, p. 253, proposes reading *aperceüt* 975, but this has not been adopted by later editions). E considers that 'Tristran tests the bow by stretching it, temporizes (in order not to alarm Godoïne), and then stretches the bow again (4443)'; but the only temporizing mentioned in the text comes not before but after 4443. The version of Muret and M⁴ therefore seems the more probable; cf., after Iseut's speech (4453–6), *Tristran s'estut, si pensa pose* 4457.

4447–51. *S'il en peüst vis eschaper, Du roi Marc et d'Iseut sa per Referoit sordre mortel gerre. Cil, qui Dex doinst anor conquerre, L'engardera de l'eschaper.* According to G. Whitteridge (*Vinaver Misc.*, p. 343), 'Godoïne, listening at the window, says to himself that if he can get safely away from this situation he will raise *mortel gerre* between Iseult and Marc'; but as there is a lacuna before 4447, we have no evidence that 4447–9 represent the thoughts of Godoïne—indeed, the context and the tenses suggest that the reflection is either that of the author or that of Iseut (who was the subject of 4445). Nor do 4450–1 represent the author's confidence that God is on the side of the lovers, in the same way as numerous passages in the first part of the romance (352, 371–80, 755–6, 909–14, 960, 2380–4 etc.); here it is Tristran, not God, who is relied upon to prevent Godoïne from making mischief.

4458–9. *Bien soit q'el voit aucune chose Qui li desplaist; garda en haut . . .* For *soit* see note on 3026–7. The fact that the verbs in the subordinate clause are in the pres. does not make it less probable that *soit* is intended as a pret.; cf., e.g., *Bien penserent fantosme soit* 4072.

4473. *Sovent ot entesé, si trait.* The editors make no comment on this line, except in so far as E, at the end of his note on 4441, adds 'Cf. also 4473'; this may mean that he understands *sovent* as 'often' and takes it as supporting his view that Tristran had stretched his bow twice. This does not seem very plausible, and it may be preferable to assume that *sovent* is a scribal error.

4474–5. *La seete si tost s'en vait Riens ne peüst de lui gandir.* E comments (II 259) '*lui* for *li* (or M⁴: *lui* "se rapportant à un nom de chose")'. The 'or' is obscure: *lui*, referring to *la seete*, is scribal for the fem. form *li* or *lié* (Muret in fact corrected to *li*); but it is also an instance of the use of the strong pers. pron., governed by a preposition, to refer to a thing. This is comparatively unusual in O. F., but occurs elsewhere in the text, e.g. *Cil mont est plain de pierre atoise; S'uns escureus de lui* (sc. *du mont*) *sausist, Si fust il mort* 922–4, also, before infin., *Du mesage ot Tristran parler, Au roi respont de lui porter* (sc. *du mesage porter*) 689–90.

4479–80. (*Esmerillons . . .*) *De la moitié si tost ne vole; Se ce fust une pome mole . . .* E cites this couplet (II 11) as the sole instance in the text of a rhyme between blocked open *o* and free open *o* (*Vowels*, nos. 15, 20). But although *vole* represents vŏLAT, phonetic representatives of the strong forms of this verb such as **vuele* > *veule*, with diphthongized free open *o*, do not seem to occur; rhymes like that in the text are normal in O. F., e.g. in Chrétien de Troyes *volent* : *tolent* (*Yvain* 843–4), *vole* : *parole* (*Yvain* 157–8, *Erec* 4867–8).

Index

The references are to line-numbers; the figure given is the number of the first of the lines cited in the lemma of the note in which the word, form or other phenomenon is discussed, not necessarily that of the line in which it occurs in the text. Classifications, corrections and interpretations implied by entries in the Index are often to be understood as topics of discussion rather than statements of fact.

atent: l'a. scribal for *se tret* 4363
atorner v.refl.: *soi a. de* (or *a*) 155
atret scribal for *a tret* 4408
Audret see Andret
aus scribal for *eus,* in nom. function
    2345
autre adj. expletive 1479, 2203, 4131
averez fut. 5 of *avoir* 2340
avoé p. part. 1030
avoir v.a. in sense of *faire* 755; in
    sense of *trover* 1091; case after
    a. a non 1177; auxil. of refl. vb.
    2236; impers. (*i*) *out demandé* 2058;
    n'avoit en eus que+infin. 2121
avriez scribal for *avroie* 2236

balence sb.: *metre en b.* 1110
ballier v.a. 3128
barnage sm.: *tuit li b.* as nom. pl. 3395
baudré sm.: *quant qu'a soz son b.* 3114
bel adj.: *estre b. a aucun d'aucune chose*
    3242; *estre b. a aucun (de ce) que . . .*
    109, 3255
bien *lit* scribal for *berbiz* 3973
bien tost adv. 515, 3093
biere sb. 4131
bliaut sm. 2882
boce sf., *bocele* sf. 3300, 3821
bocel sm., *bocet* sm. 3353
boche scribal for *boce* 3300
botele scribal for *bocele* 3300

c- scribal for *s-* 4131, 4180
Case-system, see Declensional irregu-
    larities
ce pron. obj. elided before vb. 1862
celui scribal for *celi* 3559
ceres scribal for *serres* 4131
chaz pres. subj. 1 of *chacier* 3067
cline scribal for *cl(u)igne* 576
clore v.a. 3936
com, con: com a seignor 160; asseverative
    or exclamatory 1239; *con que* 2717
Condition expressed by subjunctive
    alone 2251, 2801

Conditional clause 'postulating the
    thing denied' 211
Confiscation of Tristran's arms 204
congié scribal for *son gré* or *son sez* 4285
Conjunctions miscopied by scribe
    1382, 1649
connillier sm. 1204
conplaindre v.refl. 432
conplaint scribal for *conplainst* 432
consel, conseillier d'aucune chose 2340
consentir scribal for *conseillier* 3112
contenir v.refl. 2633
contor scribal for *conteor* 1265
corage sm.: *venir a c. a aucun* 2711; *a son*
    c., en son c. 1467
Costentin 2385
çou que, ce que 2717
Couplet, breaking of 147, 303, 783,
    982
coutel sm. (*de lance*) 3478
covienge scribal for *covient* 649
criembre v.a. 3188
cro pret. 1 of *croire* 306
croire v.a. 1173
cuir sm.: *bote le c. fors* 4051

de prep.; introducing logical subject
    1115
dechacier v.a., *dechaz* sb. 1771, 1880
Declensional irregularities 139, 1177,
    1837, 1877, 1909, 2604
defors adv. 2043
degerpir v.a. 2243
demalaire adj. 2821
demener v.a. 2295
demorer scribal for *sejorner* or for
    esfreer 2121; v.impers. 4369
deraisne sb., *deraisnier* vb. 131
desevree sb. or p. part. 2945
des que conj. 2020
desroi sb. 1399
destroit sb. 1399
desus prep. or adv. 2882
desveier v.a. 89
Deu: por D. 147